DFS - AINRING

Deutsche Forschungsanstalt für
Segelflug.

(German Glider Research Station)

Reported by

Lt. Colonel John A. O'Mara

C.I.O.S. TARGET 6/2

DIRECTED MISSILES

Combined Intelligence Objectives Sub-Committee
G-2 Division, SHAEF (Rear) APO 413

The Naval & Military Press Ltd

Published by

The Naval & Military Press Ltd
Unit 5 Riverside, Brambleside
Bellbrook Industrial Estate
Uckfield, East Sussex
TN22 1QQ England

Tel: +44 (0)1825 749494

www.naval-military-press.com
www.nmarchive.com

In reprinting in facsimile from the original, any imperfections are inevitably reproduced and the quality may fall short of modern type and cartographic standards.

TABLE OF CONTENTS

	Page No.
Foreword	3
Introduction	5
Part I - Survey of Research Work at DFS, Ainring and translations of reports by DFS Personnel prepared at the direction of the investigators.	6
Part II - A Preliminary Survey of German studies of Mathematical Pursuit Curves by Prof. Tibor Rado.	184

Appendices

A. Interrogations and reports by investigators.	146
B. Reports by DFS personnel.	153
C. Index of scientific papers published by DFS, Ainring research workers prior to Allied occupation.	214

Personnel of Team

Lt. Col. J.A. O'Mara	USAFE
Dr. Tibor Rado	USAFE
S/Ldr. H.M. Stokes	Air Ministry
Dr. R.W. Porter	U.S. Ordnance

FOREWORD

1. This report is a survey of the research and development work done at DFS Ainring by a small group of men whose most significant contributions were in the field of guided missiles. Also included is a summary of German investigations of mathematical pursuit curves by Prof. T. Rado of the University of Ohio.

2. The report does not purport to present the definitive results of scientific investigations (though much original well-substantiated material appears). The narrative matter, in the words of the research workers, describes the scope of the work and the approach to the problems assigned to the DFS. The product of interrogation and the papers written by the scientists at the direction of the investigators give (in most cases) preliminary results and the status of the projects at the time of occupation.

3. Sufficient material is included to give adequate basis for (a). An understanding of the volume importance and trend of the research program of the DFS - Ainring. (b). An estimate of the possibility of future contribution to aeronautical (and of course military) science by the research personnel at Ainring.

4. It is believed that this report cannot be studied without the conclusion being reached that men of the calibre of Stamer Fischel, Fölsche, Höhndorf, Lutz, Ruden, Assmann and Krocht stand high in the world of scientific men. The question arises, are they to continue to use their fund of knowledge and their brains, if so, for whose benefit?.

5. The war of 1939 - 1945 clearly established the scientific brain (even those apparently devoted to the purest of "pure" science) as war military potential. Deprived of research facilities the potential is less, but in an era in which the spectroscopic analysis of stellor atmospheres by means of telescopes contributed to the knowledge which led to the atomic bomb, the definition of facilities voluable to an aggressive power is difficult. Scientific knowledge is military power.

6. Clearly German science must be curbed, but how? The war of 1914 - 1918 was closed out with a peace treaty which sought to prevent the rise of German Air Power by forbidding powered flight. The result was as ludicrous as it was tragic. They simply turned to gliders and determined, rescourceful men laid the foundation for the Luftwaffe, which made the war last $5\frac{1}{2}$ years, and for the guided missile which challenges the victors.

7. Diplomats and military governors are even less likely to dream up a clause in a document that will prevent the eventual development of weapons. The new forms of propulsion control and explosive make it more absured than ever to attempt legal differentiation between friendly and unfriendly science.

8. Scientific progress is, however, simply the product of mans mind. The surest, in fact the only defence against German scientists of the stature of the top men at Ainring is to remove them. To exterminate them is politically impractical and to live is to think.

9. The problem is then ; How can the hundred ranking scientific brains in Germany (of which three might come from Ainring) be best employed to (1) maintain and increase the United Nations technological advantage over their late enemies and (2) add to the sum of human knowledge. It is the belief of majority of those who have been in closest contact with these Germans since surrender that enough evidence now exists to screen the hundred men, and to establish them in or near allied research circles under conditions which would inhabit return to Germany or contact with the wrong elements in that country. There is a challenge here, but only this way lies full utilization of the world's scientific capital under United Nations direction as one of the fruits of victory.

INTRODUCTION

After the first world war, glider flying became a matter of great interest in Germany. In 1924, the Forschungs Institut für Segelflug (Glider Research Institute) was founded, and Georgii, then Professor of flight meteorology and aeronautical research at the Technische Hochschule in Darmstadt, became its first director. The institute was soon moved to Darmstadt and its name was changed to Deutsche Forschungsanstalt für Segelflug (German Glider Research Station) referred to by the letters DFS. It became one of the ten major aeronautical research institutes in Germany.

Later on, the name of Ernst Udet, the famous pilot of the first world war, was added to the title of the institute. In 1939, it was moved to Braunschweig, and then in the summer of 1940 to Ainring in Upper Bavaria.

The original purpose of the institute was the study, on a scientific basis, of the possibilities and of the uses of gliders. However, the scope of the institute was constantly widened, and at the time of its occupation by the Allies it was sub-divided into several research units devoted to studies in a number of fields in aeronautics. The DFS had, when fully developed, the following general objectives.

(a) Study of the scientific foundations of technical developments in aeronautics in general.

(b) Testing of scientific principles involved in the construction of specific devices originated by industrial firms.

(c) In case several devices were proposed by industry for the same purpose, the DFS acted as an impartial umpire in determining the respective merits of competing devices.

Thus the final development and production of aeronautical devices and of aircraft was outside of the scope of the DFS

DFS - Ainring

PART I

For clarity, each division of DFS is treated separately in Part I although in some cases it would seem that certain projects were assigned rather arbitrarily. Also, certain cases of overlapping between the DFS divisions occur (especially between the institute for aeronautical equipment and the department for high frequency, and between the laboratory for special engines and the department for engines).

The purpose is not so much to give an exhaustive treatment, but rather to give a general view of the status of the problem, as conceived by the Germans, for the benefit of those American scientists who many choose to devote their talents to this important topic. For completeness, this part of the present report also includes relevant contributions of German scientists not connected with DFS.

Organization of DFS. (See chart) page   ).

    Director: W. J. O. Georgii (Prof., Dr., Dr. Eng.)

    Deputies (Scientific: Temme (Dipl. Eng).

              (Management: Stamer (Eng)

Institute for aerodynamics. Director: Ruden (Prof. Dr.)
Institute for glider construction. Director Kracht (Dipl. Eng)
Institute for flight tests. Director: Stamer (Eng)
Institute for aeronautical equipment. Director: Fischel (Prof. Dr.)
Institute for physics of the atmosphere. Director: Höhndorf (Dr)
Department for high frequency. Director: Folsche (Dr)
Laboratory for special engines. Director: Eisele (Dr).
Department for engines. Director: Sanger (Dr)
Photographic section. Director: Harth (Dipl. Eng).
Central workshop. Director: Erbskorn (Eng)
Administration. Director: Rauber.

Survey of Research at the DFS.

1. For a proper understanding of the position of DFS in German aeronautical research, a general description of the latter may be welcome. The following description of the organization of German aeronautical research is a translation of B18 by Director Georgii. The accompanying chart is based on this description. Thus it appears that DFS was one of the ten major aeronautical research stations in Germany.

Report On The Organization Of German Aeronautical Research.   B 18

From 1933 to 1942, Aeronautical research was carried out by the Department for Aeronautical Research of the German Air Ministry. This department controlled the Institute for Aeronautical Research of the German Air Ministry. This department controlled the Institute for Aeronautical Research, and was directed by Minister director " Baumker. In order to give research a free hand and to place the direction in the hands of scientific personnel the Aeronautical Research Department became in May 1942, an independent civilian Government department.

The direction was placed in hands of four of the leading personalities of the original department. Their capability was borrowed by their retention of their original posts in the Research Institute.

The four Directors Appointed in May 1942 were:

1. Prof. DR Prandtl Göttingen, chairman.
2. Prof. DR Seewald Aachen, deputy chairman and member of the management committee.
3. Minister Director a.d. Dr Baumker, member.
4. Prof. Dr. Georgii Ainring, member.

In November 1943 Prof. Georgii was appointed deputy chairman and a management committe member in place of Dr Seewald.

The Research Department had independent control of the Aeronautical Research institutes. The Air Ministry assigned the yearly allowance for the Aeronautical research and the upkeep of the research institutes.

The problems to be tackled by the Research Institutes were decided by the research directors. The research institutes could, with permission from the research directors, work on sufficiently urgent problems of their own.

To take care of the different research problems the directors appoited experts who coordinated the work of the different department and the research workers.

The following experts were appointed for the separate sections.

1. Research division. Dr. Lorenz.
   Flight (aerodynamics, flight mechanics, aircraft construction).
   Dr. Jennissen.

   Engines (piston engines, special engines) Dept. Ing.Gebhardt.
   Electro-physics (high frequency, physics) Dr. Rössler
   Armament and flak: Dr. Voss.
   Materials : Dept, Ing Hayer.
   Chemistry: Dr Bunde.
2. Supply and Traffic.
   Instrument Supply, aircraft supply, research materials Expert:- Dipl.Ing. Wolff.
3. Design: New construction and repair work of research service stations:- Expert: Dr. Schwaiger.
4. Administration: Assesor v. Welser, maintenance of aeronautical research.

From each research institute problems were passed by the research directorate to the Universities and high schools, which came directly under the ministry of education.

The research problems consisted of basic research, practical research and pre-development to industrial development or instrument manufacture. These problems were set by the directorate.

The industrial development and the industrial application, however comes under the technical board of the RLM, in particular under its Development Branch. The results of the research were described by the Aeronautical Research to the department for development by the technical board of the RLM. The aeronautical research also received suggestions for research from the technical board and the Department for development of the RLM.

The research directorate compared with the ministry of education is likewise an independent Research service station as in the case with the research Directorate was in comparison with the RLM. The research Directorate was in charge of the execution of the research at University and high school Instutions. The expert was assisted by the so called specialist section chiefs, the latter being drawn from the circles of University and High School Professors. The number of specialists section chiefs was 35. The specialist section chiefs being in charge of the research Directorate, were taking of their personal and scientific branch in dealing with university and high school institutions. To give an example they had Prof. Serladr of Munick, as specialist section chief for physics, Prof. Thyssen Berlin for Chemistry, for high frequency Prof Esau, Berlin.

Also the Research Director made use of the scientific advice for his sphere of duty given by the specialist section chiefs of the Research Directorate. In this connection he was in constant touch with Prof. Gerlach, Prof Thyssen and other professors of natural science.

A substantial part of the Research Directorate was the Planning Board under the supervision of Prof. Osenberg. The planning Board in charge of securing and providing for the scientific personnel, including the exemption from Army services.

The german Academy for Aeronautics Research and the Lilienthal company for Aeronautics Research were independent institutions of the Aeronautic Research.

The German Academy for research was operated on the principles of the old scientific Acadamies (Göttinger Academy of sciences, Heidelberger Academy). Renowened personalities of the Science of Aeronautics and the general natural sciences were assigned to the Academy. They had one meeting each month. Here the men members lectured on the new results of their research.

The Lilienthal Company for Aeronautic Research was a combination of personalities of science and industry. Their organization lead the character of an association where membership is obtained by payment of a fee. The Lilienthal Company had regular meetings where certain spheres of duties were discussed.

The main office for scientific reports was annexed to the Lilienthal Company, the former has been responsible for the issue of all reports since the outbreak of the war.

Prof. Dr. Georgii.

ORGANIZATION OF GERMAN AERONAUTICAL RESEARCH

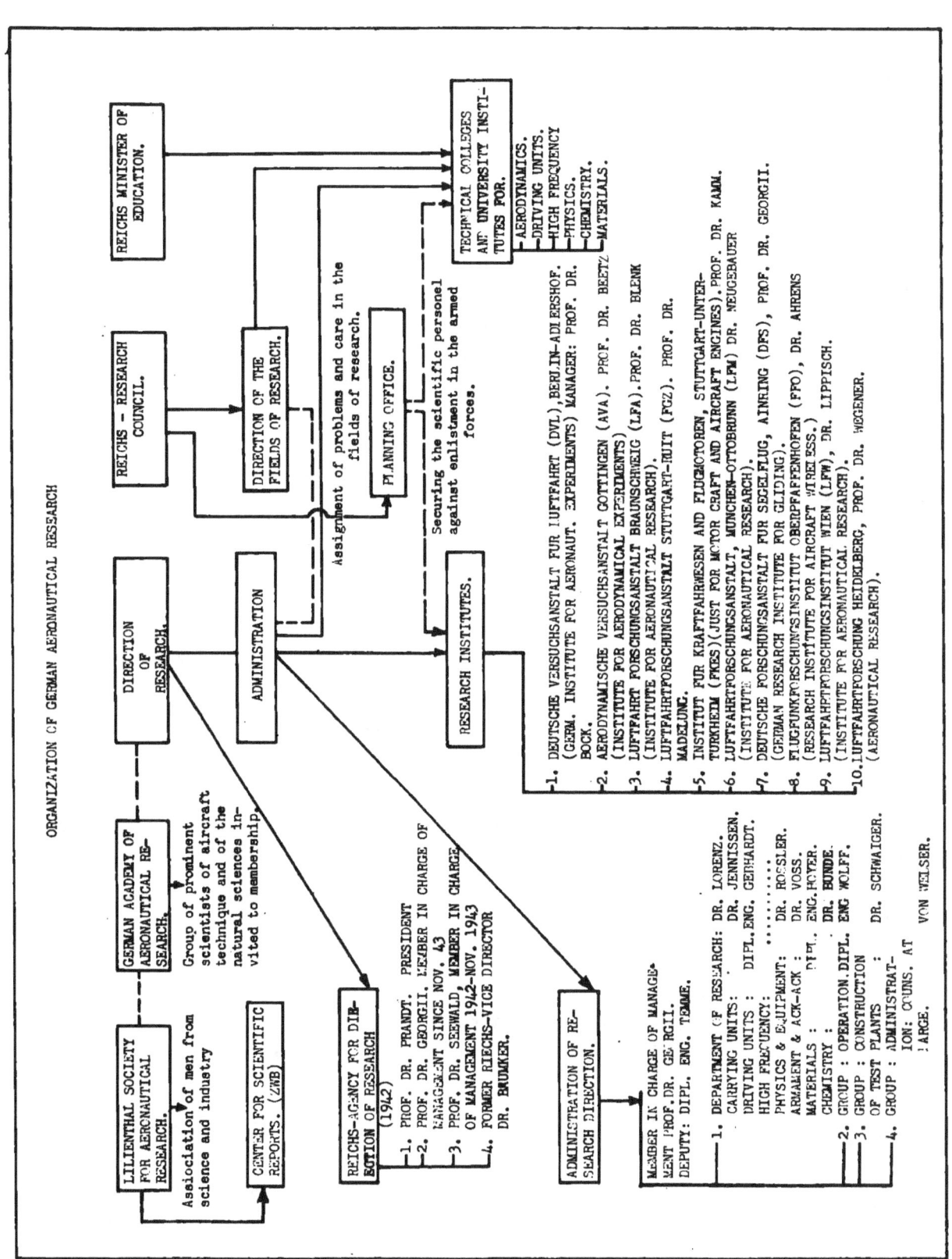

2. The research was carried on in the individual divisions, but the director, Georgii, was interested in glider flight in general and his own work is best reported separately. The following is a translation of his report on glider projects:

Gliding Research and Techniques.

1) Possibilities of gliders.

The possibilities of thermal gliders, and thus making use of the convection currents in the air were unfolded from the actual scientific and practical flying point of view during the years 1928-1938.

It can be shown, that the heating up of the air brought about by the energy of the sun and the latent energy contained in the air through the absorption of water vapor thermal upward currents extending vertically upwards to a great height can be produced by suitable presently known release processes.

It has been shown by gliders, that in the thermal glider the whole of the troposphere can be traversed (In 1938 a glider flew through a thundercloud at an altitude of 8200 m. Furthermore these flights have provided the valuable information that the vertical velocities of the air in thunder can reach 30 m/sec (measuring values).

It is also important for engine aircraft to know about the occurence of such great vertical velocities, as flight through such regions of up currents for fast aircraft doubtless means a critical stress, even more so that the so-called "bumpy gradient" i.e. $\frac{dw}{ds}$ the variation of the vertical velocity w over the strip S is very great. In accordance with measurements the vertical velocity can extend over the strip $s = 100$ m from $0^m/sec$ at $30^m/sec$.

Ascending and descending movements of air of great intensity can lie right next to each other and bring about a large bumpy gradient.

The possibilities of thermal gliding have been examined by the writer of this report in several expeditionary flights:
1925 in Columbia (S.A) and in Guatemala
1934 in Brazil and Argentine
1939 in the Libyan Desert.

Gliding tests were also planned for the tropical regions of the Atlantic Ocean. Through these flight tests the possibilities of gliding in various climates was established.

a) The temperate zones (55° - 40° lat) during the summer months offer a good gliding possibilities.

b) The sub-tropical zones (40° - 25° lat) during the whole year and even in the winter (rainy period) almost to the same extent as in the temperature zones. In the summer (dry season) daily. It is worthy of note, that in the subtropical zones during the summer the heights which can be reached in a glider are limited to 3000 m. On account of the thermal layering of the atmosphere (monsoon layering).

c) In the tropical latitudes between the actual tropics there are good possibilities for gliding almost every day.

d) For gliding possibilities over water the difference of temperature between the water and the air is essentially decisive. If the water is warmer than the air, the possibilities for gliding are good. This is reversed when the water-air temperature difference is negative.

New ways of gliding.

The possibilities of motorless flight are not limited to thermal gliding. In 1938 new ways of glidings were discovered, as the so-called wave-gliding. The fundamentals of the means of gliding depend on the formation of stationary waves, thus those remaining on the surface of a flowing medium caused by the obstruction of the bed of the current. The waves form best when the speed of the flow approximates to the speed of the wave. On account of this the waves become stationary. With the approximatetion of the two-velocity values the wave amplitude grows. Besides this it is dependent on the width of the obstruction (especially favorable proportions: Width of obstruction $b = \frac{\lambda}{2}$ or $= \lambda$, wave length $= \lambda$). The exact theoretical solution of this problem of the stationary wave formation depends on the obstructions to the flow. In the atmosphere such waves can occur behind ranges of mountains on the margin of the treposphere and the stratosphere. They are established on many mountain ranges in Germany and have been glided over (Riesen Mts. Thuringer Forest, Teuteberg Forest, Hartz and above all the Alps). They occur behind mountain ranges in every country during suitable wind currents.

Scientific examinations have shown that these waves extend high-up into the stratosphere and makes gliding in the stratosphere possible, thus above 10,000 m. During the scientific examination of this problem by the DFS in the alpine region in the Autumn 1940 an altitude of 11,460 m was reached in motorless flights by the pilot Klockner in the up-current of a large wave. The plane could have reached still greater heights, but the pilot had to abandon the flight on account of the lack of oxygen. In a sufficiently long strip of mountains these waves have extended a very great distance (150-200 km). Apart from the effect of height on man the flight is neither difficult nor dangerous. Trials were carried out by towing the glider into the region of the wave and then after releasing it from the engine aircraft it climed on the up-current of the wave.

From the tests it is anticipated that a height of 20,000 m, possibly more can be reached by wave gliding. It is also considered that waves of this type can occur not only on the mountain ranges but also under definite atmospheric conditions as well as over a plain. The examinations being conducted by the DFS had to be interrupted on account of the war.

In stratosphere gliding there doubtless lies a research problem which is very important and therefore should have been solved. The execution of this stratosphere gliding demanded certain technical assumptions in regard to the glider. Oxygen respiration with a mask is not effective over 12,000 m. It is, therefore, necessary for a glider to possess a pressure cabin if it is to fly in the stratosphere. The DFS has developed such an aircraft but it has not yet been tested. Technical safety measures for an emergency jump from great altitudes ($>$ 15 km) have already been prepared by the DFS.

2) <u>Technical use of the glider.</u>

The technical developments made originally carried out for gliders are of importance for special use in an engine aircraft.

The further development of towed flight (high towing of a glider by means of an engine aircraft) has led to multiple possibilities of use. The original towing methods with a steel rope 80 m long was further developed by the German DFS for the rigid towing of gliders i.e. for an indirect coupling of the glider on the engine aircraft. The coupling consists of a ball link on the engine aircraft and the glider (DFS coupling). Rigid towing has been proved much more simple from the aeronautical point of view. Hard bumps are felt in the flight. The pilot in the glider actually only needs to use the aileron to maintain an upright position in stable flight.

In rigid towing the cargo glider (10 man glider) DFS 230 is flown with the Ju 52, Do 17, He 111.

Rigid towing makes possible blind towing, i.e. towed flights in cloud and at night.

The rigid towing of several gliders behind one another (chain towing) is not possible. Tests abandoned on account of the instability of the towing aircraft. After the introduction of rigid towing this method for coupling two aircraft together in the air in flight suggested itself.

These flights were carried out with a Focke Wulf "Weibe" and a small two engine touring aircraft of the Gothaer Waggon Fabrik (Go No. 2) A simple coupling device was constructed which had withstood a great number of flights. The process should be developed further for the transfer of fuel from one plane to another while in flight. The design was worked out, but never put into production. It was considered that a bomber could take its accompanying fighter in tow with it and couple and uncouple every time. These tests got no farther than the preliminary development stage, they were never put into use.

Further application of towed flight was shaft-towing and towing of a bridge gangway for the transfer of liquids.

With shaft-towing an auxiliary flying body (small wing surface) was coupled on to a rigid shaft (10 m. long steel tube) on one of the fastest aircraft (Me 262) to carry the additional load (fuel, bombs) of the Me 262. Far reaching tests were carried out but not put into use.

An extensive simplification of towing methods were developed by the DFS.

Mistel towing (Pick-a-back towing.

On wing surfaces of the aircraft to be towed the towing aircraft was placed, which could release itself at any time during the flight from the towed aircraft. The first tests were carried out with a "Klemin" aircraft Kl-35 on a DFS-23. For the take-off this aircraft unit was towed up into the air with a tow-rope by a Ju-52. In the next tests a FW "Steesser" was packed onto a DFS 230. This unit could already fly under its own power without losing height but had to have a towed take-off. Finally an Me 109 was fixed on a DFS 230. This unit could take-off itself and fly. Flight was completely unrestricted. The pilot in the lower aircraft scarcely needed to touch the controls. The separation of the two aircraft in flight succeeded and was without risk. It was also possible to land the Mistel unit without separating the two aircraft.

Mistel towing doubtlessly represents the simplest method of towing with the most manifold possibilities of use. (e.g. Bomber and fighter on the wing surfaces of the bomber. Further: Application for Beethoven Ju 188 Me 109)

With the afore-named methods of towing the possibilities of application of towed flight are not yet exhausted. In many other tests (carrying tow) the methods for taking up a glider (DFS 230) from the ground by an aircraft (He 111) should be mentioned.

As a further possible technical use the glider may be used as a piloted model aircraft for testing the flight characteristics of types of aircraft patterns before the first large scale completion of the pattern. This method, which promises great possibilities of application has been very little used up to now. Although the glider research dept. has many times demonstrated these possibilities of application, the recognition of the value of these possibilities has only penetrated in the last year on the part of the Germans. The development of tailless aircraft in this field was not successful.

3) **Use of Gliders as Scientific Research Apparatus.**

The use of gliders for the systematic measuring of the vertical velocities of the air has been explained in 1.

For further scientific work the cargo glider DFS 230 has proved extraordinarily valuable as a flying laboratory, as in this motorless aircraft there is sufficient space to install measuring apparatus and instruments of every kind on a large scale and for service personnel. A load of 1200 kg can be carried.

The great advantage of motorless flight is that a long completely undisturbed flight can be performed, which enables exact measurements and tests to be carried without noise, vibrations and disturbances or danger of fire. The DFS 230 was therefore the most suitable test carrier for the television control tests of the DFS. Further the first systematic aero-electrical measurements in the free atmosphere were carried out with the DFS 230 at any chosen place (circumference of thunderclouds) at any height.

The main problems in respect of glider research on the ground of the foregoing work was as follows:

1) Producing a stratosphere glider for altitudes of 20,000 m.

2) Use of the glider for problem for flight techniques.

   a) Manifold application of towed-flight methods.

   b) Use of the glider as a piloted model aircraft to study the flight performance and characteristics of new types of aircraft patterns.

3) Use of the glider for science.

   a) Supplementing wind tunnel measurements by free flight measurements up to great heights (Mach No. 1)

   b) Use of the glider as a flying laboratory (Television control, electro-optics, aero-electricity etc).

> Translation of Report by
> Prof. Dr., Dr. Ing. Georgii.

3. Georfii gave to our investigators a brief review of the work at DFS. However, a better picture may be obtained from reports prepared, at the request of our investigators, by most of the heads of the various DFS divisions.

4. Institute for aerodynamics. The director, Ruden prepared detailed reports (see enclosures B11, B 12) whose translations follow

B.11.

Prof. Dr. Ing. Habil Ruden   Ainring, 6-12-45

Examinations on the Paul Schmidt-Argus Tube.

Title of the Research Process

Examination on Jet Tubes.

The first construction of the Paul Schmidt-Argus tube had an exposed inlet. The high lead resistance had the result that the tube at the air speed of 600 km/hr did not deliver a practical thrust. With the help of catch diffuser calculation the undersigned gave an inlet casing, with the result, that after its installation the effective thrust still amounted to 80% of the stationary thrust. The inner form of the inlet remained unsatisfactory, its difficulties were in the transition from the circular mizzel cross section to the square cross section of the flap-box. The insufficient airing of the corners resulted in rapid burning of the spring-values. With model-experiments such inner forms were developed, which guaranteed a better airing of the corners. Due to this measure the grade of effectiveness was not considerably improved.

For study of stationary currents in the flap-box demonstrative experiments in the smoke-channel were conducted a special test stand for quantitive measuring of the flap-box losses could not be undertaken.

RUDEN

Prof. Dr. Ing. Habil Ruden. Ainring, 6-12-45

Catch Diffusors

Title of the research process

1. Transmission of the even catch-diffusor theory to rotation symmetrical catch diffusors.

2. Wind channel examinations on tails-forms

3. Examination on catch diffusors

4. Theory of the effect of air currents on oblique catch diffusors

5. Shallow water examination on the Mach influence on catch diffusors

6. Examination on inner-forms of the catch diffusors.

The work of the institute for aerodyhamic and flight mechanic of the DFS on catch diffusors originated from examinations of the undersigned on level catch diffusors. In the year book of 1940 reported theory allowed the calculation of symmetrical catch-diffusors for given velocity ratios of the muzzle velocity for velocity of flow and given maximum super velocity. The maximum super velocity always appears at delayed muzzle-flow in the outer spare of the catch diffusors and it must be kept, with regard to the Mach number influence, at approximation on the sonic velocity, within small limits. Explaining the matter further, it must be said, that under a catch diffusor every arrangement is undersoot, which has the duties of leading a part of the outer air into the aircraft. To this category belong all cooling intakes, engine cowling, intakes of special power units and suction hoods of all types.

The continuation of the original work consisted mostly of completing the theory and the particularization of simple calculation methods. If the original theory was patterned on the advanced calculation of catch diffusors for a certain velocity ratio of the muzzle velocity for velocity of flow, the extended theory could also give the pressure distribution at different muzzle velocities, as the one which was based on the design. These arrangements had the assumption of symmetrical catch-diffusor forms at direction of the on-blowing current. In the mean time wind channel examination showed, that the pressure distribution at oblique on-blowing of the symmetrical catch diffusors showed fast undesirable suction points. In order to avoid this, theoretical examination over oblique on-blown catch diffusors were conducted. A concluding theory could not be provided, however, useful estimates were obtained.

The next step was the transfer of the even theory on rotation symmetrical catch diffusors. Considering the relationship of the rotation symmetrical and even potentials simple conversion calculations could be given, for which confirmation in the wind channel is still outstanding. Because the tail-form of the catch diffusor is not included in the theory, a series of tests with different tail forms were conducted in the wind channel. It showed, that the tail form has very little influence, as to resistance, and also on pressure distribution of the catch diffusor.

When approaching the sonic velocity, there appears in the nozzle and also in the outer spare of the catch diffusor pressure thrusts which influence its intake ability and its resistance. In order to find a solution has the type of pressure thrust formation the shallow water analogy was exploited and several photographs of the current were taken in a temporary shallow water basin, F final examination were to be conducted in a larger basin.

With the ideal catch diffusor the delay of flow is shifted into the free flow before the diffusor. With the result of thick appearing walls, when the super speed on the outer contact must be held at a minimum. In order to make the wall thickness suitable for further pressure increase a part of the current delay is shifted with the technical application of the catch-diffusor to the inner space of the inlet the form of this inner-diffuson will remain free. The next device would be, to choose a normal conical inner-diffusor. Its grade of effectiveness at steeper expansion is bad and the maximum grade of effectiveness at greater expansion of about $8° - 12°$ is at the most ol 8. The reason for this is the strong pressure increase which the boundary layer has to overcome on the walls. It was the problem of the research, to produce a diffusor which showed little or no pressure increase along side the walls. Forms of this type were first reported from Hara and Nisimura. With these forms a strong pressure minimum appears at the end of the diffusors, which unfortunately is accompanied by a strong cross current. Of i.e. a cooling-black fellows on air inner diffusor. The cooling-grid must turn the current more than $60°$. This is only possible with small grid-partitions of the cooling grid under great losses from the institute of the undersigned the problem was started, to produce these forms, which avoid the low pressure point at the end of the inner diffusor. Also the cross current is reduced under pressure. Actually i.e. The maximum necessary turning is limited to $60°$ at an expansion ratio of 1:2. For this ratio, closed formulas for the inner contour could be given. The form of the inner-diffusor can be determined through step-like approach with other expansion ratios.

The theory of the catch-diffusers give in every case only explanations on free rotating, pronounced idealistic forms. Its application in the technique still requires numerous special examinations and consideration. i.e. a pre-switched boundary layer is of deciding significance for the intake capacity of the catch diffuser.

The institute of the undersigned was consulted numerous times by industry in order to gain support through advice and wind channel experiments. The advice was also desired, if neither even nor rotation symmetrical catch-diffusers with oval cross-sections were applied. Difficulties were encountered when the muzzle-chene^2 did not lige vertically to the on-flowing direction (Catch diffusors with swept back wings).

In conclusion it must be said, that research in this field made considerable progress, however, many questions of the technic still remain unanswered.

RUDEN.

Prof. Dr. Ing. Habil Ruden   Ainring 6-9-45

Slip-stream Examinations

Title of the Research process.

1. Theory of the wing surface in the slip stream.

2. Wind channel measurements of the wing surface in the slip stream.

3. Wind channel measurements on control surfaces in the slip stream and descending current of the wing surface.

4. Slip-stream examination.

5. Theory of the slip-stream on the windmilling oblique on -blown propeller.

The slip stream examinations of the undersigned are based on the theoretical work on the influence of dissimilar dynamic-pressure distribution on wing surface profiles and this work deals exclusively with the level profiles. This study had the surprising result, that the profile thickness has an influence of the first order onlift and moment, when the dynamic pressure distribution various cross-wise to the direction of the span. It is understood that the effectiveness of the angle of attack and the zero-lift angle is dependent on the dynamic pressure distribution and must be pre-calculated according to the previously named work. With wind channel measurements the theoretical statement could be confirmed and supplemented. Skilful connection of the previously mentioned examination with the consideration of Kenig (Durand, aerodynamic theory, vol. IV or the work of Vandrey, the space problem of interference between wing surface and slip stream could be solved satisfactorily. Wind channel examinations which were only partly concluded and whose evaluation is not completed, confirmed this view.

All theoretical consideration which were completed up to this date had the hypothesis of leaping (unsteady) change of dynamic pressure. Recently new expressions have been formulated which are applicable on straight linear but steady dynamic pressure variation. It remains to be seen, if the pre-calculation of the slip-stream influence on the wing surface is quantatively improved.

If the propeller is blown-on at an oblique angle, the slip stream is diverted toward the oblique propeller axis. The usual impulse expressions returned these diversions incompletely. For this reason examinations were started, which would describe the diversion of the slip stream more accurately, but mainly in the vicinity of the propeller surfaces. The theory which works with the pressure potential, however is limited to the nominally loaded propeller.

The application of these examinations on the flight mechanic showed that three partial problems were successful:

1. Prediction of lift increase through the slip-stream during take off, especially the application of these calculations on the take off of sea planes.

2. Prediction on the influence of the slip-stream and wing surface work on the static longitudinal stability of normal tail-aircrafts. It had to be considered, that the work of the wing surface at approximately the Mach number 1 is expanded to a great degree through thrust waves and accordingly exerts increased effectiveness on the elevators. Prediction of variations of load at increased speed and throttling and sudden change of the wing surface wash through release of flow and Mach number influence.

3. Application of the slip-stream examination on the dynamic lateral stability of multi-engined aircraft with twin lateral controls. It was proved, that the static lateral stability was influenced to great degree through shrinking of the lateral controls, when the lateral controls assume certain positions toward the slip-stream. Because the damping is changed very little or not at all through this measure the possibility remains, to change the ratio of the half-lift period to the oscillation period in a desired way

with completed aircraft through a simple measure. The theoretical considerations were confirmed in the wind channel through oscillation experiments and found its application in the He 219 and others.

RUDEN.

Prof. Dr. Ing Habil Ruden   Ainring 6-11-45

Examination of grids (title of research process)

The installation of string axial blower and exhaust turbines in TL power units animated the examinations on axial Fleigeliader (?) and especially on the reciprocal influence of the grid profile. (The calculation of the axial blower is based on the conception, that the star-like arranged profile series, which is limited by two co-axial close adjoining cylinder sections, is equivalent to an even profile grid). On the reciprocal profile influence of the even grids foundational work of Schilhause and Weinig is available. However it is limited to use of their profile. Even in previous work the undersigned established a considerable influence of the profile thickness. The calculation however assumed large grid division. In a new, but not completed work this limitation could be removed. Demonstrative experiments in the smoke channel confirmed this theory. It was proved, that a profile grid of thin, straight, tin profiles does not divert the current, when the profiles include the angle of attack with the direction of air-flow, however a diversion of the current appears immediately, when the profiles remain symmetrical and retain the angle of attack zero, but finally become thick. The new theory could also remove a second deciding condition, namely, that the profiles have only nominal angle of attacks against the center directi(of flow and are only slightly curved. Both are conditions, which only have any value with the tight grid division of the axial blower and turbines at a lesser number of the completed type. The new theory should be of great significance for the correct pre-calculation of axial circular machines.

RUDEN

Prof. Dr. Ing. Habil Ruden.   Ainring 6-11-45

Examination on the influence of the surface roughness on laminar profiles.

Title of the research process

1. Roughness examinations on the DFS 230
2. Research glider DFS 332.

In order to determine the roughness influence of natural camouflage paint on a special equipped cargo glider of the DFS 230 type, boundary layer, Nachlauf (Wash?) and pressure distribution measurement on a wing section were conducted during flight. From this section the profile polares were determined. The result was, that the washable camouflage paint ("night-black" which was used on night fighters at that time, caused an air increase in resistance of app. 25%. This extraordinary pronounced increase in resistance originated largely through the sharp movement of the reverse-point on the pressure side. The ascertained polars assign each ca-value a certain velocity. With the velocity the Reynolds-number necessarily changes so that a varied Reynolds number belongs to a varied value. With the critical Reynolds number appears the above reactioned movement of the reverse point and manifests itself in a sharp change of resistance in the course of the polars of the rough profile (the reverse point movement was ascertained through special boundary layer measurement). In connection with these examinations a larger camouflage paint series was tested with the result that such a paint could be applied, which, with sufficient light absorption was less rough than the camouflage paint "night-black".

The maximum speed of the DFS 230 is limited to a little over 200 km/hr for reasons of stability. A compulsory upper limit resulted for the highest obtainable Reynolds number, which could only be pushed a little over the critical Reynolds-number of the even plate. The DFS 230 was not suitable for the examination on the influence of the surface roughness and even less, for the examination of laminar profiles. Construction of a special research-glider with greater speed was suggested, which should provide at the same time profiles variations by a simple method. The suggestion provided for a twin fuselaged aircraft with moveable center wing and was given for construction to the sister-Institute for glider-flight (Dipl. Eng. Kracht, DFS 332). The flight examination on the influence of surface roughness and on laminar profiles were to be continued after completion of the DFS 332 from the institute of the undersigned. In order to hasten the work two research gliders were ordered at the same time and one was to be at the disposal for the institute of the undersigned and the other one for the institute for flight mechanic and aerodynamics of the DVL.

RUDEN.

Prof. Dr. Ing. Habil Ruden   Ainring 6-11-45

Theory of the Fuselage.

(Title of the Research Process)

The usual calculation of pressure distribution on fuselages which were not ellipsoid, dependent on singularity process where the signularities are distributed length-wise on the (straight linear) fuselage axis or on the surface. Because this process is very difficult at the present time, its practical application is limited to rotation symmetrical fuselages.

A new process free from both inconveniences was available originated by my collaberator Prof. F. K. Schmidt. It resulted from the strict solution of the potential problem for ellipsoid (straight and oblique blown-on) and determines the pressure distribution of now ellipsoidical fuselages according to a method which is related to the interference calculation of astronomy.

With this process one does not only include all rotation symmetrical types of fuselages which cause into the question but all fuselages which do not have circular cross-sections and even curved center lives, in other words all types which may appear in the aircraft construction. This process is tested extensively on example calculation, however the combined presentation is still outstanding

RUDEN

Prof. Dr. Eng. Habil Ruden　　　　　　　　　　　　Ainring 6-9-45

Examination of Ground Effects

Almost all previous examination of ground effect are limited to the knowledge of the influence of currents by the ground. According to this, a ground effect is only to be expected for the wing surface of finate span. In a theoretical work the undersigned could prove, that even the problem of the wing surface of infinite span showed a noticeable ground effect. As in the problem of the wing surface profile in the vicinity of unsteady dynamic pressure changes, the finite profile thickness has here a most important influence on lift and pitching moment. A series of tests were conducted in the wind channel for the test of this theory, which the theoretical result confirmed. As secondary result the wind channel test contains a comparison of different processes for the representation of the ground effect and these examinations were conducted with a ground plate and also with a polished wing diaphram. As expected, the ground plate due to its formation of the boundary layer gave unsatisfactory values. The wind channel examination was extended for establishing error possibilities which can originate from inaccurate regulations of the wing diaphragm.

RUDEN.

Prof. Dr. Ing. Habil Ruder

"Falling Off" Investigations.

Title given by research Management.

1. Flight measurements on the He 280 (Polar, "falling off" measurements)

2. Research aircraft P 1068.

The question of "falling off" cannot only be solved in the wind tunnel because the course of the breaking away of the flow is essentially influenced by the dynamic behavior of the movements of the aircraft. On this account the flight measurements indicated below are taken by the institute for the purpose of studying the question on a larger scale. For examining the "falling-off" behavior the research management placed at our disposal the He 280, which is a twin engine aircraft. It was only constructed in a few V patterns and was never put into mass preduction. Two of these aircraft were handled over to the DFS for research purposes. The polars of the He 280 were measured before flight without the TL engine. The measuring process was largely the following: The He 280 was towed up to a height of 5000 m, detached from tow and then flown out in stationary stages of speed. The polars were ascertained by the falling speed method, in which the indicated drift angle was carefully maintained at zero, at the same time however, the landing even method was tried, which is essentially quicker and cheaper because it permits all the polars to be measured in a single flight. As already known, characteristic differences of the two poles are given. It does not appear possible to achieve a complete agreement, even if one applies corrections, which takes into consideration the hysteresis of the instrument pointer and the dependency of the lift on the angle of attack during the unstationary variation of the angle of attack. Particularly with the landing run method an essentially higher ca max is given than with the falling speed method.

The real problem, namely the "falling off" investigations were in the first place on the He 280 in its delivered condition. The wing surfaces were not particularly smooth and the shape of the wings was just as the manufacturer had left them. The edges of the wings were essentially elliptical. The profiles were Piercy-Günther profiles. The designing engineer intended the thickness and nose radius to be reduced lineally outward. Through the elongation a minimum at about 82% of the half the span occurs in the nose radius as well as in the thickness of the profile.

The "falling off" investigation in which the formation of flow was made discernible by filaments of wool, shows how, the breaking off of flow begun steadily in the region of the above mentioned minimum, whereby the left side has the advantage through an insignificant difference of shape. The "falling off" process itself is largely determined by the speed of operation of the elevator. If the operation of the elevator was so slow that a noticeable difference remained between the breaking off to the left and the right, the aircraft would tip in a wild manner and lose a few hundred meters height, before it could be caught. The process was most clear if the elevator was held in the position in which the tipping toward the left began. If the elevator was drawn rapidly through the critical region, the aircraft goes into easily controllable stalled flight. It still has to be noticed that the results remained fundamentally the same, whether the tipping process was introduced at a drift angle of 0 or the drift angles of + 5° and -5°.

The program further provided for the systematic alterations of the shape of the profile. The most simple technical solution was to vary the profile by filling it with a foamy substance and smoothing in the manner required. The fact that definite, though small, changes of the moment of inertia occur was consciously taken into consideration. By changing the shape of the profile the course of the radius of the leading edge along the span and also the course of the profile thickness systematically changed. Fundamentally, however, the sharp-cornered leading edges were excluded although at times they were applied to finished aircraft and provided a very effective means because a sharp leading edge constantly reduces the profile drag. The above mentioned investigations have for the most part been tested in the air and evaluated. Only their systematic working now remains.

Further investigations on the influence of the engine nacelles should be carried out with the He 280 and above all the influence of the inertia moment. This program could not be put into effect to date.

The wing of the He 280 is characterized by a straight leading edge. High velocity research has now shown that the sharply swept back wing is superior to the unswept back wing on approaching Mach Nos. 1. On the other hand one knows that the "falling off" behavior is worse immediately behind swept-back wings than is the case with wings with a straight leading edge or right in front of the sweptback wings, it was necessary to extend the "falling off" investigations to wings with a sharper sweep back (sweep back angle + 25°, + 05°, - 25°). For this purpose the project P 1068 was selected by the undersigned in common with the Firm Heinkel.

This aircraft, which in the final production should likewise have a TL engine, was designed in a reduced scale model (1 : 2) as a glider with wings of varying sweep-back, and handed over to the sister institute for gliding (Kracht) for construction. The measuring of falling off peculiarities should have been undertaken by the institute of the undersigned (i.e. Ruden) in the usual manner on the He 280. As the P 1068 has not been completed yet, these measurements are still outstanding. In consideration of technical development the matter is a very urgent one.

RUDEN.

Prof. Dr. Ing. Ruden　　　　　　　　　　　　　　　　　　　　　Ainring 9-6-45

Static measurements of flight characteristics

(Title given by the research management)

In 1944 the DVL, in conjunction with other German research institutes, made experiments to compile models for testing flight characteristics. The result was that no clear opinions existed concerning the required flight characteristic. In order to remove these obstacles a series of known good performing and a series of poorly performing planes were to be examined through models belonging to the DVL.

The institute to which the undersigned belonged received a part of this task developing first an apparatus which was to make possible to carry out measurements on all possible types of aircraft. Besides control-force measuring apparatus instruments for measuring speed, angle of drift, static pressure, and the angular velocity around all three axes were installed. This apparatus was first installed in the K 125 and measurements were carried out according to the T.O. for same. Further measurements were considered for the HE 111 and Me 163. They were never carried out. The DVL had planned similar measurements on other types of which the Me 262 was the only one that had been more or less completed.

RUDEN

Prof. Dr. Ing. Ruden　　　　　　　　　　　　　　　　　　　　　Ainring 9-6-45

Lateral Stability investigation

on the DFS 230

Professor Scheichting published a work a short time ago on a simple theory of lateral stability with free controls. The simplication consists in permitting only two degrees of freedom "rotation about the high axis" and the degree of freedom "rotation about the lateral control axis" The toleration of this simplication is to be tested in flight.

The test was carried out with two shapes of lateral control surfaces and an even sided stabilizing unit with a rectangular edge. With both these stabilizing units the rotatine axis of the control surfaces is brought into three different positions.

In order to ascertain the fundamental theory sufficiently accurately, the yawing stability was ascertained independent of the drift moment and the deflection of the lateral control surfaces in flight.

The stability investigations included the photographing of oscillations about the high and longitudinal axis of the aircraft. Oscillating periods and damping were evaluated. Results showed very little deviations from the simple theory with fixed control surfaces. It cannot thus be expected that the theory would satisfactorily reproduce the stability with a free control surface.

RUDEN.

Prof. Dr. Ing. Habil Ruden. Ainring 6-9-45

Examination of Tow Procedures

Title of the research process:

1. Pole-tow

2. Tow apparatus for carrying heavy loads.

In the course of time various tow procedures were developed from the DFS according to need. Accurate examination on stability and performance requirement were not undertaken. In flight tests were in most cases sufficient.

In the meantime the question of suitable balance of the tow procedures become more urgent so that it became necessary to start examination on performance requirement, stability and flight characteristics of the individual tow possibilities. The undersigned had the aim to report the flight mechanic of the tow flight in one comprehensive representation. If the examination consisted of a supplementary accurate test of the two squadron with tow-tope, rigid tow, carrying tow and mistel tow the institute of the undersigned had a leading part in the development of the pole tow. The pole tow is different from all types of towing because only one coupling point is allowed. This procedure followed by the Fa Fieseler, was not successful, because due to the tolerance of the grade of free rolls, static and dynamic stability around the longitudinal axis was not assured. If the grade of free rolls is omitted, a faultless tow with pilotless tow apparatus is possible. This pole tow apparatus was designed for all uses. In the foreground stood the carrying of bulky loads and the auxiliary tank for fast aircrafts (Me 262, Arado 234). The natural oscillation of the pole caused an oscillation of the tow apparatus to appear at high speeds, which made the continuation of the flight in tow impossible. When the actual frequency of the pole is considerably increased and increase of this critical air speed is possible.

RUDEN

Prof. Dr. Ing. Habil Ruden   Ainring 6-11-45

Project "Eber"

The project "Eber" was worked out from the institute of the undersigned under commission of the research management. The "Eber" is a short range fighter similar to the "Natter" but with the difference of the "Natter" where the self start from the ground is abandoned. More consideration was given to start and raising the apparatus in pole-tow with help of the Me 262 or the FW 190. At the altitude of the bomber squadron the "Eber" was to be released at a distance of 5-10 km behind the squadron and speeded up with r-apparata. At a greater height than the bomber squadron of approximately 300-400 m. The run was calculatively sufficient in order to reach and attack the bomber squadron which was assumed with a closing speed of at least 100 m/sec. A second attack was possible through the power resume of the installed r-apparata. The equipment of the "Eber" consisted of a salvo-gun and heavy armament of the pilot. At first it was considered to carry out one attack as a ram attack. Closer examination persuaded as to drop the ram attack (compare the report ram-attack) and perform two attacks. The project was not completed owing to the lack of production capacity and also to the limited capacity for use. The consideration originated from the fact that the union fighter and "Eber" at comparably small performance loads of the tow aircraft experiences a loss of speed of approx. 100 km/h. With strong air superiority it must be reckoned with that the tow union will be easy prey for the enemy if the latter attacks from greater height.

RUDEN.

Prof. Dr. Ing. Habil Ruden   Ainring 6/9/45

Load Discharge

Approximately two years ago the question of low altitude load discharge was presented to the institute. The experiment, to find a way with the help of rocket brakes, was accomplished but the application of this process was out of the question because the low altitude discharge became impossible due to tactical reason.

The institute continued the development of the load discharge with rocket brakes from high altitudes and applied two methods which were both successful. The first method provided for exact altitude measurement and release of the rocket brake after a certain drop-period, the second method worked with an advanced ground feeler which releases the R-brakes when touching the ground.

                                        RUDEN.

Prof. Dr. Ing. Habil Ruden   Ainring 6-9-45

Examination on glide and snow skids

On new projects the question arose if the landing gear of the intercepter fighters, which anyway has to abandon the self-start, should be emitted and replaced with simple skids. In order to obtain more accurate values on the friction co-efficient, a whirling arm was used to determine the friction of wood on wood, steel on wood, rubber on wood and the corresponding values were determined on a concrete foundation. Of special interest was the effect of simple water lubrication studied at the time snow skids were examined and for the clarification of the processes, considerations and measurements were conducted.

                                        RUDEN.

Prof. Dr. Ing. Habil Ruden.   Ainring 6/12/45

Ram Attack Examinations.

Recently the question on the prospects of success of the ram attack appeared time and time again, and at the same time the problem of how the pilot can be saved, had to be solved.

The mechanical process of ramming was studied on a model experiment where a falling weight hit a cylinder shaped aircraft fuselage representing structure. These examinations were to determine the magnitude of the thrust impulses, the effective duration and the energy requirement, which at least can now be estimated.

To protect the pilot from unbearable accelerations (100 g and more) a push seat must be provided, which reduces the thrust point over a damped spring or a suitable energy destroying construction (i.e. a rope, which splits a board lengthwise during the thrust process). Construction difficulties were encountered in the accommodation of sufficient spring tracks. Finally further consideration on the rest-body, its movement and on the exit of the pilot had to follow for the purpose of baling out a catapult seat with parachute was planned, which is very promising, but unfortunately has not bee manufactured or tested

RUDEN

Prof. Dr. Ing Ruden   Ainring 12-6-45

Gliding Bomb Projects.

The first rough drafts showed the gliding bomb with its relatively large density, was expected to have many special difficulties in flight stability. Two things limit its accuracy of hitting the target. The first: conditions of take-off from the carrying plane; two: small inaccuracies in construction. In order not to endanger the carrying plane the gliding bomb will have to be dropped at a flying speed which is less than its stationary trajectory. It means that the flight will have to be started with phygoid oscillation which in itself will mean that a change of the main point of impact will result from it. The precalculations for this change resulted in the first theoretic examination. A second task concerned itself with tolerable insymmetrical construction which appeared to be possible in the pretended picture of impact. The result as that gyro-control was unavoidable.

The introduction of gyro-control also solved the stabilization difficulties immediately. Its further development was given to the institute for air equipment (Prof. Fischel).

The best solution for the frame was an "all wing bomb" having a wing with small side ratio. The characteristics of such frames, especially the study of wings with small side ratios, were given great attention in the wind tunnel at the institute. A conclusive adaption, however, is still outstanding.

                                                      RUDEN.

Prof. Dr. Ing. Habil Ruden   Ainring 6/9/45

Rope Release Device

(Problem of the research Management)

A Berlin company suggested a droppable bomb, suspended on a rope of 1000 m length and parachute for the purpose of a bomber obstruction and the research management commissioned the institute of the undersigned for its consideration. The tests proved, that the parachute only has a chance to survive the opening thrust, when a rope release device with a suitable brake drum is installed in the bomb. The generation of heat is so great that a cooling system must be provided. Therefore the undersigned suggested a vaporization cooler calculatively a water volume of approximately one liter was sufficient.

Although the complete construction was so complicated that a mass production could not be recommended, at least one apparatus, which was already completed should be tested. This test was for the purpose of giving a decision for the reoccuring suggestions. Due to little interest and the fuel shortage the tests were not performed.

RUDEN.

Prof. Dr. Eng. Habil Ruden   Ainring 6-9-45

Project "Natter"

The project "Natter" was worked out by the La Baibem, Waldree. The "Natter" is a flight apparatus which is started from the ground with the help of R-apparatas and a Walter power unit for the purpose of attacking bomber squadrons flying overhead. The DFS conducted several pre-examination to determine the flight characteristics of the "Natter" and provided personnel and equipment in Waldsee tests. The test of the flight characteristics were to be conducted in carrying tow to an altitude of 5000 m and at this altitude to change over to normal rope-tow for measuring important mechanical flight factors. The change-over from carrying tow to rope tow did not succeed, because strong angle of incident oscillations appeared so that the pilot lost control over the "Natter". Therefore a flight was started whereby the "Natter" was brought to an altitude and then released. After the release the "Natter" was dropped to 2000 m in order to assume the required speed, then flown out in a horizontal flight to minimum speed (Alfang polar) and dropped an additional 1000 m and tested in several flight curves. The speed was to be registered during this procedure. Due to the failure of the measuring apparata the readings of the pilot had to suffice. After finishing the measuring flight the pilot baled out of the "Natter" and saved himself with a parachute.

As result of the flight a good controllability around all axis, sufficient Ca max. and sufficient stability was proved. An additional flight which was to determine more accurate stabilities could not be conducted.

In the meantime several ground starts were conducted in Waldsee over which results Dipl. Eng. Zarber should be consulted.

RUDEN.

Prof. Dr. Ing. Ruden   Ainring 6/9/45

Wind Tunnel Experiments.

Upon request of the industry a series of wind tunnel experiments were completed. In most cases these measurements were conducted by factory specialists and its developments completed by the industry. In several instances as i.e. the measurement of the Me 328, the numerous wind tunnel measurements were worked out from the institute and developed at length to important aerodynamical increase measures.

A greater test series was dedicated to the aerodynamics of the brake flaps, whereby the brake flaps were changed according to size and angle on the wing profile and studied accordingly to its brake effect and the influence on the lift and moment.

RUDEN.

Prof. Dr. Eng. Habil Ruden   Ainring 6-9-45

Shallow Water Basin

Evidently between the compressible current and the shallow water current there exists a close relationship which permits changing from one current type to the other. Despite the fact that the shallow water analogy is limited to even problems, and undoubtedly errors occur through the split between model and shallow water basin, the shallow water-tow channel however can be applied successfully. The primary effort is extraordinarily small. The velocity coming from the sonic-velocity amounts in our case to 1 m/sec. No difficulties are encountered with the shallow water basin at passage of the sonic velocity. (They would also appear, as with the wind tunnels, when the angle of the towed model with still water were set like the still model in turbulant water). The shallow water channel of the institute could unfortunately not be completed. However, several examinations were conducted numerous times in a temporary construction.

RUDEN.

Prof. Dr. Ing. Habil Ruden   Ainring 6-9-45

Free Flight Tunnel

Title of the research process:
Model Wind Tunnel.

The free flight tunnel will make it possible to combine flight movements with aerodynamic studies. A construction of this type for "Abkipp" examinations is of considerable important. Aerodynamical stabilities could be determined easier and faster in the free-flight tunnel than with test flights. In order to study the possibilities of such a tunnel, a small model-tunnel was constructed which is moveable around vertical and cross axes. Its cross section is $1m^2$, its maximum valocity app. 20 m/sec. Both sizes are too small to be sufficient for the requirements of the "prazis". Tunnel size and tunnel velocity must be measured according to the least allowable Reynolds number of the control surface. With regard to the depth of the control surface, the Reynolds number must at least amount to $2-3 \times 10^5$. Applied to the free flight tunnel, a necessary cross section resulted of app. 4×4^2 at a velocity of appr. 50 m/sec. Due to the lack of working material the development of the free-flight tunnel was not supported the model-tunnel was used for the examination of some tow possibilities.

                                                        RUDEN.

B.12.

Report on Landing Skids.

Chief Specialist: Dipl. Ing. Rudolf Kreyser
               Freillassing, Watzmannskr 21.

Publications: Kreyser, Examinations of landing skids.
              (2 part report. UM)

Examinations of snow-skis were made by Dr. Fuchs, Kramsach-Achenrain/Tirol.
A report on glide friction on snow is in existence. UM...

Report on Wind Tunnel Tests

The examinations carried out on brake flaps were published by Heinrich Voepel in the Year Book of the Deutsche Luftfahrtforschung 1940 (?)

Report on Ramming Investigations

Specialist: Prof. Dr. Ruden, Ainring Siedlung, Wielandshag
            Dr. Schapitz, Reichenhall-Karlstein 51.

A report was being worked on, one part is safe at the airport, the other part has been lost. It would take 6 weeks to complete the work with the help of two specialists (see above) one mathematician and one draftsman.

Report on Discharge of Load.

Specialist: Dipl. Ing. Schieferdecker, now at Chieming, Schreinerei Ellmayer.

Publications: Schieferdecker: Ultra short-wave Schwan-see for use up to 5000 in above the see. UM 3525.
It would take two months to complete with the help of one specialist (Dipl. Ing. Schieferdecker) and one technical assistant.

Translation of report by RUDEN

Report on Investigations of the Slipstream.

Specialist: Prof. Dr. Ruden, Ainring, Siedlung Wielandshag.
Prof. Dr. Hopf, Bayerisch Gmain, Hans Salas.
The Aerodynamist Franlein Eichmer.
Zwingenberg, a.d.b. Gartenfeld 1.

Work commenced about 1938.

Publications:

(1) Ruden: Lecture on wing profiled in proximity to desultory Nowae pressi changes, delivered at the Lilienthae Sessions on question of control surfaces in Friedrichshafen in 1938 Lilienthae report No. 62.

(2) Ruden: More recent investigations on wing profiles in the neighbourhood of desultory dyhamic pressure changes. Lecture at the Lilianthae session in Augsburg 1939. Lilienthae report No...

(3) Ruden: Theory of wing profiles in the neighbourhood of dynamic pressure changes. Year Book of the German Air Research 1939.

(4) Ruden: The NACA profiles in the neighbourhood of desultory dynamic pressure changes. Year book of the German Air Research 1939

(5) Ruden: Wind Tunnel measurements. Year book of the German Air Research 1940

(6) Ruden: On the influence of the slipstream on the dynamic lateral stability of multi motor aircraft with double keel-shaped lateral controls. Lecture delivered to the Lilienthae Session on Lateral Stability at Jena 1940 Lilienthae report No...

(7) Ruden: Wind Tunnel measurements on the lateral stability of aircraft with double keel-shaped lateral controls. Lecture delivered to the Flight Mechanics Committee of the Academy of German Air Research 1942. Publication of the Academy of German Air Research.

(8) Ruden: On the slipstream and its influence on the static and dynamic stability of the aircraft.
Lecture delivered to the academic session at Bad Eilsen. May 1944.
The print has not yet been produced. The manuscript has been lost. The re-writing of the last named manuscript would take six weeks.
Personnel necessary: one specialist (Prof. Dr. Ruden) two draftsmen and the help of the photographic section.
The manuscript for the application of the theory on spatial slipstream problems with the additional help of the Koning-Vandrey Theory has likewise been lost. The re-writing of this manuscript together with the evaluation of the partly available wind tunnel measurement for testing the theory would require two months.
Personnel necessary: 2 specialists (Prof. Dr. Ruden and Franlein Eichner) Two mathematicians, one draftsman and the photographic section.

The manuscript on the obliquely on-blown weakly loaded slipstream may likewise be partly in existence. It would take about four months to complete the work. Personnel required: 1 specialist (Prof. Dr. Hopf) 2 mathematicians and 1 draftsman.

The theory of wing profiles in the neighbourhood of linear dynamic pressure distribution only exists in statements. It would take four months to complete the work with one specialist (Prof. Dr. Ruden) one mathematician and one draftsman.

Report on Calculations for Tactical Flight Mechanics

Specialist: Prof. Dr. Ruden, Ainring Siedlung Wielandshag
Prof. Dr. F. K. Schmidt, Reichenhall Hohenzollernstr 15.

A preliminary report on straight accelerated flight movements and on accelerated curved flights was in preparation. Under the assumption that insufficient basic material is available the completion would require six weeks. Personnel required: two specialists (see above) two mathematicians, one draftsman in conjunction with the photographic dept.

Report on the Paul Schmidt Argus-intake

Specialist: Prof. Dr. Ruden, Ainring, Siedlung, Wielandshag
Dipl.Ing. Frolich, Ainring, Feldkirchen Behelfsheimsiedlung

The experimental work on the inlet were given to Dr. Eisele for inclusion in his report. A film was made of unstationary movements in flap boxes which is probably to be found amongst the material safe at the airport.

Report on the Free-flight Tunnel

Specialist: Prof. Dr. Ruden, Ainring Siedlung Wielandshag
Dipl. Ing. Ruchti, Darmstadt-Eberstadt, Boelckestr. 45.

Prof. Ruden edited a record of the main work carried out, which may have been lost.

Fundamental drawings and designs of the main work were worked out in cooperation with Prof. Ruden of the construction management of the DFS (Ing. Brannig, Ing. Drenkelfort). It cannot be established yet, whether they are still available.

Report on Falling-off Investigations

Specialist: Stud. Assessor Runkel, Freilassing Ludwigzellerstr 24.
Publications: Runkel, Falling off Investigation with the He 280 V7
UM 3530/2

The second named publication reports on the aircraft He 280 in the condition as delivered. Pressure distribution measurements on a section of the profile of the He 280 and likewise impulse measurements were not published. The same applies to the "falling off" investigations with changed nose radius and changed profile thickness. The completion of these reports would take two months each. Personnel required: 1 specialist (Stud. Assessor Runkel) three mathematicians, 1 draftsman in conjunction with the photographic dept. The data for this was moved to Ebnermuhle and have meantime been secured at the airfield.

The investigation indicated in the main report on the influence of enging nacelles and of inerta ellipsoids assumes the return of the measuring devices and would take about three months to execute in favorable weather conditions. The "falling off" investigations for swept-back wings after completion of the aircraft P1068 would take six months in favorable weather conditions. Personnel required would be the same as for investigations of the DFS 232.

The Report on Glide Bomb Projects.

Publications by Gobel FB and Plato-Jank FB, house reports by Schieferdecker. Lennertz, Feder and four wind tunnel reports. It is not known whether the basic data still exists.

  Report Project Natter
       Project Eber
       Rope Launching device.

Specialist: (1) Dipl. Ing. Tacher (Project Natter)
     (2) Prof. Dr. Ruden and Dipl. Ing. Schieferdecker (Project Eber).
     (3) Dipl. Ing. Schieferdecker (Rope launching device)

In all these cases no reports are in existence. They could each be produced in 4 weeks by one specialist and one technical assistant.

Report on the Shallow water basin.

Specialists: Prof. Dr. Ruden, Ainring Siedlung Llielandshag
      Dipl. Ing. Frolich, Ainring, Feldkirchen, Behelfsheimsiedlung.

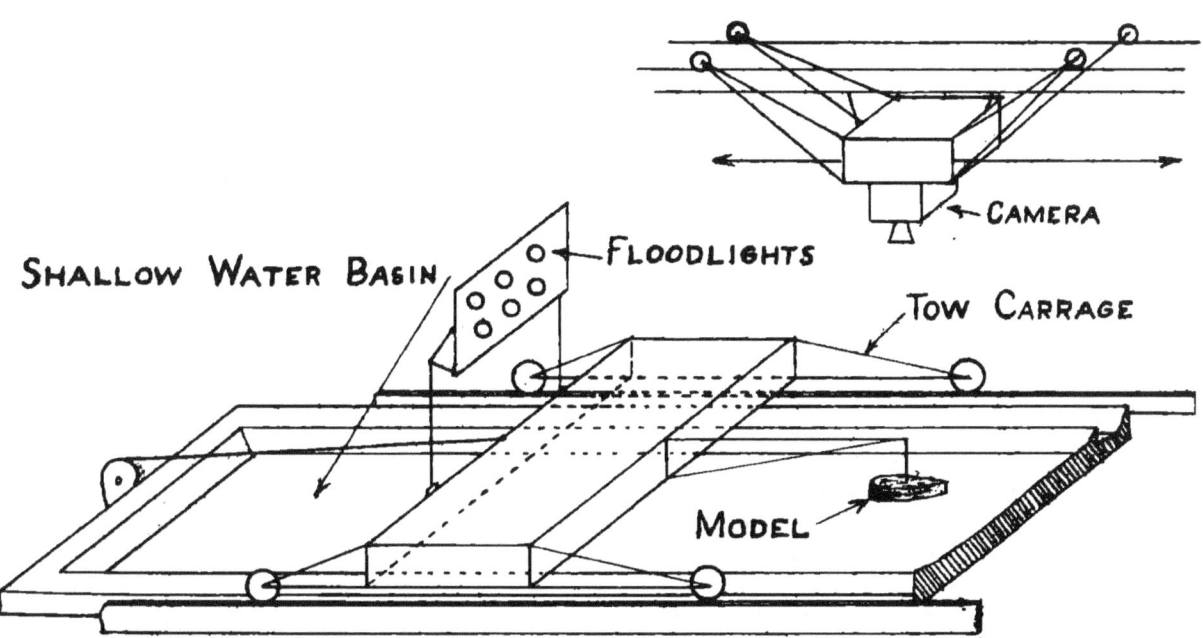

Construction of the shallow water basin see sketch. Two house reports by Dipl. Ing. Frolich are in existence on the shallow water basin. They are to be found together with some photographic material safe at the airport.

Report on Manual control measurements.

Specialist: Dipl. Ing. Zacher, Prien Flugplatz
Dipl. Ing. Herbert Hartmann, Freilassing, Salzburgerstr. 37
Publications: Hartmann: Wash on Wings (Comparison between Flight Tests in the wind Tunnel and in Theory)
Diploma work of the T.H. Munich.

There is still an incomplete report on Control force measurements which would take six weeks to be completed by one specialist, one technical assistant and the help of the photographic dept.

Report on Lateral Stability investigations on the DFS 230.

Specialist: Dipl. Ing. Zachen, Prien Flugplatz.
Ing. Hans Breirkenaner, Reichenhall-Noah, Jagerhans.

The tests have been concluded. The report partly finished. It would take 6 weeks to complete it with two specialists, two mathematicians and one draftsman.

Report on measurements of Static flight characteristics.

Specialist: Dipl. Ing. Kreyser, Freilassing Watzmannstr. 21.

The report on the measurements on the KL25 was worked out. It would take 6 weeks to complete it with one specialist, (Dipl-Ing Kreyser), one technical assistant and the help of the photographic dept.

Report on investigations of Towing methods.

Specialist: Prof. Dr. Ruden, Ainring Siedlung Wielandshag.
Dipl. Ing Schieferdecker, now at Chieming
Schreinerei Ellmayer.
Publications:
(1) Schieferdecker: Roll stability of chained attachments for firing investigations UM 3526.
(2) Measurements during which towing UM.....

A farther report on the measuring flights with the Arado 234 could be completed in 3 weeks, assuming that sufficient data is still available. Personnel required: one specialist (Dipl. Ing. Schieferdecker) and one technical assistant.

The comprehensive representation of flight mechanics of towed flight would take about 4 months. Personnel required; 1 specialist (Prof. Dr. Ruden) 1 mathematician, 1 draftsman, in conjunction with the photographic dept.

Report on Investigations of the influence of
superficial roughness on laminar profiles.

Specialist: Dipl. Ing. Runkel, Freilassing Ludwigzellerstr. 24
Prof. Dr. Ruden, Ainring Siedlung Wielandshag
(for laminated profiles)
Investigations commenced beginning of 1940
Preliminary completion spring 1944

Publications:
(1) Kretz: Investigations of profile drag on rough surfaces.
TB Vol. 8 book 4 1941
"Air Force blue" (closer designation in the publication) and
"Washable Black" were examined (Production Firm Temperol)
(2) Runkel: Profile drag and boundary layer measurements
on the NACA 23012.
Profiles with smooth and rough paint work.
TB Vol. 11, Book 8 1944.
(3) Runkel: Foemel: Casual investigation of the roughness
and capacity for reflection of black, washable
paint. Investigations and information 3512.

Examinations were made on Temperal paint, other paints that were
produced by the firm Gebr. Schmidt G.m.b.H. (Printing ink Factory,
Berlin) in contract to the DFS and paints produced in the institute
itself. (Pigments: Graphite and carbon black, obtained from the
firm Riedel de Hain, Berlin, Oranienburg lampblack; Binder:
"Indula" of the Munchener Industrie und Lackfarbenfabril (Lacqner
works) G.m.b.H. and "Dextrisol"

The nests with the research glider aircraft after preparing all the
necessary camouflage paint and laminar profiles would take six
months in faverable weather.
Apparatus required: 1 touring aircraft, e.g. He 111, a research
glider aircraft DFS 332. Personnel required: 2 pilots, 1 aircraft
assembler, 1 measuring engineer, ground personnel for the maintenance
of the aircraft, 1 manual worker to install the apparatus, 1 specialist
(Dipl. Ing. Runkel).

Report on Grid Investigations

Specialist: Prof. Dr. Ruden, Ainring Siedlung Wielandshag.

The manuscript of the work has been completely lost. The theory is
supported by diagrammatically represented potential functions. On
essential part of the diagrammatical representation is not available.
The residual functions, in particular the bestimations of the
residual values of the infinite series must be re-calculated.
Completion of the work would take 4 months. Personnel required:

1 specialist (Prof. Dr. Ruden), 4 mathematicians, 2 draftsmen in connection with the photographic section.

The demonstration pictures in the smoke tunnel have also been lost. To reproduce them, assuming that the smoke tunnel is in working order, would take about 2 months. Personnel required: 2 experimental engineers, in conjunction with the photographic section.

The Report on investigations of Ground Effect.

Specialist: Dipl. Ing. Conard, Litzelberg Attersee No. 22.
Post Kammer-Schorflung, Oberdonan.
Work commenced Summer 1943
Preliminary completion: Autumn 1943
The investigations concerned the individual wing near the ground. They ought to be supplemented by investigations on the ground effect on elevators, which is to be found at the same time as on the wings in a downward current. An aircraft body without fuselage was contemplated.
Publications: Conrad: Wind tunnel investigations on ground effect. The manuscript was forwarded to the German Aircraft Research for publication.
Further investigation requires a wind tunnel with a special balance suspension. The balance suspension had already been prepared in Darmstadt before the occupation. If it is still useable it must first be tested. Assuming that this is possible. The investigations would take about 2 months. Personnel required: Wind tunnel staff, consisting of 3 measuring technicians, 2 calculators and a specialist (Dipl. Dr. Conrad).

The Report on "Fuselage Theory"

Specialist: Prof. F. K. Schmidt, Reichenhall
Hohenzollernstr. 15.
Work commenced Autumn 1943.

The investigations have been concluded as far as the production of the manuscript. For producing the printed work would take about six weeks. Personnel required: 1 specialist Prof. Dr. F. K. Schmidt, 2 calculators, 2 draftsmen in conjunction with the photographic section.

Report on Catch Diffusers.

Specialist: Prof. Dr. Ruden, Ainring, Siedlung Wielanshag.
Dr. Walter Bredel, Turk B. Marzell No. 66.

The commencement of the work goes back to the year 1939 in which the undersigned formulated the theory of level Symmetrical Catch Diffusers. The thoery was treated further according to the needs of practice. Special difficulties occur when boundary layer material enters the nozzles. Suction was recommended as a remedy, however, in most cases the more simple discharge fillet. Both measures require almost constant special investigationd in the wind tunnel. Theoretical deliberations for this are not yet available but statements promising success could be made.

The so-called unsymmetrical Catch Diffusor of the theory not only gives the only data for all catch devices with compulsory slopping construction, but it governs also the catch devices which are blown on lbiquely (slanting angle of attack). Unsymmetrical types of construction occur with leading edge intakes (Mosquito) and with belly and wing radiators, as well as with all inlets which are attached close to the fuselage or wings. TL engines closely combined with the fuselage were recently especially largely discussed because good wing qualities have been almost completely ruined by the construction of engine nacelles on the wings.

A problem of flow which has not yet been entirely explained arises from the leading edge intake on swept back wings, even if the conception of vertical flow, which must necessarily be formed inside such inlets are available.

The difficulties of the theoretical treatment of the unsymmetrical catch diffusor lies in the fact that the theory apparently compelled the catch diffuser to be pursued indefinitely, to give useable methods of calculating. This resulted in the deflection of the field of flow by oblique on-blowing about the angle of attack. How for the remedy of a grid alters the interesting inlet flow is still unexplained. Theoretical statements with catch diffusers which finally remain away from the flow, had not yet met with success.

In Ruden's institute the rotation symmetrical problem was solved by transferring the level form to the rotation symmetrical form. The manuscript for this may still be available with Dr. Brodel. (The AVA Gottingen, Dr. Kucheman) has taken up the rotaion symmetrical problem. Dr. Kuchemann has for this purpose tabulated the field of flow of the ring boxtex and the welling ring. But for oblique on-blowing he could unfortunately not use this method. In Ruden's institute special value was placed on the so-called best watch diffuser. By this is understood the catch device, which, under the above-mentioned conditions possesses the smallest retraction (Retraction is the ratio of the outer diameter to the diameter in the clear of nozzle section). The best catch diffusor has now a very sharp nose, which is always a disadvantage, it the ratio of the nozzle velocity to the speed of on-blowing is greater than 1 (with the TL apparatus it occurs in this case at the take-off).

The problem now consists of selecting the nose rounding in such a way that the take-off thrust is not noticeably reduced and at the same time that the retardation is not essentially increased. Naturally the high-speed characteristics of the catch device must be maintained. Profile investigations of the DVL have recently proved that a small nose radius is an extraordinary means of increasing the critical Mach No. How far this applies to the best catch diffusor must be explained by a wind tunnel test in the high speed wind tunnel. Photographs of flow in the shallow water channel should be obtained for this in the necessary preliminary study. On the conclusion of the work there is little to be said on the whole problem under the assumption that the material was not destroyed in the occupation. The following work can be completed:

(1) Transfer of the level theory to the theory of the rotation symmetrical catch diffusor. This would take about two months with 1 specialist (Dr. Brodel), 2 calculators, 1 draftsman.

(2) The theory of obliquely blown-on catch diffusers.
Time required: About four months.
Personnel: 1 specialist (Prof. Ruden) two calculators and draftsman.

(3) Theory of interior diffusors with constant course of pressure
Time required: Three months.
Personnel: 1 specialist (Dr. BRedel) 2 calculators.
1 draftsman.

(4) Wind Tunnel investigations on the shapes of sterns.
Time required: 2 months.
Personnel: 1 specialist (Dipl. Ing. Conrad) 2 draftsmen, 1 calculator.

(5) For the investigation of the Mach influence the completeness of the shallow water canal has to be assumed. After this is completed about 3 months would be necessary to complete the examination.
Personnel required: 1 specialist (Dipl. Ing. Frolich)
1 experimental engineer, 1 photographer.

On the theme "Catch Diffusor" the following publications were made:

(1) Ruden: Level, symmetrical catch diffusors Year book of the German Air Research 1940
(2) Ruden: Wind tunnel investigations on level, symmetrical catch diffusors.
Year book of German Air Research 1940
(3) Ruden: Wind tunnel investigations or rotation symmetrical catch diffusors: FB 1227
(4) Ruden: Catch diffusors. Lecture delivered at the Munich Work Session on the aerodynamics of Engines 1941. Report of the Lilienthae Society No....

(5) Brodel: on the theory of Level Catch Diffusors FB.....
(6) Brodel: Short summary outstanding work
        FB.........OR   UM..........

The theory found application in the inlet of the Jumo 004 TL engine. The specialists of the firm BMW-Spandau, BMW Munchen, Daimler-Benz-Backnang, Junkers-Jumo and Junkers IFA Dessau, Focke Wulf Bad Eilsen, Argus Reinickendorf all worked on it. The institute gave a lot of advice to Dr. Schilo the Reich's power-unit contractor.

- - - - - - - -

5. Institute for glider construction (see 1.3). The director, Kracht, did not turn in a promised report, but enclosures a2, a4, a10, a11, give a quite detailed picture, based in part on statements by Kracht. Some relevant remarks concerning glider flight at extreme altitudes are contained in the document listed under C50. For glider flight see also 3.2.

6. Institute for flight tests. The director, Stamer, prepared two reports (enclosures B14, B15) whose translations follow. See also enclosures A2, A10, A11.

Institute for Flight Experiment of the   B-14
DFS (Institute F).

The institute for flight experiments worked on the task of various problems especially to solve the practical flight operations by means of flight tests (showing large models)

Primary consideration was given to all imaginable towing methods which through combining of available aircraft types promised hopeful use for numerous purposes.

Primary consideration was given to all imaginable towing methods which through combining of available aircraft types promised hopeful use for numerous purposes.

The thoughts, which led to the presentation of the problem, were in most cases the ideas of the institute F.

SUMMARY

1. Rigid-tow
2. Multiple-tow
3. Carrying-tow
3a. Bomb-tow

4. Starting-tow
5. Mistil-tow
5a. Mistel-requirement-cargo-carrier.
5b. Cock chafer wings
6. Long and rigid tow.
7. Brake-landing
8. Catch-tow
9a. Rope bomb
10 P.A.G.
10a. Water-PAG
11 Vorspann tow
12. Buck-shot
13. Dive brake for LS
14. Rope-intake-winch.

Work of the Institute for Flight Experiments.

Institute F. of the D.F.S.

1. **Rigid tow problem:** Obtaining dependable blind-tow possibilities for cargo-gliders with the best possible relief for the pilots.

Reason: Long-rope tow to be employed only with good view over the rope length. Great demand of space when positioning two squadron on the ground. Difficulties during flight in flight formations. Accidents through rope-release. Breaking of rope at rough weather. Pilots fatigue at rough flights and over long distances. Difficulties with interphone communications between the aircrafts.

Test Method: Development of rope angle indication. Changing rope position due to vertical air-movement. False indication. Shortening of the tow-rope length to visual distance. Drive to rope length of 1.50 to 2.00 m. Increasing aeronautical difficulties and increasing fatigue of the pilots. Development of a so-called rigid tow coupling for tow distances (rear of motor aircraft to front of cargo-glider) of about 1.50 m.

Results: Complete blind-tow ability. The pilot of the glider corrects his position around the longitudinal axis according to the control surfaces of the aircraft. Affords considerable relief to both pilots. The pilot of the aircraft does not have to consider the towed glider. He can bank sharply, throttle suddenly or give full throttle, change altitudes suddenly or fly in fight formations etc. The pilot of the towed glider merely works the aileron but otherwise he is towed like a weather flag. Smallest demand for space on the ground. No release of the rope. Simple, interference free inter communication with brake coupling. Measuring ratio at least 3:1.

Final Technical Solution:

The tail of the aircraft carries a ball cover, in which, in the form of a ball-cup link, a ball is placed. Between ball-cover and ball a brake lining is installed. The impact pressure between ball cover and the ball is changeable according to the weight of the glider and grade of roughness of the air. The ball supports a moveable arm, which is damped on its side movements (by the mentioned brake lining) and limited through the edge of the ball cover. The coupling in the moveable arm is turnable, permitting the towed glider free rotation around its longitudinal axis. The coupling is perfected as a ball-cap coupling. The coupling half on the moveable arm is turned 45° opposite the bow of the towed glider. Both couplings hold a cross-like stone which seems like a Kardan link with closed couplings. Un-coupling can take place from the aircraft or the towed glider.

2. Multiple Tow

Problem: Towing of oversize gliders for which large aircrafts in sufficient numbers are not available. (evtl. towing of aircrafts with engine defects).

Reason: Transport of heavy equipment in special gliders, delivery of damaged aircraft to factories, etc.

Test Procedure: Securing various long towing ropes on the center of gravity on the aircrafts and schooling of the pilots, the multiple tow procedure is very simple.

Final Technical Solution: Single coupling on the glider. Securing the center of gravity (precise securing below the center of gravity) of the aircraft.

3. Carrying Tow:

Problem: Towing of considerably high-loaded aircraft (example: jet fighter) by slower aircrafts with additional lead capacity.

Reason: Starting help for jet fighters. Saving of fuel for start and climbing of the jet fighter. Leading the jet fighter to the bomber current.

Test Method: Towing the acrobatic suitable "Hawk" (glider) under Ju 87. Demonstrating the high surface lead of the Hawk through negative incidence (Austelling lift). Rope tension with a flight-weight of the Hawk of 800 kg to 3000 kg. Vertical tow under Ju 87. Towing of the Ju 87 (with removed propeller) under the He 111. High surface load demonstrated through lift. Tow of the "rudder" under He 111 for measuring purpose.

Results: Towing with a hemp rope or a damping link in the steel cable, the carrying tow is possible without any special difficulties. According to its surface load and its angle of attack, the towed aircraft assumes a position of rest and the pilot has to keep the rudders in a neutral position. Setting the towed aircraft on the ground (landing) in carrying tow was also possible. Radio or wire telephone communication between the 2 aircraft is desirable.

Technical Solution: Securing on the carrier aircraft below the center of gravity, on the carried aircraft above the center of gravity by means os a pivot-hanger on rope-bay.
Normal start, however the carrier aircraft takes off first and picks the towed glider at a rope angle of 50-60 degrees from the ground.
For towed gliders without landing gear (i.e. Nadder) a front wheel carriage was developed, from which the glider was picked up.

3a. "Bomb Tow"

In the described manner for "carrying-tow" a bomb without wings was started on a front wheel carriage and towed on a rope.

Reason: Keeping the landing gear free from the bomb load during the start.

3b. "Seal" (Robbe)

In the descfibed manner for "carrying-tow", a pilotless small winged flying body was started, towed and landed. Flight weight about 2000 kg. Towing aircraft He 111.

4. Starting Tow (lift-tow)

Problem: Starting help for extremely high loaded aircraft is provided, whereby a towed, lightly loaded glider takes over part of the load of the engine aircraft.

Reason: Starting difficulties on small airdromes without concréte run-ways.

Test Methods: Towing a DFS 230 overa Do 17.

Result: Rushing of the towed glider over the 90 degree position with a greater rope length. The visual difficulties from the towed glider to the engine aircraft below.

Technical Solution: Securing the rope of the Do 17 over the center of gravity and on the towed glider below the centér of gravity with a damping link in the rope. Vision window on the bottom of the DFS 230.

Remark: The promising problems were not completed because on 2 other places similar work was started (Flight technical specialist groups, Gothaer Waggonfabrik) and duplication of the work was to be avoided.

5. Mistel Tow:

Problem: Towing of cargo gliders with considerably high loaded and faster engine aircraft (example: fighter) through a combination of the two aircraft to an aggregate. Examining at the same time undetached landings and detached procedure in the air.
Examination of mistel-tow possibilities of pilotless carrying aircraft through the influenced servo machine in the carrying aircraft from the above aircraft/ Combination of bomber and fighter aircraft (Burdjager).

<u>Reason:</u> Nominal effort when towing cargo-gliders, complete blind-tow ability, possibility of pilotless tow, better defense and smaller shorting down possibility at return of the tow-aircraft.
With the Burdjager combination greater depth penetration of the fighter. Protection of bomber squadrons. Increase of start performance of the bomber.

<u>Test Methods:</u> Test flights with joint landings and detaching in air with the towed-on aggregat OFS 220 and KI 35 through the Ju 52. The same with the aggregat DFS 230 and Fw 56 self-starts and flights with joint landings and detachment in the air of the aggregat DFS 230 and Me 109.
Flights were conducted with 2 pilots (above and below). The test with pilotless DFS 230 were not accomplished. The continuance as combination Ju 88 and Me 109 (Beethoven) were taken over from the Institute S of the DFS.

<u>Result:</u> Flying unusually simple. Detaching without difficulties is obtained when through the mechanism, at the moment of detaching an increase of the longitudinal dihedral angle is reached. Joint landings without incidence.

<u>Technical Solution:</u> On mounted aircraft with under carriage, the under carriage is used as support. The rope pyramid with gorspannung tension should be secured in a fashion that the under carriage shock-absorption is eingefahrenem and loses its tension when uncoupling and increases the longitudinal libedral angle. A simple tail support, which folds in direction at the flight and only at actual increase of the congitudinal dihedral angle uncouples itself.
Mounted aircraft with or without installed under carriage support through solid or moveable support and also tail support and mechanism for forcing an increase of the congitudinal dihedral angle during detachment.

5a. Mistel-Requirement-Cargo-Carrier:

A pilotless carrier aircraft was developed and combined with the FW 190. Ad additional load about 600 ltr. fuel and 1600 kg load cargo were provided (for increase of depth penetration). A test of this aggregate was not completed.

<u>Remarks:</u> For all Mistel types the carrying of fuel to the point of detachment was planned for the aircraft below (increase of depth penetration).

5b. Cock Chafer Wings:

Theoretical considerations were conducted on the advantage of dropable, with additional fuel filled wings for normal aircraft of all types and for aircraft with special power units.

The dropable wings were to form a double layer resp. 1½ layer with the main aircraft to the point of detachment.

6. Long and Rigid Tow:

<u>Problem:</u> The aerodynamical advantages of long tow were to be connected with

the advantages of rigid tow, that during flight, according to need long or rigid tow could take place.

Reason: The approximate aerodynamical disadvantage of the rigid tow opposite the long tow is about 10-15%. Rigid tow is required only during bad weather or fatique of the pilots.

Test Methods: A kite-winch, later a winch for this purpose was developed and installed in the engine aircraft and during flight change from long to rigid tow and again to rigid tow took place. A rigid tow frame was developed for this purpose. Test patterns were the Ju 52 and DFS 230.

Result: Choosing the change of tow procedure in flight is possible. Special difficulties do not appear, but with the exception of certain critical rope length, which have to be passed over quickly.

Technical Solution: Installation of a gasoline auxiliary motor operated rope-winch in the engine aircraft. Automatic speed regulation and switching off of the winch. Application of a rope-cap device (special development) for emergencies. Substitution of the Kardan coupling by the tow rope.

7. **Brake Landing:**

Problem: Landing of cargo-gliders in unprepared areas the roll distance (glide distance on the ground) should be reduced to a minimum, independent from the prevailing ground conditions.

Reason: Long roll distances reduce the employment of cargo gliders, due to the unsuitable terrain and in many cases injure the occupant through obstables.

Test Method: On the nose of the aircraft type DFS 230 rockets, at first Sander Leinen rocket and later driving gears so-called fog-throwers, were installed. At the beginning the rockets were ignited one after the other and later all at one time.

Result: At negative acceleration of about 3g. the roll distances could be reduced from about 200 m to about 20 m.

Technical Solution: Installations of a so called rocket box in the fuselage nose of the DFS 230. At the same time, 3 ignited fog-throwers - driving glass together pushed 1500 kg for a duration of 3 seconds.

Remarks: For single operations, the use of smoking powder material at the moment of stand still affords the occupants good fog protection against aimed fire. The morale effects of the burn-noise on the persons in the vicinity of the landing is noticeable.

8. **Catch Tow:**

Problem: It was contemplated to pick up empty (or full) cargo gliders from the ground by engine tow aircraft, without landing at the ending aircraft. Also simple leads were to be picked up.

Reason: A normal pick-up tow of cargo gliders is often impossible due to the condition of the terrain and landing places. It is often wished to pick up simple loads from terrain which does not permit a landing.

Test Methods: With the Ju 87, it was tried to pick up a rope of about 300 m. length Anbremsen (?) It showed that the quantity of the straight layed out rope cannot be speeded up at the required rate without Überbeanspruchung?. Also the resting quantity of rope-drums, etc. seemed too large, and the pick up with air speeds under 180-200 km/h had to be abandoned. The tests were successfully completed with a rope extension-apparatus which was developed for this purpose. First test carrier Ju 87 and Hawk, Later He 111 and DFS 230.

Results: After catching of the rope (also possible at night) the acceleration takes place automatically over the rope-extenso apparatus. According to catch-speed, wind and terrain conditions 80-100 m. rope is released.
The released rope destroys wood-launch whose shear resistance is in any case less than the breaking load of the rope. Acceleration about 2.5.g.
Single leads of about 10-100 kg were also picked with this procedure.

9. Catch Landing:

It was contemplated to catch landing aircraft on the runway in a similar way as the carrier wings by employing rope-extenso-apparata which are anchored in the ground. This procedure seemed to be especially useful in order to catch aircraft with engine trouble (special power units) at the end of runway. These tests were not completed.

9a. Rope-Bomb:

It was tried to tow bombs up to 50 kg on a rope under fighter aircraft in order to bring it into Bomber formations.
The bombs were secured with a rope, released unchecked and the lost meters of the free fall were checked with a small rope-extenso-apparatus of the above mentioned type. This apparatus worked without difficulties.

10. PAG (Personnel Landing Apparatus):

Problem: An apparatus was to be developed with which 3 persons with equipment could be dropped and who would stay together until they landed, also would not injure themselves when dropped into the woods and would not require parachute jump training.

Reason: Due to fast aircrafts, small exit hatches and untrained jumper there is a distance of several hundred meters between the landed personnel. Dropping into the woods resulted in injuries due to branches of the trees.

In modern aircraft is sufficient space to accommodate parachute-jumpers.

Test Methods:

Cylindrical bodies with the recording equipment were dropped on Multi-parachutes (2, 3 and 4 parachutes). They were suspended below the fuselage resp. wing-root bomb well. One and two containers for 3 men of this type were tested below the He 111 and the Ju 188. Also manned test releases were conducted.

Results:

Decrease in speed of 20-30 kg resulted with the single body on the He 111 and Ju 188, however no influence on the flight characteristic or take-off characteristics was noticed. No accident occured.

Technical Solution:

In a wood constructed cylindrical body, 3 men lying on mats were accommodated.(outer diameter 1.05m). The men were strapped in. The feet were placed against a pillow. The point of the body looked like a fin-cap, into which was placed an artificial air bag. With a landing shock of about 7-8 seconds, the rate of vertical descent deformed the cap with about 200 mm federweg(?)
The end of the body formed a ply-wood breaking cap, under which the parachutes were placed together with fin-cap and breaking cap the cylindrical part formed a rear streamlined body.

Remark:

For greater depth penetration a PAG for 2 men with a small diameter was built.

10a. Water - PAG:

A 3 man PAG was developed and built for the release on water. The apparatus was equipped with a Koenig-outboard motor and was good for 5 sea miles and showed special seaworthyness. The release proceeded without defect.

11. Vorspann (?) Tow:

Rigid tow of an over loaded Go 242 by an He 177 with full load. The engine performance of the He 117 was not sufficient for start or for climbing.

Reason:

The normal multiple tow (as described under Pos. 2) cannot be used for rigid tow.

Test Method:

At first the Go 242 was towed on a short rope behind the He 117, whereby

the He 77 obtained a longer rope span by an Heinkel 111.
The Go 242 was rigid towed behind the He 177 and the He 111 performed the span in the same method.

Result:

The start and climb help in the form of one or several span aircraft for rigid tow formation or overloaded single aircraft is possible without considerable difficulty.

Technical Solution:

Installation of a tow coupling in the nose of the He 177, telephone communication of the 3 pilots with one another. The aircraft flying in front serves as lead aircraft to the point of detachment.

12. Buck-shot: For extensive use a rocket projectile was to be built from available parts which could be landed from short tracks from the underside of the wings.

Reason: It was desired to fire a whole bundle of projectiles at one time instead of having the rapid fire of an automatic weapon in favorable position. Also after the discharge to avoid the ballast of numerous weapons in the aircraft.

Test Methods: In order to stabilize the Sander Leinen rocket, various wing types were developed. As projectile a 4 cm dia. flak combination incendiary grenade was provided and replaced during the test procedure by an equally heavy full projectile. The flight bodies were discharged from a stationary groundgun carriage and launched from an Me 109 for test purposes.

Result: The results were not measured, because the same problem was worked on at a different place without knowledge of the DFS.

Technical Solution: Over the rocket body a 6 winged Leitwerk was pushed and fastened. For a head a 4 car full projectile with a threaded ball was screwed on. One of the Leitwerk wing edges had a "T" shaped profile and the flight body was carried on this wing in a 300 mm track. The ignition was electrical through a bridge-igniter with powder base inserted in the nozzle.

13. Dive Brake for LS:

Problem: Cargo-glider with full load were to be forced down very steep with a high rate of vertical descent, without the course speed going beyond the max which is described for reasons of security.

Reason: The employed brake parachutes for obtaining this aim showed numerous disadvantages and interference possibilities.

Test Method: Dive brakes were developed on which brake-grids were extended on the surface and underside of the wings in a way that the air forces approximately equalized themselves. In other words, the hand forces were reduced. The brake grids extended over large parts of the wing surface and underside, that outside the brake effect through air resistence the lift was destroyed at the same time numerous test flights were conducted with these test brakes.

Results: It was possible to put the test carrier DFS 230 with 1000 kg ballast vertically on its head without going beyond the allowable highest speed. The brakes could be kept extended at the landing and they effects a shortening of the landing procedure.

Technical Solution: The grid on the surface, near the main span, opens from back to front, the grid on the underside, which is placed somewhat to the rear, opens from front to rear.
Operated through hand levers with several pump motions. Opened brake is self locking.

14. Rope Intake Winch:

Problem: For aircraft tow operations, especially tow solving operations, the dangers and interferences of rope release should be avoided.

Reason: Rope releases endanger ground personnel, result in uncontrolled flying over the area with danger of collision, delay operations, etc.

Test Methods: A rope winch was developed, which was driven by the slip-stream with Schalenkreuzradern (?) and at the moment of detachment of the towed glider rewound the rope within 30-40 seconds.

Result: Wearing out of rope was reduced. The danger for ground personnel and other aircraft was removed. Time and fuel was saved.

Technical Solution: The winch was installed in the aircraft in such a fashion that a cup of the Schalenkreuzrades (?) was exposed to the slip-stream at all times on the underside of the fuselage. The rope was led to the outside of the tail of the tow-aircraft. A Kappvorrichtung (?) was installed on this plane, in order to Kapp (?) the rope in all positions in emergency cases. The end of the rope carried over the towing ring a leather funnel with the point in the direction of the flight, to avoid swinging of the rope. In order to avoid uncontrollable rope intake and jerking of the rope with the slackened rope during towing, a brake or lock was provided which the pilot could control test carriers He 72 K 135, He 46, Hs 126.

Translation of Report by Ing. Stamer.

B.15.

Institute for Flight Experiments.
Reichenhall 6/24/45

Addition to the brief report of the Institute F of the DFS

1) **Rigid tow.**   Specialist Stamer/Kiefel

Presentation of problems by Inst. F of the DFS. Problem is concluded for:

         Ju 52   DFS 230
         He 111   DFS 230
         Do 17   DFS 230
         He 177   Go 242

examined with negative result:

         Hs 126   DFS 230
         He 111   Go 242

In latter cases the measuring ratio and performance overage is too unfavorable.

The towing construction with changeable shock absorption in flight, should be in effect within 2 months. Report of ZWB "Rigid tow"

2) **Multiple tow.**   Specialist Stamer/Kiefel

Presentation of problem by RLM/Messerschmitt.

Problem is concluded for:

         DFS 230 with max. 5 He 72
         Ju 52 with max. 3 Ju 52
         Ju 52 with max. 3 Me 110
         Me 328 (giant) with max. 3 Me 110

The problem is concluded.

Report by ZWB "towing by attaching to several aircraft"

3) **Carrying tow.**   Specialist Stamer/Kiefel/Pape

Presentation of problems by Inst. F of the DFS

Problem with the systematical explanation of carrying-tow possibilities is concluded. Measurement would be desirable (performance balance). Required time about 2 month.

Report by ZWB "Carrying tow"

3a. **Bomb tow.**   Specialists Kiefel/Willhoft.

Presentation of problem by RLM.
Problem with systematical explanation of the bomb tow possibility is concluded.
No Report.

3b. **Seal (?)**   Specialists Stamer/Pape/Lowinger.

Presentation of problem by RLM
Problem, with tow and landing of a small winged construction of the DFS 230 is concluded. With the build-in radio transmitting lay-out in a landable streamlined body, the problem stood before its conclusion. A new beginning of this work to its conclusion (without construction and structure of the radio transmitting lay-out) would take about 2 months.

4. **Rigid tow.**   Specialist Stamer/Kiefel/Hamacher.

Presentation of the problem. Inst. F of the DFS.
The problem was interrupted after test-flights with the Do 17 and DFS 230.
Required time for conclusion and measurements (performance-balance) 4 months.
No report.

5. **Mistel tow.**   Specialist Stamer/Kiefel/Deginus.

Presentation of the problem Inst. F. of the DFS.
Problem with systematical explanation of the Mistel towing possibilities is concluded.
The "To take on board again" of the fighter is still to be explained.
ZWB - Reports on "Mistel-tow"

5a. **Supply-cargo carrier.**   Specialist Stamer/Kiefel/Deginus

Presentation of the problem through RLM.
Problem was not concluded.
Approximate time required. 1 month for flying, 2 months for flight measurements (performance balance)
No report.

5b. **Cockshafter wings.**   Specialist Stamer/Zitter/Rudolph

Presentation of the problem by Inst. F of the DFS.
Only theoretically treated at the present time. Flight experiments and flight measurement. Required time about 4-5 months.

6. **Long and rigid tow.**   Specialist Stamer/Kiefel.

Presentation of the problem.
The problem was concluded with the explanation of the procedure and development of coupling and winch.
ZWB Report "Towing with any changeable rope length up to the rigid tow"

7. <u>Brake-landing</u>.   Spec. Stamer/Kiefel

Presentation of the problem by Inst. of the DFS
Problem concluded for the DFS 230
ZWB-Report "Brake-landing"

8. <u>Catch-tow</u>   Spec. Kiefel/Gerlach

Presentation of the problem by RLM
The problem stood before its final conclusion. About 3 months will be
required for additional tests and partial measurements (acceleration and rope
strength)
Report was submitted to ZWB - but not published.

9. <u>Catch-Landing</u>   Spec. Stamer/Kiefel

Presentation of the problem by Inst. F. of the DFS
Only consideration was given for a project.
Accomplishment of tests - about 3 months

9a. <u>Rope-bomb</u>   Spec. Kiefel

Presentation of the problem by RLM
The problem stood before its conclusion. Releases with 50kg bombs and
FW 190.
Remaining work about 1 months time.
Report was submitted to ZWB but not published.

10. <u>PAG</u>   Spec. Stamer/Kiefel/Walter

Presentation of the problem by RLM
The problem was worked on by 2 and 3 men. Concluded for 3 men.
For 2 men - PAG required time: about 1 month.
The report was available in the form of a D Air T (Instructions for use)

10a. <u>Water-PAG</u>   Spec. Stamer/Kiefel/Willhoft.

Presentation of the problem by RLM
the problem stood before its final tests.
Required time for the rest of the work about 1 months time.
Report was not available.

11. <u>In Front of tow</u>.   Spec. Kiefel/Koech.

Presentation of the problem by RLM
Experiments were conducted for the principal explanation of the procedure with
Go 242 - He 177 and He 111.
Measurements for performance balance would require about 2 months time.

12. <u>Buck-shot</u>.   Spec. Stamer/Kiefel/Gerlach

Presentation of problem by Inst. F of the DFS
Experiments for the explanation of the possibilities is concluded.
ZWB - Reports were returned.

13. **Nose-dive brake.**   Spec. Pape.

Presentation of problem by Inst. of the DFS
The brake for the DFS 230 was finished and available and was tested.
The report was not completed.

14. **Rope intake-wind.**   Spec. Stamer/Kiefel

Presentation of the problem by Inst. F of the DFS
The problem was concluded for various patterns.
Required time for a new pattern about 2 months.
ZWB - Report was not available.

                            Translation of Report by Stamer.

- - - - - - - -

7. Institute for aeronautical equipment. Reports were submitted by
the director, Fischel, as well as by several workers in his institute
(enclosures B2, B6, B7, B8, B9, B10) whose translations follow. (See
also the enclosures A2, A10, A11)

                                B 2.

DFS Institute for Aircraft Equipment.   Ainring Airport

Prof. Dr. Ing. Edward Fischel.

The great duty of the Institute was to create a scientific basis for flying
and to perform preliminary technical work in the field of flight equipment
to lend support to the technical difficulties which arise and to execute
judgement as a neutral place.

The institute was founded in May 1939 and at the beginning of the war was
moved from Darmstadt to Brunswick and later to Ainring.

Important work was carried out as given below:

A) Work in the field of automatic control

I. Formulation of the theory of the automatic control of air and water
craft. The theory served the purpose, by reason of its characteristic
data for calculating the stability of controls and aircraft. It was
formulated once in special consideration of the automatic control
apparatus, whereby simplified conditions were selected for the controlled
aircraft and at another time in consideration of the special characteristics
could be introduced for the automatic control apparatus. This subdivision

was necessary in order to clarify a very complicated problem. In connection with this the following work occurred:

The theory of control with constant rudder displacement.
The theory of control with the extreme control position (Right left control)
The automatic longitudinal stability of aircraft.
The automatic lateral stability of aircraft
The automatic depth stability of torpedoes under water.
In addition there was work of a special nature, e.g:
Automatic lift stabilisation of aircraft above the angle of attack flaps.
Influence of the rotation of a flying body on damping and control characteristics and still more similar problems.

II. Development of an apparatus for reproducing the movement behavior of automatically controlled air and watercraft for the purpose of stability tests or calculation control.

As the numerical evaluation of the stability calculations required much time, a mechanical electric apparatus was constructed, which permitted the oscillation behavior of an aircraft to be examined on its three axes. Corresponding to the number of partial oscillations of the whole movement, mechanical oscillating systems were used, which were coupled together in an electrical manner corresponding to the effective proportions. The oscillations of the three axes could be registered on an oscillograph.

III. <u>Development of a primitive control for glide bombs.</u>

The object of this development, which was actually begun in 1940 was to create an automatic control for glide bombs with the minimum technical expense. For the rudder of the aircraft was coupled directly to the positions or direction of the measuring gyro and the influence of rudder forces on the gyro compensated by a servo-unit, which was controlled by the inidental gyro precision. The control was built into experimental frames and tested in experimental flights in 1941.

IV. <u>Equipment of a cargo-glider with fully automatic control and remote contsol for television tests.</u>

For the examination of television problems in connection with pilotless aircraft a cargo glider (DFS 230) was provided with an automatic 3 axis control and a remote control and handed over to the DFS Dept. H for tests to be carried out.

V. Many automatic controls were examined by industry in relation to their unrestricted functioning under vibration, low temperatures and general functioning.

In addition in accordance with the problems given in the introduction on advice was given by industry.

B) Work in the field of remote-controlled flying bodies directed against land and air targets.

I. Theoretical and diagrammatical work.

For remote controlled flying bodies the theory and design of their trajectories was formulated and executed and particularly for the "target-covering" and target finding apparata. Under "target-covering" is implied a process, in which the bomb-aimer guides the flying body between himself and the target and keeps it in this line. The corresponding curves were called "target-covering curves" or often on account of the three positions of the observer, bomb and target, named "three point curves". The paths taken by the target finding apparatus and apparatus with television equipment were designed as "sequence curves" or "hound curves". The paths were, as already mentioned, mathematically and diagrammatically treated and in special consideration of the limited capacity for movement of the flying body. By the attacks of such bodies on marine and air targets the possibility can occur in the middle of its flight path generally shortly before the target, that the bomb does not achieve the necessary curvature and therefore does not hit the target exactly or flies over it. The errors were calculated for special cases. It was, also considered how to remote control the target finding apparatus in flying bodies in order to guarantee its stability and hitting the target.

II. Model tests with target covering, television and directional beam methods. Flight tests for testing flying bodies with an without propulsion and for studying their control as well as the possibilities for use are costly and require time. They can be considerably reduced by using a model apparatus built for this purpose, although they are not entirely unnecessary. For this reason model apparatus was developed for the target covering, television and directional mean procedures.

The apparatus for glide bombs (as Hs 293) reproduces the fighting space on a scale 1 : 1000 and consists actually of three wagons which run on the floor of a large room and represent the target, the glide bomb and the bomber. On the largest wagon sits the bomb-aimer and guides the bomb placed on the second wagon with the help of a joystick over a cable. The third wagon bears the target, which controlled from a different point can carry out evasive movements. The equipment is so made that the bomb aimer can guide the bomb in the same flight curves as in actual use. The flight mechanical properties of the bomb are reproduced with extensive accuracy by the apparatus, but not so exactly as with the model apparatus which was provided for flak rockets.

An apparatus was developed to study the conditions of approach against ships of television bombs, which consisted of two wagons. The larger wagon represented to television bomb, as at that time there was no television equipment at our disposal the bomb aimer stood on this wagon and observed the target on the focussing screen of a normal camera. The smaller wagon carried the target, the silhouette of a ship. The conditions of approach were only examined in the horizontal plain the model impressions were registered and evaluated in relation to their accuracy of hitting the target.

The directional beam methods, methods by which the bombs were held automatically in the beam, were also subjected to model tests. To produce the directional beam a searchlight was used. A small wagon which carried the photo-cell and by which this was controlled, represented the model bomb. The apparatus only permitted movements in the horizontal plain to be examined. As with directional beam methods the psychological behavior of the bomb-aimer plays a secondary roll. The apparatus was not in the position to essentially enrich the results calculated during its construction. For the problems of flak rockets, which were of special important, an apparatus was developed which would bring not only qualitative but quantitative results.

The matter was thus investigated as follows:

The model apparatus for flak rockets made possible the examination of remote controlled rockets, which approached their target on target covering curves. The approach was reproduced on a scale in space while the time appeared in true dimension. The total problem of the reproduction splits up into two sub-problems:

1) The reproduction of the rockets in regard to their aerodynamic behavior, their control and special characteristics and

2) The reproduction of the path and the problems connected with the possibilities of use and of the psychological behavior of the person controlling it.

In model flak rockets the experiment was now undertaken for the first time of representing the characteristic properties of the rockets to the greatest extent and at the same time representing them in space. The greatest value was placed on this of making this as accurate as possible and to create at the same time such a slack construction in which all type of seizures and variations were possible. The model apparatus was constructed in the following manner: for the purpose of a guidance equation the moments balance of the moments effecting the rocket were calculated in a series of electrical and mechanical calculating machines. The rudder angle is controlled by a bomb aimer by means of a stick and agrees with the control adjustment. The bomb-aimer selects the stick angle by reason of his optical observations of the trajectory of a small model rocket, which moves as accurately in a model flying space as the stick-controlled rockets move in actuality. It is the duty of the bomb-aimer to guide these model rockets on a target covering curve to an independently controlled target. The immediate position of the rocket in space is given from the moments balance on a system of coordinates fixes on the ground and by which the differential equation of the trajectory is solved in a mechanical manner in a calculating machine.

From this calculation one gets the trajectory vector in accordance with dimension and direction whereby in special cases the dimension is suggested as the time program. By breaking up the vector into its three components in a "kartesischen" system of coordinates one obtains the three partial velocities with which the model rockets must be moved into order to run through the right trajectory.

As the guidance equation as well as the moments and trajectory equations contain the specific equations and remote control dimension, it is necessary to make this adjustable to the general usefulness of the apparatus. Corresponding devices on the actual calculating machines would make this possible. By changing the calculating machine it is thus possible to study the question of 1) while the psychology of the bomb-aimer and the possibility of use can be observed or registered while the projectile is pursuing its trajectory. The apparatus is 50% finished, the remainder being in the assembly stage.

The 4 model apparata mentioned above can likewise be used for instruction and practice in connection with guided missiles.

c) Work in the province of high frequency and telegraphy.
The institute only carried out incidental work in this field and was not specifically intended for high frequency. Thus the following problems have no direct connection with each other.

1) High wind measuring by means of radio soundings:

To determine the velocity of the wind at great heights in accordance with direction and size an apparatus was developed which consisted of 3-4 directio findings stations, which measures an electrical balloon sounding by means of an "adcock" frame. The measuring stations transfer their observations to a central point, which ascertains the momentary values by means of graphs. The apparatus was finished in 1941 and placed at the disposal of the RLM.

II. Development of ultra acoustic timing links.

The object of this development was to delay rectangular impulses of 2 and more microseconds period up to several keeping them as true to shape as possible by cutting out the influence of temperature during the course and by avoiding multiple reflection. The problem was solved in the following manner:

The impulses to be delayed were modulated to a carrier frequency of several millicycles, the value of which corresponds to the actual frequency of a supersonic crystal of 10-12 mm diameter. The supersonic impulse given by the supersonic crystal is radiated into a liquid. After passing through the liquid column, the length of which corresponds to the desired delay (V = 1500 m/s are 15 cm strip length = 100 microseconds delay) the impulse is received and rectified by a second crystal. By mixing liquids with positive and negative temperature coefficients of sonic velocity (e.g. water and alcohol), the period becomes independent of the temperature. True to shape transmission was attained by the corresponding damping of the crystal, whereby frequencies of +/- 400 kilocycles were measured.

For the purpose of adjusting the periods the strips were made adjustable in length.

Position of the work:

Fundamental examinations concerning the influence of temperature, frequency, sensitivity and technical development with regard to the crystal holder, construction of the strip and regulatability concluded.

III. Development and testing of methods for anti-chaffing of radio measuring equipment, special panorama sets by means of acoustic timing links.

The impulses radiated from the radio measuring apparatus as well as those reflected from the aircraft inside the chaffing cloud are conducted after reception direct from a sonic strip of the intermediate frequency of the receiver and delayed here at an integral multiple X of the period of the impulse succession frequency, so that the n th and n + x th impulses can be connected against each other directly or after rectifying by a lower frequency.

By using Dr. Fack's method with an opposing circuit for the impulses reflected on the chaffing cloud, a total extinction of the "coil" occurs, while the impulse reflected on the machine can no longer disappear on account of the "doubling effect" and can thus be used for measuring without being disturbed by chaffing. All firing signals disappear also by this method.

Position of the work:

Testing strips for 2 ms in operation in the laboratory, trial strips for practical use for about 6 ms with temperature coefficient regulator in course of construction, experimental circuit on the radio measuring apparatus nearly completed.

IV. **Blind landing procedure.**

Object of the procedure:

Continuous indication in the landing aircraft of the distance from the landing point in potential or current values, as well as the indication of the deviation to left or right of the line of approach. Combination with electrical altimeter for straight flying on the glide path, later cutting out steering for a fully automatic blind landing.

Use planned for single engine fighters on account of the low cost for the airborne equipment (only a small auxiliary set of about 4 tubes necessary) Principal of method for E-measuring at the landing point:

Synchronized impulses of 20 micro seconds period were radiated from two impulse transmitters erected in front of and behind the landing place in the direction of the line of approach, and the temporal overlapping measured. The zero values of the temporal overlapping is at the landing point. Indication of E-measuring in connection with electrical altimeter on a duel instrument so that with the pointer covering a straight glide path can be pursued to the point or by control on a cathode ray tube, so that in conjunction deviation from the line of approach the position of the machine and its direction of motion can be read off at any time.

Position of the work:

Base for E-measuring constructed on the Aimring airfield and synchronization with acoustic timing links carried out. Successful experimental execution of the method.

Practical E-measuring commended at the measuring base, flight tests in course of preparation.

V. Testing a navigating method.

At the end of 1944 we were asked by the RLM to test a navigating procedure which had been constructed by Siemens of Berlin. It consisted of measuring bases, which fixes the direction from which an impulse from the object to be measured is gauged. The place should be diagrammatically ascertained from both directions. The erection of measuring bases which was originally under-taken in Berlin followed here, but the testing was not carried out.

VI. Development and construction of command sets with impulses.

For remote controlled bodies a remote-control method was developed by industry, which modulated a high frequency carrier with four sound frequencies, to transmit command signal right and left, above and below. It was feared that after a brief use that this procedure could easily be jammed on the part of the enemy by ascertaining the wavelength. Therefore a method was developed which worked with highly-keyed impulses. The impulses were of a very short period to make them difficult to find out.

A device was developed on the "Start-stop Principle" which is described in greater detail in the appendix to this report. In this apparatus the time for putting through the command signal cannot be abbreviated any more by the inertia of the mechanical construction elements. Thus ideas were cultivated and tests executed for constructing commando sets on an inertia free basis for this purpose. The interval of the impulse which establishes the command in a known manner, is determined by a timing link. For this purpose ultra-acoustic timing links (Section II) can be used, or continuous magnetic bands, on which th impulses are magnetized.

D) Work in the province of infra red and ultra violet.

Tests were undertaken to develop a so-called infra-red television set for the temperature range of minus 20 to 60 degrees, which however, in the first stages only permitted a very course screening of the picture. The radiation maximum of bodies with actual temperatures in the given range lies at about 10 microseconds. The following apparatus was constructed to exploit the range of the spectrum. Behind a lens a number (approx. 100 to 200) thermo-elements are arranged, the tensions of which are scanned about 8 to 25 times per second and control the intensity of the cathode ray of a cathode ray tube. The tripping of the cathode ray is so influenced by the scanning device, that for every thermo-element a definite point is constantly coordinated on the cathode ray tube. It is thus possible to make an invisible picture, projected on the surface of the thermo-element visible to the eye (See scheme diagram 1).

In accordance with scheme diagram 1 a testing apparatus was constructed to try out the fundamental ideas. Making use of the full sensitivity was only possible under very favorable testing conditions, as the first series of the thermo-cells still had too great a difference in sensitivity. It could, however, be recognized that the housing was not suitable and further that compensation was necessary for the radiation which resulted from the difference of temperature between the camera and the mean temperature of the picture. In lengthy examinations the corresponding fundamentals were explained and in accordance with the experience gained a first set designed. Production was commended, but the apparatus could not be completed (See plan diagram 2 of the new set).

During the use of test apparatus the following was ascertained:

1) The range of the infra-red television set is approximately the same as that of a standard mirror actinometer with the same opening ratios and the same receivers with the same degree of amplification.

2) Mechanical scanning can be constructed with sufficient operational security.

3) The interference level could be reduced to approx. 2 micro V. with corresponding precautions so that potentials of more than 3 micro V, which are given off by the receiver-elements under the effect of incidental

radiation could surely be proved.

4) With a correspondingly extended focus there arises the possibility of solving not only navigational problems but also night fighter problems.

5) The thermal columns developed for the apparatus are primarily sufficient for further development it would be desirable to increase the sensitivity of the receiver.

6) The amplifier is suitable for the purpose.
The development of the infra-red television set has come up against great difficulties. They can, however, be overcome as far as is known from the tests.

II. Apparatus for examining thermal processes.

In order to comprehend heat conductance and diffusion processes occurring in the thermo-elements for infra-red television sets, an apparatus was built to reproduce such processes hydraulically, with which heat conductance problems that were difficult to solve or unsolvable mathematically could be represented and evaluated in a simple manner. Such problems are for example; conductance of heat in cylinders, balls, discs, bands etc. With requisite intermittant supply of heat. Determination of temperatures ratios in blast furnaces, the zones of influences for which frequency hardening of turning and cutting steels and the like.

The same apparatus was equipped as an electrical set, whereby the results could be made visible in the form of a curve on a cathode ray tube. With this method of execution a point number sufficient for practical proportions thus a corresponding number of measuring positions can be carried out. The accuracy of the evaluation of the problem in question obtained with this apparatus can thus ensue with the desirable approximation.

III. Physical fundamental tests to extend the sensitivity of infra-red photo-cells in accordance with the long wave field with the help of secondary emission.

No essentially complete success.

IV. Impulse lamps for ultra violet rays.

The susceptibility of wireless command sets to interference has caused the RLM to seek a more definite means of communication and to give instructions for the development of ultra-violet impulse lamps. For such high pressure lamps, which give light impulses shorter than one microsecond with a current intensity of 10,000 and more amperes, fundamental examinations were carried out for the purpose of raising the intensity and operational time. A sample lamp was constructed. With an impulse lamp of industrial origin transmission tests were carried out in connection with the command sets described above.

E) Work in the province of gyro apparatus.

The work in the province of gyro apparatus was preponderantly of a theoretical nature. The following work was actually, executed:
The theory of a gyro was formulated, which lacked torsional acceleration. The cause was established of why a free gyro (positioned gyro) runs out of course under the influence of vibration. The theory was formulated and executed.

The theory of a supported gyro was formulated, which as mentioned under A/lll was used for constructing a control. Besides this a platform was used for a telescope for the observation of the parts in motion. They were used to obtain a stabilized telescope with which night fighters and remote controlled bombs could be observed from the machine.

The so-called cardan errors of the directional gyro and artificial horizon were calculated and the results proved experimentally. Under "cardan errors" is meant the variations of the indications of a gyro in relation to the actual values. Different forms of artificial horizons were considered and the principle elucidated on models.

F) Work on special fields.

I. Examination of the magnetic behavior of steel construction type aircraft in relation to the most favorable place for installing remote compasses.

II. Development and construction of remote compasses on the induction principle with the smallest measurements and provided with special compensating devices.

III. Development of an exhaust meter.

In order to determine the air surplus coefficient during combustion in Lorin engines with an inertia of 1 to 2 seconds, a CO_2 meter was put in hand. With this apparatus use was made of the fact that the transmission velocity of sound in exhaust gases is influenced by the H_2 and CO_2 content. By measuring the sonic velocity in accordance with the interference method with automatic setting and indication the variations of the stochiometrical mixture should then be given if they become greater than $+/-5\%$. The temperature should likewise be automatically compensated.

IV. An automatic parachute release dependent on height as a defense measure against deaths through air accidents.

V. Humidity gauge for great altitudes in accordance with the electrical bridge procedure.

VI. Development of a glow-relay with complete operational assurance in the shortest ignition time (for command sets).

These are essentially the tasks which were carried out under my supervision

Reichenhall   Translation of Report by Prof. Dr. Ing.

3.6.45.   EDUARD FISCHEL.

APPENDIX

Electro mechanical remote control command, sets for four commands:

A) Principles and general requirements for development.

     The command set was developed for the remote control of armed flying bodies. It works on the "Start-stop" method and can be applied to highly keyed frequency carrier transmitters, light flashing and guidance transmission. The effect of foreign disturbances is made as difficult as possible. Glow relays were used, which allowed the discharge delay to be reduced (ignition assurance, ignition velocity) with an ionisation electrode.

     The following measures were taken to make the susceptibility to disturbance a more difficult, to ensure operation, with the lowest expense of space and material and to avoid narrow defile parts on the part of the receiver (consumption).

1) Use of impulse time procedure limiting to a minimum the number of necessary commands, (4 commands) limiting to a minimum to number of impulses necessary for each command. (For our Command 2 impulses, 1 initiating impulse and 1 executing impulse) and limiting to a minimum the period of the impulse by introducing grid controlled gas discharge tubes at the position of the electro-magnetic relay. The time after which a new command can be given is determined by the time of the command with the greatest impulse interval and the preparation time necessary for a coming command. This amounts to 37 ins. i.e. it is possible to give 27 commands in a second with the apparatus. With frequency carrier and light flashing transmission the alternating value of the impulse sent out amounts to about $10.^6$ and with control transmission to about 10^{-4} sec. On the receiver side these impulses are lengthened to about 5×10^{-3} so that simple, non polarized electro-magnetic relays can be controlled.

2) High keying of the transmitter, i.e. increasing its capacity to a multiple one for giving signals. The greater intensity at the

receiving tube improves the ratio to the interference level. The receiving apparatus can be selected with lower sensitivity, so that the danger of interference by the enemy is reduced.

3) The most accurate synchronization of the receiver with the given and rectifier of the scanning latitude of the receiver on the impulse breadth of the giver. With the stop-start method limits are drawn by the inaccuracy of the start as a result of the scattering of the attraction periods of coupling and the initiating relay.

B) <u>Construction of the Apparatus.</u>

The apparatus consists of the command given with a guide stick and the command receiver, which is controlled over the conductor frequency carrier or light flashing transmission. The command giver consists of an impulse giver with transmitter contact track loop, slide coupling, and propulsion engine as well as an electrical part. The command receiver consists of an impulse distribution with receiver contact track, loop slide coupling and propulsion engine, as well as an electrical part with the glow relay associated with every basic command. The contact tracks carry the laminae allied to the initiating impulse and to each individual command impulse.

C) <u>Method of operating the apparatus.</u>

Both propulsion engines run uninterruptedly with contact revolution; the slide coupling carrys a constant friction moment on the loops held by the armatures of the initiating magnet by anti-resonance cams. The loops of the giver stand just in front of the initiating laminae of the transmitter contact track, while the loop of the receiver rests on the initiating laminae of the receiver contact track. By deflecting the guide stick a relay allied with the selected command closes in the command giver, whereby current is supplied to the laminae of the transmitter contact track corresponding to the command simultaneously the same current is supplied to a glow-tube in the initiating magnet circuit. The glow-tube ignites. The armature of the initiating magnet attracts and sets the anti-resonance cam of the slide coupling, by which the slide coupling is switched on for <u>one</u> revolution. The loop also makes this revolution and passes over the fifth laminae of the transmitter contact track.

When the initiating laminae allied to the giver command, tension impulses occur by the discharging of the appropriate condensers, which reach the receiver by remote transmission. The initiating impulses occurring at first reaches the initiating laminae of the receiver contact track at the ignition electrode of a glow relay on the initiating magnet circuit over the loop. Its armature attracts and releases the slide coupling for <u>one</u> rotation. At the same moment, in which the loop passes over the laminae corresponding to the given command, the second impulse occurs (command impulse) and is conducted to the ignition electrode of the allied relay. The glow relay ignites and with allied auxiliary protection (Hilfschutz) switches on the command. The armature of this Hilfschutz remains attracted and holds the command until a new one appears. If no other command is wanted the guide stick is returned to the output position, whereby only the initiating impulse is put through and the command put through is extenguished.

D. Possibilities for further development.

1) Command graduation. This can be achieved by measuring the time which elapses between the switching on and off of a command, e.g. by the association of the time angle by means of one or several stages of work.

2) Making interference more difficult. With frequency carrier transmission a duplication of impulses by means of transient wave conductance can be used for making interference more difficult. The pair of impulses of the command giver are unretarded once on the transmitter side and retarded once over an electric chain conductor and then carried to the transmitter. From every individual impulse there occurs thus a double impulse from the pair of impulses, which are radiated over the frequency carrier transmitter. On the receiver side the control of the individual impulses is made in a reverse manner by a similar chain conductor in combination with a coincidence tube.

Further possibilities of making interference more difficult occur through varying the delay time of the chain conductor.

DES - Ainring

Abteilung G 5　　　　　　　　　　　　Ainring. 26 June 1945

Abteilung G 5 of the Institute for Air Equipment (Abteilung for Theoretical Investigations)

Scientific Collaborators:

1. Braunschmidt, Dr. Studienrat　　　at present, Passau am Inn
2. Golling, Dipl. Ing.　　　　　　　Freilassing. Lilienthalstrasse
3. Greinel, Dr. Ing.　　　　　　　　Ainring - Siedlung
4. Leisegang, Prof. Dir. Dr.　　　　at present, Jena (Thuringia)
5. Seebach, Dr. Studienrat　　　　　probably: Munich, Walhallastrasse 1
6. Simon, Dr. Ing. Flugkapitän　　　Bad-Reichenhall, "Sonnenbichl"
7. Sinn, Ing.　　　　　　　　　　　probably: Öhringen bei Heilbronn
8. Vogg, Studienrat　　　　　　　　 at present, Pfarrkirchen/Niederbayern
9. Sponder, Dr. Ing.　　　　　　　　Salzburg, Gaswerkgasse
10. Stinshoff, Dipl. Ing. head of Abteilung　　Ainring - Wielandshag

Problem Elaborated

Stability of Automatically Controlled Flying Bodies

Lateral Stability

A gliding body was to be put into up and down flight and laterally-guided flight by means of a primitive steering apparatus. It had only an aileron. Lateral stability was secured with the help of a supported gyroscope without turn-indicator, in which by proper choice of back-slope of the measuring axis good maintenance of course and damping properties were obtained. The maximum of stability was ascertained theoretically and verified by practical experiments.

The advantage of back-slope is the simultaneous control of the vertical and longitudinal axes. At the same time there results a primitive method of initiating and performing flight in a curve. (Report by Sponder: Control Effect, summer 1943). There is the additional advantage that flight out of trim does not occur, as it may when one control is used for the vertical axis and another for the longitudinal. In continuing the work on lateral movement, the properties of automatically controlled flying bodies were studied at the start, if, as in the case cited above, they were intended to contain only a measuring axis.

In that connection the following questions were cleared up: Control on the aileron or rudder; back-slope of the measuring axis; Back-slope of the damping gyroscope; force of gearing-ratios; Influence of the properties of the body (for example, wind-vane stability, sliding roll moment, etc.). These problems were calculated for the flying bodies DFS-D2, HS 293, BV 143, LT 950, BV 246, and V1.

The following mention may be made of the results:

Basically the control on the rudder for stabilizing laterally movement is especially favorable for bodies of medium and large span, since in these cases by proper choice of back-slope and gearing-ratios dampings for vertical and longitudinal axes or aperiodic character can be obtained. The magnitude of the sliding roll moment exerts influence and it must have a minimum magnitude, but a certain magnitude must not be exceeded, since lateral movement in such a case becomes dynamically unstable.

High wind-vane stability and effectiveness of rudder are always favorable. Damping of the oscillation of the longitudinal axis is approximately proportional to the back-slope of the position-gyroscope, in so far as one may, in view of the strong coupling of the two axes, speak of special oscillation of one axis. Since all the mathematical results depend closely on the aerodynamic properties of the bodies, only the influence of the variants can be given here. On the back-slope, however, an illustration may be given in order to characterize it:

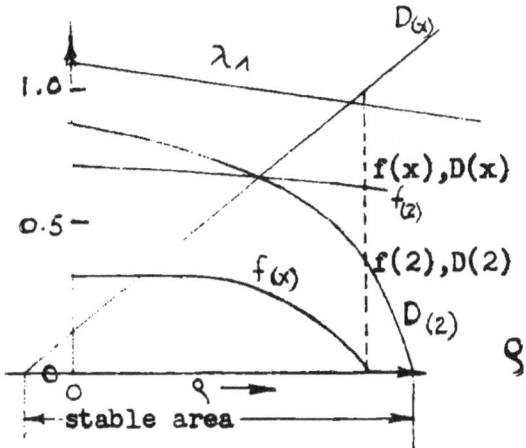

χ_1 = real root, designates the inward swing of the path of the center of gravity

= frequency and damping of the longitudinal axis

= frequency and damping of the vertical axis

ς = back-slope of the measuring axis

A back-slope of the damping gyroscope is advantageous if the control itself shows strong dragging properties; that is, if the rudder-movement in an oscillation shows strong phase-differences as against the impulse of the position-gyroscope.

The coupling of the vertical and longitudinal axis always means a strong reduction in damping for the vertical axis, so that especially in case of wide span it is necessary to be sure that the gearing-ratio of turn-indicator is good. For flying bodies the areas of stability were as a rule first specified, in order to provide a comprehensive survey; in such cases the possible variants were included in the calculation. The result was a diagram of the following character:

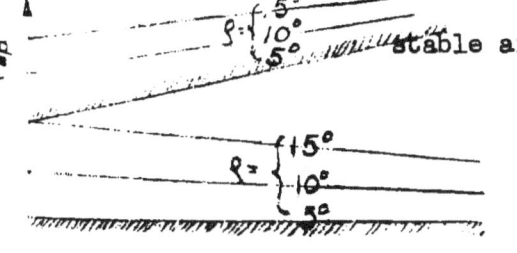

$C'LB$ = coefficient of sliding roll moment

$C'NB$ = coefficient of wind-vane stability

The results, only briefly mentioned here, found practical application in the testing of the flying bodies V1, Lt 950, and Bv 246, which, because of theoretical preparations, we were able to make fly perfectly by means of a few measures of a general character.

Control on the aileron can always be exercised in practice; in such a case one need only choose correctly the wind-vane stability of the vertical axis and the gearing-ratio values of the control. A great increase in the damping of the indirectly controlled vertical axis, however, cannot be so easily accomplished by these means. The oncoming yawing-moment of the aileron, which can change its warning-sign according to the angle of incidence, plays an essential part in this matter. But by correct choice of the type of aileron the yawing-moment can be made to have a favorable significence, and good damping is accomplished for the vertical axis also. It is also important that the coupling moment, as well as the turning roll moment and sliding roll moment shall not assume too high a figure, if dynamic stability is to be assured, and for this reason narrow spans are favorable. The back-slope of the position-gyroscope, depending on the body must amount to at least 5 - 10°. If the back-slope is greater, the dynamic stability becomes better, but ability to maintain the course decreases, and at the same time curves are commenced and flown with extraordinary ease. It is true of steering on the rudder as well as on the aileron that curves are flown only by banking without slides.

Deviations from the course as a result of disturbing factors (such as being out of trim, or defects in construction) occur with both types of control. The magnitude of deviation depends on gearing-ratios and properties of the body. In general a body with an aileron is better able to overcome disturbing moment affecting the longitudinal axis, while one with a rudder overcomes moments around the vertical axis with less deflection of course. Experience shows that the greatest disturbing moments occur because of the surfaces, in other words as moment around the longitudinal axis, so that if a high degree of accuracy in the course is required, aileron-control is more successful. For the rest, the overcoming of disturbing moments must be considered in connection with the special characteristics of the body, so that it is possible that the ratios will differ sharply.

Longitudinal Stability.

In collaboration with the Technische Hochschule Darmstadt the different possibilities of gearing-ratio on longitudinal position were examined and the behavior of the body in relation to gearing-ratio of, for example, altitude, longitudinal position, variometer, damping gyroscope, velocity at angle of incidence, etc., was calculated. (see 15 partial reports of the Technische Hochschule Darmstadt).

Several distinctive conclusions may be mentioned: A gearing-ratio for altidude (Höhenaufschaltung) has a scooping-up effect on the phygoid oscillation and also, to a slight degree, on the oscillation at the angle of incidence. A gearing of the variometer would damp the phygoid oscillation, but mostly fails in consequence of the fact that there is no variometer sufficiently delicate. A gearing of the position-gyroscope provides the best damping for the phygoid oscillation, but requires a turn-indicator for the oscillation at the angle of incidence. In principle, of course, the differentiation of the position-gyroscope can also be used in place of a turn-indicator. The gearing of the angle of incidence has no influence on phygoid oscillation, but has the effect of a position-gyroscope where oscillation at the angle of incidence is concerned.

A gearing for velocity works similarly to one for altitude; both increase the frequency of the phygoid considerably, decrease the amplitude, and closely connect the two oscillations. Mixtures of the above-named magnitudes are, of course, possible, and by the properly selected combination of impulses of altitude, position, and turn indicators it is possible to attain well-damped courses for longitudinal movement as well as for phygoid oscillation and oscillation at the angle of incidence.

In a special case a study was made of whether gearing for longitudinal position on the flaps of the wings had a beneficial effect on the controlability of the flying body. It was to be established that the longitudinal position once set up would produce an inclination of flight-path independent of velocity. For this purpose the flying body was trimmed to such a form that an alteration of the flap-angle produced no additional moments, but the longitudinal axis of the body always coincided with the flight-path. In practice it was proved by this method that an artificial eye or target-finding instrument can be installed without an after-trim-former (Nachtrimmvorrichtung). The whole installation has the effect of a normal position-gyroscope construction with additional gearing at the angle of incidence.

In a special work an investigation was made of the possibility of steering large aircraft with the help of the Flettner control, almost without power and without additional mechanical help; and the conditions for it were established. (Report by Sponder)

Stability of the Depth-Course of a Water-Torpedo.

On the basis of theoretical investigations it was established that the main cause of the instability of the torpedo is the strong alteration of buoyancy in case of a deflection of the rudder. The Whitehead tail-piece is better for stability than the Wollwich tail, because it produces a greater alteration of moment for the same alteration of buoyancy. The most desirable thing would be a control at the head of the torpedo, by which absolute dynamic stability could be attained at the start. This type of control is used in the bow in the automatic stabilization of the submarine.

Gyroscopic Research.

In a report entitled "Errors of Indication in a Free Gyroscope Suspended on Gimbals" the indicator values of a free gyroscope arranged in any manner in aircraft are calculated with the help of transformations of coordinates. An exhaustive investigation is concerned with the indicator-errors in those arrangements of course-gyroscope and horizon which have practical importance (Report of DFS, Ainring, von Seebach).

The installation of the supported gyroscope, mentioned at the beginning of this report, is being theoretically investigated. It is shown that in case of oscillations about the other axes of the flying body there occurs a deviation of the gyroscope, and consequently of the flight-path, to one side. The effect which had already appeared during the test was explained in this way.

FB No. 1965: "Investigation on the Deviation of a Free Gyroscope Suspended on Gimbals, under the Influence of Nutation." The deviation of a free gyroscope suspended on gimbals, resulting from nutation, was studied experimentally and theoretically, and remedy measures were discussed. (Seebach - Weidmann)

On-off Control.

A large programme was carried out for the study of on-off control for a system with one degree of freedom. Systems with and without self-damping were considered, and later the influence of the whole angle and a switch delay. A practical method of specifying previous control systems of flight mechanics by formulae, curves and graphical presentation. In practice no measure of enduring amplitude is allowed, so that a black-white arrangement with temporary damping and also backlash is possible.

In further work the additional aerodynamic resistance due to the effect of the on-off control on the rudder was calculated, though in practice it has no significance. This was confirmed by calculation of the lift/drag ratio for and tests on the BV 246, which is the flight body with the best lift/drag ratio. Hence, bodies with steady on-off control were dispensed with, since no measurable difference in lift/drag ratio was apparent.

Influence of acceleration on the damping of flight bodies.

Normal rocket drives give an additional damping of greater or lesser strength. But apart from this damping there is, during acceleration, an amplitude decrease due to increase of the reestablishing forces. This damping is only apparent, for it consumes no energy, and when the body settles down at a higher velocity, the amplitude regains its initial magnitude.

For several bodies such as the Natter, Enzian, V2, etc., the control installation is considered and the gearing ratios calculated for practical demands.

Flight paths.

The results of investigations on the flight paths of controlled Flak rockets by tracking methods are given in report VB 1930 by Dir. Dr. Leisegang. In this report were formulated the conditions for a hit, the hit probability with no restraint of the prescribed conditions and the demands on the flight body for attaining a maximum possible range.

In report VB 1823 the hit errors were calculated for a flight body fired at a slowly moving target such as a ship through an inaccurate following of the dog curve. In both reports much weight is given to practical considerations. In an action observation the necessary radii of curvature for the onset of a fighter on an enemy aircraft were decided, the attacker flying in from any direction.

For special bodies such as the Natter and HS 117 curves of pursuit were fixed in practical observations and the hit probability and limits of application determined. For this, the aerodynamics of flight bodies and the dependence of speed on the type of flight were taken into consideration.

The fighter project X 4 was the first remote control installation by radio from the attacker. The possible ranges of application, hit probabilities and demands on the flight body and armament were determined by path tests.

Control of rotating bodies.

The bodies X 4 and X 7 rotate during flight. The upper and lower limits of rotation velocity, between which the body is still under control, were determined experimentally and also the in-swing during a single frequency control. From these experiments the rate of rotation was calculated. It was found that it was critical that, because of wind vane stability, the body possessed a frequency in the neighborhood of the most favourable rotation frequency, which led in some cases to the starting of oscillations and a headlong fall. This could be understood from a theoretical standpoint and also means of overcoming it found.

The body X 7, which has a particularly simple type of remote control, gave difficulties in the initial part of its path. Several starting possibilities were tested and the minimum initial velocity determined. The control possibilities and consequent hit probability were also found.

Gearing of the target seeking head.

The first step in applying the fighter project X 4 or Flak rockets was to provide for a remote control by tracking methods. A further aim was to control the last part of the path by means of a target-seeking head.

In particular for the X 4 basic demands were laid down for the head, gearing ratio and possible initial course errors, in order to have a firm basis for developments. These demands are such that, if for a range of 2 to 3000 metres the target seeking head has a limit of address (ausprechgrenze) of at least 1 Km, then an initial course error of 5° can be allowed.

It is further presumed that the fighter instrument has a minimum radius of curvature of about 2 Km and a cone of fire of 30°.

In a further development it was established that consideration of the exact angle of incidence of the projectile is not needed provided it is less than about 2 or 3°. Under the above conditions the impact error is never more than 4 or 5 m and lies in the range of action of the rocket.

Until the target-seeking head takes over, the flight path must be height controlled, and this is done in the case of the X 4, by means of an additional pick-off on the gyro which is already installed. A large lateral deviation cannot occur on account of the rotation of the projectile.

It was decided to provide time and swell magnitude (Schwellwert) switches for switching in of the target-seeking apparatus.

The use of the target-seeking apparatus for Flak rockets presented greater difficulties, for its catching range and distance must be considerably greater. The tests required and the angles and distances needed were determined by considering the flight mechanics of rockets.

For the instrument HS 117, in order to keep the enemy's mode of interception in its simple form, a limitation was to be placed on the use of the rocket in the sense that it was to reach the enemy only in its after-flight (Nachflug). If at the same time as the steering after the cover-procedure one directs it behind the opponent, one may cause the target to appear theoretically on the longitudinal axis of the rocket as the limit of address

($Ansprechgren_ze$) is approached. The conditions for this case were defined for the individual firing situations, and the possibilities

of applying them were tested. At the same time, in order to
counterbalance sighting errors which appeared, processes were
studied which contemplated a gradual retrimming (Nachtrimmen) of
the angle of interception (Auffasswinkel) which first appeared, and
their applicability was established. By use of the above-mentioned
restrictions and remedy measures it would have been possible to
make use of target-seeking heads which were on hand or in view.
The first usable infra-red instruments were to attain ranges of
about 2 km. with the cone of fire from $\neq 10°$ to $-10°$, which for
the above-mentioned case of the HS 117 is sufficient to compensate
for possible errors in finding and striking the target, if one
does not place too great demands on the projectile in respect to
flight mechanics. (UM No. 3544 and 3547 by Dr. Greinel, and
Combat Observations).

For a hit from other positions than the after-shoot (Nachschuss)
the primitive method mentioned above is not feasible. In the
Wasserfall weapon, therefore, the intention was to direct in advance
the target-seeking head, which by itself had only a very small
range of measurement.

If one intends to use a target-seeking head not only in the after-
shoot or in the major range of the after-shoot, the primitive mode
of gearing is no longer feasible. By installing a turn-indicator
whose impulse twists the axis of the target-seeking head toward
the longitudinal axis, or, what follows the same flight-paths, by
gearing the differentiation of the target-seeking impulse so that
the target-seeking head itself must be stabilized, the use of the
projectile can be considerably extended. By this method of gearing, the projectile flies its own angle of lead, which in the final
analysis makes the flight-path straight and free from acceleration.
In this way it is possible, as it was intended in the investigation,
to level out even defensive movements and major errors in dropping,
and also mistakes in trim and likewise the angle of incidence, and
to make hits in spite of them.

The use of such a gearing ratio will be used primarily for attacks
on fixed or slowly moving point targets, e.g., ships.

In the last case a small installation error of $1°$ in the target-
seeking head would lead to a miss.

In parallel investigations the effect of the control gearing ratio
of the target-seeking head on the dynamic stability of the projectiles was considered.

In general it can be said that, for larger distances, the target-
seeking head acts like a positional gyroscope, but its approach

to the target is equivalent to a high control gearing ratio and would always produce finally dynamic instability. In most cases, however, the instability limits lie so near the target that they present no difficulty. This is true for direct and hand gearing of the target-seeking head. If the latter is only used for correcting the general path, as a compass is used for course correction, then it has no influence on the stability. This application is only for target-seeking apparatus of greater scope and is only possible in certain special cases (Radieschen).

Ainring, 26.6. 1945.

Stinshoff

B.6.

Further details concerning the report of the institute dated 3.6.1946.

The further information consists of partial reports of my co-workers, which are given in connection with it and the following supplementary notes.

As the titles and numbering of the reports are taken from memory, no guarantee for the unconditional accuracy can be given.

A/1. (a) In 1940, I made a summary covering the whole field of automatic control, which appeared in the file of the German Air Research Department, RLM, under the heading "The full automatic control of aircraft".

(b) The theory of control with fixed control surfaces (Ruderhartlagen) worked on by Dr. Greinel, Dr. Leisegang, and Dipl. Ing. Golling was produced at this time and on account of its curve and numerical data afforded an easy view of the problem being dealt with. (Dr. Leisegang lives in Jena, the two others in Freilassing).

(c) Automatic depth control of torpedoes.
Calculatory orientation tests with different combinations of control elements. Commenced: March 1942 completed Autumn 1943. Two reports, one final report published by Dr. Joh Schedling, Physicist of Bad Reichenhall, as a house report of the DFS. The theoretical treatment of the problem was discontinued as without parallel experiments, the tests appeared abortive. A resumption of such tests in Gotenhafen, which was favored by the RLM, was rejected by us on account of the great distance between Ainring and Gotenhafen.

(d) For all the usual problems and works, see the report of Dipl. Ing. Stinshoff, Ainring-Wielandshag.

II. Apparatus for the repetition of movement behavior of automatically controlled aircraft.

This gives the short designation "Oscilloscope". The first complete apparatus was developed and constructed in the period between January and May 1942. On account of other more urgent work, the apparatus was only qualitatively needed and not measured and gauged in detail, so that for quantitative measuring, it would have to be examined. The further development occurred only when working capacity permitted it. Dr. Vieweg, T. H. Darmstadt, who with industrial support, built apparatus has its value. Ing. W. Ramsbrock, of 2 Riedelstr. Bad Reichenhall, worked on the oscilloscope. The following reports have been published:

(1) By. H. Temme: The fundamentals of the oscilloscope (?)

(2) By E. Fischel: DFS House Report 32 "The Integration of linked differential equations in physical ways.

(3) By W. Ramsbrock: DFS-HM3534 "Further development of the oscilloscope (?)

III. See Appendix - Dr. R. Muller, Bad Reichenhall on "Primitive Control"

IV. Equipment of a loaded glider for television tests. On account of the overloading of German Industry the three axial control was installed in our workshops and used in flight by our engineers.

No special importance is attached to this problem.

V. For Section V, see the report of Dr. R. Muller. B/I Theoretical and graphical work on remote controlled flying bodies. See the report of Dipl. Ing. E. Stimshoff.

II. (a) Model tests with the target covering procedure.
The tests have been completed and included in two reports.

(1) ZWB. Report 1830. "Model tests with glide bombs in accordance with the target covering procedure".

(2) ZWB. Report 1831. "Experiences of tests in accordance with Report 1831"

By the same Authors.

(3) ZWB. Report 1832. "The trajectories of guided flying bodies at the course level by E. Fischel. Work carried out in 1941 and 1942. Dr. Ing. Karl Bach lives in Bad Reichenhall.

(b) Model tests in accordance with television procedure. Carried out and completed in 1943 by Karl Staiger of Reichenhall-Marzoll. Publication ZWB 1897 - Title as heading.

(c) Model tests in accordance with the directional beam procedure. Abbreviated Name: Feuerlilie. The construction of auxiliary apparatus was carried out, improved design was however, broken off, as a control; would be superfluous for the treatment of the problem carried out mathematically and the expense for an elaborate experimental apparatus could no longer be borne. Commencement of work began in 1943. Cessation December 1944. Several reports are in existence as house reports. Author: W. Brinkmann, who lives in Ainring-Perach.

Note: The physiological influence of guided missiles (Lenkschutzen) occurs only to a small extent with the directional beam procedure. For this procedure, model apparatus was used in the same sence as calculating machines and for which we all had ideas.

(d) Model apparatus for flak rockets. Commencement and completion of work.

Wasserfall: The qualitative apparatus was commenced in May 1943 and completed in February 1944. The quantitative apparatus was commenced in February 1944 and is not yet completed.

The Wasserfall apparatus is representative of the study apparatus for "Krenzflugler"

The "Ebenflachner" commenced in August 1944, the theoretical preliminary work completed in December 1944.

Completion report on "Wasserfall" UM 3508 and illustrated report. UM 3558 on the quantitative apparatus.

An uncompleted manuscript manuscript report is in existence on the "Rheintockter" which would take two people about 10 days to complete. An almost completed manuscript is in existence for the "Ebenflachner" in particular "Enzian" which would take one man about three days to finish.

The following men worked on these projects:

> Dr. Johann Schedling, Physicist, Reichenhall.
> Dr. Richard Walker, Mathematician, Teisendorf.
> Friedrich Schogl, Physicist, Teisendorf.
> Dr. Herbert Lange, Physicist, Reichenhall.
> Heinrich Janzus, Engineer, Piding.
> Felix Garten, Engineer, Reichenhall.

The completion of the apparatus "Wasserfall" for quantitative tests can be of fundamental importance in respect of representation by models, as this apparatus permits a possibility of estimating the limits of model technique in regard to the accuracy of the copy. The importance of other work on Ebenflachner apparatus lags behind.

C/I. High wind measurements by means of balloon soundings. The development and construction of the measuring process were carried out in 1939-40 by Dr. J. Folsche, who lived at that time in Gross-Gmain. A sketch of the equipment was available as a DFS house report.

II.) This work is described at length in a report by
III.)
IV.) Dr. H. Born (See Appendix).

V. Research of the navigations procedure "Ewald".

An exact description of the procedure is not available. At the moment, this cannot be carried out as the leader of this group, Engineer Hofner is unreachable. He has not returned from a business trip which he undertook shortly before the occupation of Munich. It is probable that he has gone to relatives, who live in Diesen on the Ammersee. Several of his co-workers are also unattainable, as the group was not composed of actual DFS personnel but of those latterly nominated by the RLM. Reconstruction can only be carried out in conjunction with Hofner. Besides this, the assurity of a frame for Fighter Guidance (EKT) to be found at the Dortmund Airport, would be essential. Difficulties in executing the procedure were not expected if the reflection of the transmitting impulses in the atmosphere remained unimportant.

VI. Command apparatus with impulses.

The exact position of the work was given in Appendix I of the main report. Commencement beginning of 1941. Completion end of 1944.

A final report is in existence as U and M of the DFS by Dr. R. Fleischner and J. Erz: "Electro-mechanical remote controlled command apparatus for four commands" (Darmstadt system).

The main work was done by: Dipl. Ing. Josef Erz, Bad Reichenhall and Ing. Helmut Bachmann, Bad Reichenhall.

The importance of the apparatus lies mainly in its flashlight transmission, as during radio transmission without additional equipment, it is easily disturbable.

Thus the coincidence procedure was undertaken in parallel-development, which, however, has not yet been completed. Two types of apparatus were provided, a smaller type for two commands and a larger type for four commands for flak rockets. As construction element for the coincidence procedure, Dipl. Ing. Erz suggested the magnetic band, and Dr. Berg constructed the supersonic course strip. The apparatus with the sound strip "Mosaik". As the recent removal caused damage to the improvised test equipment, it will have to be reconstructed, taking several months. The work on "Mosaik" lies in the province of Dr. Folsche and thus not in my Institute.

D/I. Infra red television apparatus.

Work commenced about the beginning of 1942 and has not yet been concluded. Position: After numerous tests with a test apparatus, the first apparatus was designed and submitted to the workshop for construction. Spare parts for this apparatus are available, but a final report has not yet been made. Completion would take six men (3 scientific workers, 3 mechanics) about 9 months. The need for materials is no longer a consideration.

Men working on this:

Dr. Ing. Werner Hohenner, Bad Reichenhall

Electro Ing. Walter Hoeke, Bayr-Gemain.
Dipl. Ing. Hans Seilmeier, Piding, Bad Reichenhall
Ernst Borchers, Freilassing, Datzmannstr.
Norbert Ningler, Precision Mechanic, Freilassing.

Importance of work: The test has a considerable importance as at the time it was only known passive procedure for the means of orienting temperature radiation. In spite of much preliminary work on the greatest distance practically obtainable, no statement can be made.

II. Apparatus for the examination of the thermal processes. Work began about the beginning of 1943 and ended about the end of 1943.

Final report as a house report of the DFS designated as "apparatus for the examination of special heat conductivity problems" by Dr. L. Geilung. An apparatus was constructed and with it a series of questions arising in the course of the work on infra red television apparatus were solved. At the beginning of May 1945, the apparatus was in serviceable condition at Ainring. Work carried out by Dr. Ing. Leonhard Geiling, Freilassing.

Importance: The apparatus can be used for similar problems in other provinces and with a low working cost, results can be obtained which cannot be obtained mathematically or only with considerable more work.

III. <u>Work on Infra Red</u>.

Exact position of the work is given in Dr. Fleischner's report.

Part I of the report: Work commenced at the beginning of 1943 and completed at the beginning of 1944.

Main work carried out by Dozent Dr. Richard Fleischner, Bergweg 6. II Reichenhall.

Importance: The method of adapted infra-red by means of electrical light, is a new method of testing, which has arisen from earlier work. This work is not without prospects under favorable working conditions.

Part II of the report: Work commenced beginning of 1944 and discontinued the beginning of 1945. No final report available.

To complete the work, three scientific workers and one technical assistant would be necessary. Cost of material - unimportant.

Principal Workers: Dozent Dr. R. Fleischner
Dipl. Ing. Edmund Pirch, Piding.

Importance: Prospective tests to adapt infra-red by means of electric light.

IV. Impulse lamps for ultra-violet rays. See the report by Dr. Fleischner on: "Principal tests on impulse lamps".

Commenced 1.10.1943 and not yet concluded. Manuscript partly in existence.

    Principal workers: Dr. Gunter Glaser, Geislingen/Steige
                     Ing. Leiss, Geislingen/Steige

Importance: Fundamental research for the construction of technical flashing lamps with accessories and receiver. Testing equipment was prepared, but it was lost in transit on the way to Ainring in an air attack. It would take two months to complete the final report.

E. Province of Gyro Apparatus.

I. The theory of rotary acceleration gyros. Mainly dealt with in my file: "fully automatic aircraft control".

II. Examination of the loss of course of a cardan suspended free gyro through the effect of nutation. This problem was executed by Dr. Weidmann and Dr. Seebach and published under this title as FB No. 1965 in 1944.

    Dr. Phil Weidmann, Bad Reichenhall, Col di Danastr.
    Dr. Ing. Seebach, Reichenhall-Marzell.

III. Stabilized Telescope.

    Commenced the middle of 1941, completed summer 1944.
    No final report available, but manuscript is in existence. In the course of the development four apparatus were built.

    Principal Workers: Dr. Fleischer, Reichenhall
                   Dr. Joh. Schedling, Reichenhall.

Important: Prospective development for artillery observation from lifting propellors. Discontinued only on account of lack of time and workshop capacity.

IV. Several works were carried out and completed in respect of cardan errors.

    (a) The cardan error of the free gyro is treated geometrically by

(b) The cardan error of the free gyro is handled mathematically by Dr. Seebach, Reichenhall/Marzoll. Published as FB Report under the same title (1944).

(c) The cardan error of the protected gyro by Dr. Seebach, published as FB report in 1944. Note: A protected gyro means a gyro whose precision axle is held in its normal position by force.

V. In the gyro technique session, several lectures were given which the union of German Engineers would like to publish. In addition to the problems designated under IV, lectures were given on the theory of protected gyros and the theory of gyros extracted by integration. Manuscripts were available as DFS house reports under the title "The relay gyro" (protected engine gyro) and "The gyro integrator". Lectures given by Dr. Seebach, Dr. Weidmann, Dr. Schedling.

VI. Artificial Horizon.

Work commenced at the end of 1944. No final report is available, only a manuscript. Work was carried out by Dr. Ing. Leonhard Geidling, Freilassing.

F. I/II. Work on the remote compass.

Work began in 1943 and a conclusion reached. The results of the tests and construction of the apparatus were laid down in two reports, which the DFS mimeographed as house reports. The workers were Dr. Ing. Geiling, Freilassing, and Ing. Helmut Deeg, Bayr-Gemain.

III. Exhaust Meter.

Work began March 1945. Position: Explanation of the fundamental possibilities of solving problems as well as preliminary work of a calculatory and designing nature. Commencement of a series of tests on changing the speed of sound by altering the CO_2 and H_2 content in exhaust gases.

No reports available yet. Completion of the work would take 5 men (2 scientific workers, 2 mechanics, and 1 aircraft assembler) about 9 months. Cost of material not important; fuel requirements about 1000 liters for basic tests.

Workers: Dr. Ing. Werner Hohenner, Reichenhall.
Chem. Ing. Ernst Kohlwein, at present a POW.
Dr. Leonhard Geiling, Freilassing.

Importance of Work: With the considerable use of fuel in the Lorin engine, such a type of indicating apparatus is of striking importance during the period of use.

IV. Automatic parachute release.

Work commenced beginning of 1943 and concluded the end of 1943. DFS house report as final report with the title: "Automatic parachute release".

Worker: Ing. Fritz Hering. Reichenhall.

Importance of Work: The apparatus is usable for this special purpose, for general purposes, it cannot be used without redesigning.

V. Humidity gauge for great altitudes. The apparatus was completed in the laboratory in 1943 and was handed over to Dr. Hohndorf at the Institute for Physics of the Atmosphere for testing and continuous use. The work was performed by Dr. Ing. H. Pfeifer and transferred to Dr. Hohndorf for further continuance of the work in the Institute

On the importance of the work, Dr. Hohndorf can give a sound judgment.

VI. Glow relay.

By introducing a plummet into a three-electrode glow tube, its ionization condition is defined and guaranteed by a brief operation of the tube independent of outside influences.

The experiences are laid down in a ZWB report UM 767. The author is Dipl. Ing. J. Erz, Reichenhall. The tubes were constructed by the firm of Osram, Berlin. A bigger series is in preparation. The tubes had an importance for using as ignition devices for command apparatus.

B-7

DFS - Institute for Flying Equipment.   Reichenhall 6/25/45

Partial report of Dr. Fleischer.

Principal examination on impulse lamps.

The procedure for generation of light impulses was applied many time, especially with stroboscopy and the spark kinematography.

The characterization of all these methods is the short timed discharge of a condensator over a gas-discharge distance.

The impulse lamp and the radiation is evaluated, which originates through the short-times discharge of a tension-source over a charging link (resistant, self-induction) to about 10 KV charged working condensator of about 0,1F over a sparking distance submerged in a gas filling, either through self-ignition or through helped ignition from the outside over a igniting-electrode. The character of the discharge outside the "condensation" through the working condensator depends stronly on the gas-pressure.

The problem was presented, to examine throughly the physical foundation of these intensive spark discharges dependent on the parameters of the discharge.

Examined were, dependent on the type of gas, gas pressure, electrode-spare, tension capacity, inductivity and resistance.

a) The electrical discharge over the spark-distance.
b) from the spark distance radiated radiation energy
c) the timely expiration of the optical radiation.
d) the spectrale energy distribution.
e) size and form of the light area.

These measurements were to serve as foundation for the construction of technical lighting lamps with accessories and receiver.

Research on Infra Red.

This research has the aim to determine photopathodes in the sense of "outer Photoelectrical effects, (rather great inner resistance) whose "longwave limits" lie further in the infra-red spectral area, than the known "combined photokathode layers" of the fundamental materials Cs_2O, with inclosed foreign-metal-atoms and on surface distributed metal atoms. The long-wave limit lies with these layers in the most favorable case at about 15000 $A^°$ E. The electro currents which were released through light, are however, in a space of several thousand $A^°$ - E from the long-wave limit already so small, that a technical usefulness cannot be considered on frames of over 10,000 to 12,000 $A^°$ E. Besides for application, where the optical or atmospheric absorption, or passage is of importance, these spectral areas are unfavorable. The next area of optical passage of atmosphere lies around 16,000 $A^°$ E.

The goal of research was:

I. To find a way which with the known photokathodes make accessible these spectral areas of measurement and evaluation. Or -

II. To develop photo-kathode layers, whose long-wave limit lies in the ultra red, and whose sensitivity is so high, that a technical use in the area of 15000 to 20000 $A^°$ E is possible.

In the combined photo-kathodes of a certain structure with the base material Cs_2O half conductor the light electrical depth effect leads, which appears in these layers beside the surface effects, at radiation with longwave (R > 8000 A^o - $_e$) to formation of a spare charge with final duration in certain zones of the half-conductor. When during the existance of this space charge these photo-kathodes are exposed with a shorter wave length, as the one, with which the spare charge was generated, the electrone discharge will be completely or partly blocked. A photo-electrical cell of this type with both electrode kathodes and anode, has the effect as a three-electrode tube, where by the grid is pictured through the place of the space charge in the half-conductor of the kathode. The size of the blocking depends on the space of the space-charge generating wave-length from the wave length which is to be measured. The smaller the space, the greater is the blocking. However, when the photo-electrical depth-effect has a longwave limit, which lies at a longer wave-length as the photo electrical surface effects, than by means of the above named blocking of the photo electrone-emission a spectral area of measurement and evaluation is made accessible, which lies jenseits of the ordinary long wave limit marked wave length. The conducted examinations showed however, that light, which is only about 2000 A^o E short-waved than the generating spare-charge is able to extinguish it momentarily and completely. However, this way does not permit, any essential advance in infra-red.

To Part II.

a. The technical evaluation of a photo electrone current is possible in a close to the longwave limit lying spectral area, the sharper the reduction of the photo electrical sensitivity according to the long wave limit. It is to be determined, what influence the roughening of the kathoden surface has on the course of the spectral photo electrical identification line in the vicinity of the long wave limit and on the spectrale position of the longwave limit itself. On material for the experiments, the easily obtainable and workable bismuth was chosen despite the U - V sensitivity, became it shows in metallic form and in soot-like form (bismuth black) equal crystal structure.

Bi - metallic: longwave limit at 3130 A^o - E
Bi-Black   "   "   " 3650 A^o - E

The longwave limit is on the roughened layer around 500 A^o - E moved toward the red. For the exact determination of the course of the spectral identification line in the vicinity of the long-wave limit, the energy distributions of the light sources are still missing at the present time. Similar experiments on the combined Cs_2O layers shall be conducted, because the present course seems to be promising.

b) It was planned, through intervening from the inside through installation of radio active-substances in the kathoden layer, to influence the course of the spectral sensitivity distribution. The examinations have not been started. The work was conducted from the viewpoint of full basic research without short term notice and they can only be conducted from that viewpoint. When this goal is reached the technical field of appliance will be many sided.

Translation of Report by

Dozent Dr. rer. techn.

RICHARD FLEISCHER.

- - - - - - - - - - -

B 8

DFS Institute for Flying Equipment
Department Automatic
Dr. Rudolf Müller.

Reichenhall
6.25.45.

Report on Conducted Work since the End of 1940

Problem: Automatic Munitions Control.

1. Development of a pneumatic primitive control and its test with the glide bomb D 11 which is suitable for the attack on level targets.

Since these glide bombs have to be employed in large numbers in order to achieve success, it was necessary that the cost for the automatic stabilization was reduced to a minimum. This can be obtained if one employs the known principles and the methods of mass production on these precision parts. However, one can change the principle of control, and examine, if through this change, the fundamental structure and the cost is reduced. We chose the latter way, because it suited the character of our research institute better.

Structure and Effectiveness of the Auxiliary Motor Control.

The rudder is mechanically and directly coupled on the measuring axle of the gyro and, therefore, corrects the deviation from the flight position with the smallest loss of time. The generated rudder torque through air forces, force the gyro to precision around the free axle.

Therefore, over a switch, an auxiliary motor is switched on, which counteracts mechanically the powers from the rudder, to that the precision of the gyro is maintained within small limits. Compressed air was used for starting the gyro and the auxiliary motor, because the generated powers with the cheap motor (compressed air cylinder with piston) must be large.

Data: Maximum torque - 0.4 Mkg
Duration - 2°/min
Compressed air pressure - 3 atu

About 20 pieces were manufactured as laboratory samples under employment of available compressed air gyros, and also about 8 piece D II frames were equipped. The D II frame is a 500 kg bomb with attached strongly pronounced wing area in the "all wing type" construction. Special rudders and elevators are not provided. The aileron takes over both functions, meaning course deviations are reached alone through banking and altitude deviations through synonomous movement of the aileron. For attacks on level targets, the course alone should be maintained. Therefore, a gyro was installed, which fails to rotate around the high axis. Through incline backwards (10°) of the gyro measuring axis, also the rotation around the longitudinal axis could be measured. As the rotation around the high axis was measured alone, a banking mistake due to construction inaccuracy through a change of course would be noticeable and would be corrected. Due to the delay of the correcture through the long way over the change of course, such a frame is not stable. However, if the bank is measured immediately by slanting the gyro, the frame flies stable.

Progress of the work at the end of 1941: The flight tests gave sufficient results of course accuracy for level attacks and stability, despite missing artificial damping.

Later, the problem was considerable enlarged due to the demand to be able to attack target points. Since the shop capacity was too small, the problems could not be conducted fast enough, and was after several experiments, which brought difficulties (targets with course and altitude automatic) discontinued. However, the model tests on questions of the target procedure were from a difference branch of the institute for flying equipment successfully completed.

Co-workers: Dipl. Ing. Bülte, Ainring
Ing. Schmitz, Piding
Ing. Kuhn, Piding

The two published house reports and hand pamphlets were destroyed on orders bezw. were to be found in a single copy in the DFS library.

II. Laboratory examination of the automatic pilot for the V-1.

This problem was upon request of the test department of the air-force Karlshagen in Ainring conducted. The functions of security were tested at various temperatures under the influence of periodical vibrations and by use of compressed air containing water. The difficulties were worked out in close cooperation with the Mfg. Plant, Fa Askania, Berlin. Difficulties were encountered on the packings of the servo-unit at low temperatures.

    Co-workers: Dipl. Ing. Merz, Freilassing
          Ing. Ferner, Piding.

    Completion of the work: February 1944

The reports (15 part-reports) are in possession of the test department of the Air Force Karlshagen, but partly in manuscript form. Our own examples were destroyed.

III. Development of the control of the Flak-Rocket, "Enzian"

  Our development was conducted under the responsibility of the Fa Holzban-Kissing A.G., Sonthofen/Allgän and was limited to stabilization and control of the flak-rocket, "Enzian". The rocket "Enzian" has a total weight of 1.5 with a useful load of 500 kg. The start is two-stepped, first a 4 fold powder power unit of 400 kg thrust drives, and it is released after 6 seconds. The main power unit operates about 60 sec. with 1500 kg thrust. Two axles were stabilized, the longitudinal and transverse axis. For this purpose in the experimental stage for aircraft, certain control apparata (2 ea. kn 4 gyro and 2 ea. servo-units LrM 12) of the Fa Siemens, Berlin, were used. Both servo units effect the aileron, air time contrary as aileron, then as elevator. Due to the tailless construction, the frame only showed the one rudder.

  The tests, which were in the essential part, taken over by us had the following results. The start from a 4 m moveable glide track without catapult speed-up takes place without difficulties at elevation angle of $90°$ to $30°$. The start supports (1 step) were discharged securely. The flight is stable.

  Due to the nominal working facilities, in half a year, about 30 rockets were discharged, and the considerably greater testing difficulties in regard to the function of the power units, the question on control could not be practically examined. Provision was made for: radio transmission of the commands with the set "StriBhurg-Kehl". The altitude gyre (precision) and the bank commands for changing the course by electrical ms-tuning of the bridge of the bank indicator. At a later date, the integration gyre LOK 11 of the Fa LOW, Berlin was to be used as altitude gyro; the apparatus AV 10 of the Fa Horn, Planen. The control of the apparatus should take place with the optical sight by means of a telescope and later with radio-measuring sets avoiding the density methods.

At the end of last year, the control of the entire project sent to the Fa Messerschmitt A.G. in Oberammergau due to greater capacity for accomplishing the problem. After our move to Oberammergau, the entire project was discontinued (even before the laboratory was equipped).

Co-workers: Dr. Seebach, München
Ing. Staiger, Reichenhall/Marzoll
Dipl. Ing. Merz, Freilassing
Dr. Weidmann, Reichenhall
Ing. Ferner, Piding
Ing. Schreiner, Reichenhall
Ing. Schaffer, Reichenhall

IV. Cooperation on problems of control and the target finder set of the fighter rocket X-4.

Due to the occupation of the Reich, our practical participation did not exceed the first information.

Translation of Report by

Dr. MÜLLER

- - - - - - - - - - - - - -

DFS Institute for Aircraft Equipment   Bad Reichenhall   B-10
Ainring Airport   26.6.45

Dr. Heinz Born, Physicist.

Report on the work carried out since the beginning of 1942.

I. Elimination of interference conditioned disturbances during television transmission between aircraft.

In the task of guiding glide bombs by television pictures, there occurs as a result of reflections on the earth's surface disturbing interference phenomena, which can bring about not only the stoppage of the individual pictures up to the complete destruction of the screen. Among other things, the different behavior of horizontally and vertically polarized radiation during reflection was taken for the solution of the problem in addition to the use of multiple antennas. Both the last named procedures brought partial success, but they did not allow the interferences occuring immediately before the target to be cut out entirely. The tests were carried out with 73 and 35 cm wave lengths over land, fresh water (Lake Constance) and salt water (Baltic, Kolberg-Gotland).

The work was commenced at the beginning of 1942 and concluded at the end of 1943 with a DFS house report on "The elimination of interference conditioned disturbances during television transmission between aircraft and with special consideration of the behavior of glide bombs".

Work carried out by Dr. Heinz Born, Bad Reichenhall, Luitpoldstr. 12.

The execution of the task brought only a partial solution of the problem as a result of fundamental difficulties.

II. Development of ultra-acoustic time-links.

From the idea of transmitting television pictures by means of suprtsonic waves over a thin steel wire with a view to controlling glide bombs independent of enemy and interference disturbances, the development of ultra-acoustic time-links arose quite generally. Tests were at first undertaken to transmit over steel wire of a diameter of 0.5 mm at 15 millicycles modulated carrier frequency, which led to relatively good results. Unfortunately, the coupling of the wires on to the crystal was not reproduceable and caused great difficulties for practical use. As, moreover, the transmission of television pictures resulted with final speed a sharp discrepancy occurred between the picture and the actual station which at high speeds of the jet bombs is intolerable.

For this reason, the final speed of the transmission is used to break up the impulses into several, to transmit these impulse groups electro-magnetically and then to coordinate them again into a single impulse, thus closing in a sure manner. The object of this development was to retard rectangular or similar impulse groups for about $2/\mu$ sec keeping them as true to shape as possible.

Preliminary tests, which were carried out first with wires and then with solid metal rods, on one occasion, as already mentioned, gave no reproduceable linking of the source of the sound on the crystal; on other the multiple reflections could not be eliminated by using metal rods. This gave as a result of the radial oscillations a strong dragging of the shape of the impulse. A short random test with mercury as the transmission medium with the development of liquid strips was commenced.

The problems were solved in the following manner:

The impulses to be retarded were modulated to a carrier frequency of several millicycles, the value of which corresponded to the actual frequency of the supersonic crystal or one of its odd superposed waves. This was worked out first with the third, fifth and seventh superposed wave of the crystal of 1.7 mm thickness and a basic frequency of 1.68 kilocycles thus with frequendes of 5.05, 8.4 and 11.7 millicycles. The diameter of the crystal used amounted to 15 or 20 mm. The supersonic wave impulse leaving the acoustic crystal is reflected in a liquid column, the length of which corresponds to the desired delay.

(With water, 15 cm = 100 / μ sec).

After passing through the strip, it is either received by the second crystal and rectified or reflected on a reflector disc, in order to be taken up again by the transmitting quartz as receiver. At 8.4 millicycles (5th superposed wave) in a 100 / μ sec strip length, 10% of the input potential at the transmitting crystal could be regained as output potential at the receiving crystal. By using the so-called reflecting strip, it can be brought about through the corresponding operating condition of the receiver tube, which with its grid was coupled direct to the oscillating circuit of the transmitting or receiving crystal, that the direct impulse on the anode side appears as a negative impulse, so that a simple division or path filtration of the direct impulse can follow.

By mixing liquids with positive and negative temperature coefficients of the speed of sound, the independency of the running time and the temperature is established. Mixtures of water 17% ethyl alcohol or 24% methyl alcohol were used. The remaining range of temperature of the speed of sound in consideration of the accuracy of the mixing proportions is about 1/100th of the value of water thus about 2.5 cm/sec/°C. Although the regulation of the temperature influence for many procedures can be effected in another manner, it is, however, unconditionally necessary, with all strips to use temperature compensated liquid mixtures, as otherwise with temperature gradients perpendicular to the expansion of sound, curvatures of the phase surfaces occur which make transmission extraordinarily bad.

Damping measurements on an acoustic crystal gave a frequency range at first of plus/minus 200 kilocycles, which can be fixed by corresponding damping at about plus/minus 400 kilocycles.

The strip was constructed in the following manner:

In a so-called crystal head (Quarzkopf) the quartz metallicized on both sides was inserted in a groove and pressed over a rubber ring as packing and an insulated pressure device against the support ring, the voltage was conducted to and from by a spring on the back side. This crystal head is screwed over a packing ring to a flange of a brass tube of about 25-30 mm diameter, so that one side of the crystal comes into direct contact with the liquid. By putting the three holding screws of the crystal head unequally, a small inclination of the surface of the crystal against the sound wave face can be achieved and thus multiple reflection can be cut out, as with the second reflection, the reflected impulse at determined angle values falls in the first zero position of the radiation characteristic of the receiving crystal. The support for transmitter and receiver were the same.

After concluding the basic tests concerning the influence or the temperature, frequency band, sensitivity and technical development, in regard to crystal supports, construction of the strip, a complete apparatus was constructed as a pattern, consisting of impulse lock and key The apparatus contained sound strips of 4 and 10 cm long or 6 and 10 cm long, so that an impulse, including the zero impulse can be excluded and then included in a triple group. The building of a triple group was chosen to keep down disturbances by impulse transmitters with high impulse frequency to the lowest possible extent.

The basic research was commenced at the beginning of 1944 and the construction of apparatus in September 1944 and this work was completed in January 1945 and published as a DFS house report under the title: "Development of ultra-acoustic timing links"

Work carried out by: Dr. Heinz Born
Alois Neckowski, Ing., Freilassing

The importance of acoustic timing links is general, and they have a great range of possibilities for further use, as up to now, they have only one known form of delaying electrical impulses true to form with proportionately low consumption over greater periods. In particular, the temporal comparison of two or more impulses with the help of timing links over coincidence circuits against the usual method of visual observation of the cathode ray tube has in addition to the advantage of greater accuracy the possibility of direct readings. During the retardation of very short impulses with high limiting frequency over relatively long periods e.g. ms the ultra acoustic timing links are to a great extent superiod to the electrical delay links.

III. Development of regulatable and re-running ultra-acoustic timing links.

With a view to using timing links for hyperbol navigation for the purpose of time comparison, by the use of which particularly simple conditions occur which make possible a simple control for course steering and thus flying on a directional beam and in view of the problem of automatic focussing in conjunction with radio measuring apparatus (radar) for night fighters, tests were prepared for automatic re-running timing links. Tests were also carried out for increasing the frequency range of the acoustic transmission system to retard even shorter impulses.

Position of the work: Drawings for regulatable timing links completed, construction of apparatus in preparation. Commenced - February 1945. Broken off - April 1945.

Work carried out by: Dr. Heinz Born
Alois Neckowski

Completion of the work would take two engineers and four mechanics about four months requiring supersonic crystal, measuring equipment (including three oscillographs).

The importance of regulatable timing links lies in their applicability for time measurements, in particular, for hyperbola navigating procedure. The automatic adjustment leaves the navigator free from mental work and makes possible a running automatic position signal. There are also possibilities of applying it to a great number of other procedures.

IV. Development and testing of procedures for anti-chaffing of
   radio measuring apparata - especially the panorama apparatus -
by means of acoustic timing links.

Principle of Procedure: The impulses radiated from the measuring apparatus as well as reflected on the chaffing apparatus as well as reflected on the chaffing cloud (Duppelwolke) as also from the aircraft inside the chaffing cloud are conducted after reception directly from the intermediate frequency of the receiver from a sound strip and retarded about an integral multiple X of the period of the intermediate frequency, so that one can connect the nth and nth plus impulses against each other directly by the intermediate frequency or even by the lower frequency. By using Dr. Fack's procedure of opposing connections, a total extinction of the coil occurs for the impulses reflected on the chaffing cloud, while impulses reflected on the machine no longer disappear as a result of the chaffing effect and it can thus be used for measuring without disturbance by chaffing. Strong signals also disappear by this method.

Relatively long period of about 4 - 6 ms are necessary for strips lengths of 6 - 8m. In order to obtain manageable measuring of the apparatus and to cut out curvatures of the phase surfaces as a result of temperature gradients perpendicular to the speed of sound, these periods were achieved by means of separate strips of about 1.5 m long connected in series, which were connected through a small broad band amplifier. Besides this, the development of a temperature coefficient control was begun in order to cut out entirely the very small course of the period with the temperature. For the construction of this control, the interesting physical observation was applied, that by the additional of alcohol to water, the speed of sound does not decrease but at first increases, at 1560 m/s it covers maximum to fall only with the increasing alcohol content to the value of pure alcohol (1180 m/s).

Position of the work: Commenced in November 1944 and not yet concluded. Intermediate reports were sent to the commissioner BMF at the end of December 1944 and the end of February 1945.

Testing strips for 2 ms in operation in the laboratory. Testing strip for practical use about 6 ms with temperature coefficient control in construction. Tests for the remote control of radio measuring apparatus preceded the work and together with the ZVH, Ulm-Darmstadt, should be successful.

Work carried out by Dr. Heinz Born.

Continuance of the work would take about four months and would need one high frequency physicist, one engineer, one designer and the possibility of installing the completed apparatus in a workshop. It would also need a radio measuring apparatus with service personnel.

The importance of this work lies in the cutting out of chaffing and strong signals especially for panorama apparatus. The remote control of smaller measuring apparatus can also supplement Dr. Fack's method to an extraordinary degree.

V. Testing a blind landing method.

The private patent application of the undersigned is the basis of the blind landing method, which entered the Reich patents office on the 19.4.44 under the document No. B 205928 Xl/62a with the title: "Method for the blind landing of aircraft" as well as the appropriate additional application of the 22.1.45. From these two applications, copies of which are attached, the principles of the method are given. The method ought to be used particularly for single engine fighters on account of the low expense of the side of the aircraft.

Position of the work: Commenced October 1944. Foundations laid for E-measuring on the Ainring Airfield with 2 x 1.5 KW impulse transmitters, and synchronization with acoustic timing links executed. Successful performance of tests in the laboratory, practical E-measuring commenced, flight tests in preparation.

In March 1945, the work was postponed in favor of the tasks numbered III and IV.

    Work carried out by: Dr. Heinz Born
                                 Dr. Hans Weller, Physicist
                                 Freilassing.

Completion of the work would take about 4 to 5 months and would require 2 engineers, 3 mechanics and 2 assistants.

    Material: 2 impulse transmitters for 20 μ sec and about 1 kw
                  impulse capacity 1 measuring foundation (2 transmitting
                  stations, mobile or stationary)
                  1 short wave direction finder
                  1 LKW (?)
                  1 aircraft type Fi 158 (Storch)
                  1 aircraft type Fi Me 109

The importance of this method lies in the extra-ordinary exact and above all running E-measuring of the landing point by aircraft, which in connection with an altitude gauge permits flying on a straight glide path, in which no kind of apparatus is required on the landing field. The representation of distance, altitude and side deviation on an easily visible triple instrument on the representation of the flight path on the cathode tube is just as valuable for the safety of an absolute blind landing as the data of the take-off point and the independency of the field intensity measurements.

Reports, manuscripts and designs appertaining to these reports in possession of the undersigned were destroyed in accordance with instructions.

Translation of Report by

Dr. HEINZ BORN

----

8. **Institute for physics of the atmosphere.** Report from the director, Hohndorf, is not available. The enclosures A2, A10, A11, give a picture of the work at this institute. Some of the most recent topics considered by the Hohndorf institute are described in the letter listed under C 29, whose translation follows:

C 29.

German Research Station for Gliders.

To the Research Management
of the R.d.L. and the Ob.d.L.   Ref: M. Dr. Hdf/Lo   26.3.45.

Re Proposals for Distributing Research Contracts.

The Institute gives the following reply to the three letters of the 27 Feb. 1945 in which the Research Management informed the Institute for Physics of the atmosphere of the DFS, that the commission "Stratosphere Research" is to be hurried over and the instructions for "experiments on the H20 in the atmosphere and aero-electrical experiments" provisionally replaced.

Under the assumption that a later confirmation would be undertaken by the research management, the Institute has been recently engaged on the following work, which up to now, came under this branch of instructions:

(1) Experiments on pressure nozzles at flying speeds around Mach No. 1 by means of measuring rockets. In connection with this pressure, nozzles should be examined in respect of their accuracy of their estimates of the static pressure and if the occasion arises of the flight velocity.

(2) Measuring the infra-red transparency of different forms of clouds with the heat gauging device of Zeiss with the simultaneous determination of the visibility and the cloud elements at three positions on the measuring strip, near the Ainring airport. On account of numerous new measuring experiences, the extenction coefficient for different wave lengths and sizes and drops should be determined in order to give finally in furtherance of the experiences a prognosis of the visible range of infra-red with the help of the visible range measured in the different types of clouds, as shown in UM 3556 by Bickenbach and Weickmann "The range of various heat gauging devices in cloud".

(3) Experiments on frequency detonations (wobbling) with the object of examining the effect of a detonation order in the rythmn of the individual frequency of the lifting parts of the aircraft.

The three aboce named problems have already been agreed upon by the research management the proposals for the first had not been promulgated up to this time: With commission (1) as up to this time, it was not possible to establish to any extent a binding estimate of costs: with commission (2) as up to this time, it was given under "experiments on the H_2O in the atmosphere" with commission (3) an extension is requested, because the obtaining of explosives which up to last autumn could be effected very quickly, it at present difficult owing to transportation.

With regard to the instructions on "experiments on the $H2O$ in the atmosphere" the institute would like further work to be carried out.

(4) Development of the Pfeifer hygrometer for registering the ascent of balloons. Quite apart from the importance of obtaining further fundamentals on the water content in the higher layers of the atmosphere from the point of view of engine development, the Chief of the Meterological Service and a series of observatories of the Reich Buro of Meteorology are interested in the creation of this apparatus. The further development of the Pfeifer apparatus for use in balloon registering, which was already planned with the first development of this apparatus, has later been replaced in favor of other problems. As recently, the weather advice in aircraft has demanded more and more actual foundations through observation, which could not be obtained by any apparatus known in the field of humidity gauging, the pursuance of this problem appeared to be of war importance.

In conjunction with problem (1) "Pressure Nozzle Experiments" the necessity arose to obtain still further estimates of the condition of the atmosphere along the measuring strip itself. While the air pressure for the individual altitude layers can be determined more or less accurately by calculation and comparison with distant positions of ascent, this is not possible for the temperature. It was necessary to develop a thermometer of very low inertia to ascertain its value by a wireless method (with radio soundings) at a receiving point on the ground. As bi-metals, which up to now were used almost exclusively in radio soundings, are completely unsuitable for rapid changes of temperature, the institute requests the distribution of instructions for:

(5) Development of radio sounding temperature gauges of low inertia with the help of resistance thermometers or thermo elements.

The institute requests the termination of the experiments in progress under "Stratosphere Research".

(6) The development of a density gauge in accordance with the interferometer. Up to now, the aerodynamists have determined only the essential dimensions of the air density from the air temperature and pressure. With at least equal accuracy, the density can be immediately determined with the aid of the interferometer principle. At very great heights, which can today be reached by rockets, the density of the air is so small that the ventilation of standard thermometers scarcely suffices. At these altitudes, the air temperature can be calculated from the air density and air pressure. Inversely at high flying velocities, the pressure can be ascertained from the density and possibility the measurements. Finally, this apparatus is in the position to control air pressure and temperature measurements, as it is itself independent of the flying velocities in the regions below Mach No. 1.

The institute further requests the approval of instructionson:

(7) Development of thermo elements with silicon.
It stands in the thermo tension series with the value 1000. It is thus (very essentially) better than all thermo-metals used up to the present time. The difficulty with the production of thermo elements with Si lay in the fact yhat Si cannot be processed, and that under damp conditions, it oxidizes to crystal and does not adhere to its base. A Schmidt (of the Firm Heraeus) was the first to succeed in producing a Silicon mirror in 1938/39. When he joined the Institute in 1941, the Firm Heraeus expressly gave the DFS permission for Schmidt to continue his tests for the production of Si heating elements. In the course of time, apparatus necessary for other tests was built like it which permitted these experiments to be conducted. A few grams of Silicon are

available at the DFS. The importance of these tests makes clear that this new thermo-element in accordance with the old measuring gives such essentially higher tensions than is customary with thermo-elements, that surplus trade galvanometers will suffice, where otherwise precision instruments are necessary, which can be disposed in required quantities all over the place (or rather in the aircraft).

As with increasing altitude, the air pressure falls slowly per degree of altitude (at about 40 km, the reduction amounts only to about 1 mm Hg at a difference in altitude of 1 Km) it is necessary to construct barometers, which work at great heights with tolerable accuracy.

The Institute requests the approval to develop a "Spätan Course Box" (Spätanlaufdose). This box is to estimate the pressure at previously determined altitude regions and only in this, however, with very great accuracy and small inertia.

With the aero-electric experiments, a good part of the measurements can be carried out without using aircraft, and indeed in accordance with up-to-date measurements, a close association between the disturbances of the aero-electrical field in the neighbourhood of clouds and the behavior of thermal up-currents on the ground can be avoided in as far as the space charge of the layer air masses near the ground can be taken up high with it. Institute requests approval for:

(9) Experiments on the aero-electrical ratios near the ground during the release of thermal up-currents. The experiments have the object of explaining the disturbances under, near and in cumulus clouds as a supplement to the foregoing observations in flight from measurements on the ground to create fundamentals for the examination of the local disturbances of the aero-electrical field in conjunction with question which can be of importance for electrical interval fuzes.

As a partial program of the experiments of the aero-electrical condition of the clouds, the examination of drop charges of precipitations on the ground can be executed without difficulty. Experiments of this kind have already been carried out but have been evaluated from a different point of view. The development of the apparatus for the measurements were commenced at the beginning of the war but were later discontinued. It appears possible to complete the apparatus and to commence measurements in the summer. Examinations should primarily be carried out in shower precipitations.

The Institute correspondingly requests a distribution of the contract on:

(10) The measuring of droplet charging in precipitations particularly in showers of rain.

With problems (9) and (10) questions of the wandering space charges are to be examined, while the following problems are concerned with the examination of a part of their origin.

The high space charge is known to be based upon ionization of layers of air near the ground to be led back by radio-active particles, which originate from the earth. According to every peculiarity of the ground and its capacity for giving out radio active substances, the space charge near the ground must be different. According to discussions with the research place of the Reichspost in Munich:

(a) These differences in the ground in the neighborhood of Salzburg are very great and

(b) The disturbances conditioned by them are largely the cause of gauging (homing) errors.

The Institute requests approval on:

(11) Examining of the radio active condition of the air near the ground and the radio active exhalation of the ground at separate points in the vicinity of the Ainring Airport. This problem has the object of proving the following hypothesis in collaboration with the Research Group of the Reichspost and in conjunction with problem (10): radio active substances given off in the air near the ground space charges which are carried up into the air by thermal up-currents and broken up by horizontal winds, whereby they produce those wandering disturbance points, which make the work of the direction finder at Maxglau near Salzburg so difficult.

In connection with aero-electrical experiments, the dependency of the aero-electrical field on the height above the ground can be carried out in particular with the registering balloons. Even if these methods in relation to measuring in gliders, represent a step backward, they will lead to the object in special cases, as for example, with extensive layers of cloud. The Institute thus asks for the approval of a contract on the:

(12) Development of apparatus for developing the aero-electrical field with the aid of registering balbons.

With the development of measuring apparatus for the aero-electrical experiments, a large number of individual experiments were carried out on the greatest insulators, maximum ohm resistances and the lowest grid currents, which can be obtained by using tubes. It also seems of the greatest interest for all other problems in which a small quantity of electricity is to be determined, that these measurements should be supplemental and published. The Institute requests, therefore, the distribution of a contract on:

(13) Systematic experiments on highest insultation, maximum ohm resistance, and minimal grid currents.
Examinations should be made for all on the dependency of the temperature, humidity and density of the air, as well as ultra-violet eight. These examinations are of fundamental importance for the majority of aero-electrical measurements, for their success stands or falls by the value of the insulation.

The Institute for Physics of the Atmosphere of the DFS presents as 13 plans, the proposals for distributing or extending the research contracts and gives in the appropriate letters details on the programs, etc. which are not mentioned in this summarized report.

Heil Hitler

Institute for the Physics of the Atmosphere

Translation of letter by

Dr. Hohndorf

DEUTSCHE FORSCHUNGSANSTALT FUR SEGELFLUG (DFS)
(German Research Institute for Gliding) - Ainring OBB.

Director: Prof. Dr. Phil. hon. Dr. of Eng. GEORGI.
Assistant: Scientific: Dipl. Eng. TEMME.
Operation: Eng. STAMER.

Institute for Aerodynamics: Prof. Dr. RUDEN.
a. Development of gliders.
b. Towed bridge section.
c. Towing with pole coupling.
d. Release container braking.
e. Flow calculation of diffusors.
f. Falling off of Aircraft.
g. Wind tunnel tests; (Darmstadt).

Institute for glider construction: Dipl. Eng. KRACHT.
a. Cargo glider
b. Jet propelled pursuit planes.
c. High altitude glider.
d. Research glider with laminar flow wing.
e. "Mistel" (pick-a-back) - Ju 188 x Me 109
f. Investigation of behaviour of A/C at Mach.No.1.
g. Coupling of two airplanes in flight.

Institute for Flight Experiments: Eng. STAMER.
a. Long rope towing; rigid towing.
b. "Mistel" (Pick-a-back) Ju 188 x Me 109.
c. Carrying tow
d. Pick-up-tow
e. Flight operations for other institutes.

Institute for Flight Equipment: Prof.Dr. FISCHEL.
a. Ultra-red searching devices.
b. General compass investigations in steel aircraft (theoretical)
c. Automatic stabilization of unmanned aircraft.
d. On-Off control method (theoretical).
e. Development of gyroscopic control for aircraft.
f. Stabilized telescope.
g. Torpedo stabilization (theoretical).
h. Remote control experiments with models.
i. Remote control of Automatic target seeking devices (theoretical).
j. Device for command transmission free of disturbances.

Institute for the physics of the Atmosphere: Dr. HOMINOFF.
a. Use of gliders in stratosphere.
b. Investigation of condensation trails.
c. Physical investigation of the undercooling of the water at low temperatures.
d. Icing of aircraft.
e. Investigation of atmospheric electricity at high altitudes with DFS 230.

Section for high frequency: Dr. POLSCHE.
a. Wind direction finding at high altitudes without optical sight.
b. Flight experiments with television devices for improving the image.
c. Television as an aid to remote control.

Laboratory for special engines: Dr. EISELE.

DEPARTMENT FOR ENGINES: Dr. SANGER.
a. Development of Lorin engine.
b. Development of carbon combustion chamber of Lorin unit.

Photographic section: Dipl. Eng. HARTH.

Central workshop: Eng. ERBSKORN.

Administration: RAUBER.

9. Department for high frequency. The director, Folsche, submitted a report (enclosure B 16) whose translation follows. See also the enclosures A 2, A 10, A 11.

B. 16.

Work of the High Frequency Department DFS, 1939-1945

Rigid Towing for the Ju 52 DFS 230.

I. Blind towing of loaded gliders.

A. In the branch of tests for using range finding equipment for blind towing, the short rope and rigid towing methods were tried out. Towing plane Ju 52. Loaded glider DFS 230. Length of tow-rope 80 m to 1 m.

The short rope towing plane is in consideration use with tow-rope up to 6 m long, and with the addition of brake flaps, it can also be taken through cumulus clouds. With a shorter rope length, the oscillations are not at one's command for any longer period. The rigid towed carrier developed at the suggestion of Stamer makes possible blind flying in all weather conditions. Flight tests 1939. Test flyer "Barabas, Folsche available in Report UM 624.

B. A glider equipped with PDS three axis steering was developed for the relieving of the glider pilot or for fully automatic towing and the bank difference between the two machines was fixed on a pivot arm and controlled by the steering. Unrestricted function even under bumps conditions. Tests end of 1941.

C. Long rope towing flights with touch lever apparatus which indicates the angle between the direction of the rope and the glider. Blind flights could also be carried out in bumpy weather with the aid of an artificial horizon and brake of performance and training for instrument flying.

D. Towing with direction finder 5 vertical signals. Direction finder 5 in the engine aircragy was constructed on one of the second frames on the high-control fixed tail plane and controlled by a horizontal axis. In place of the homing transmitter, the direction finding of the glider was done by means of horizontal antenna and the value transferred to the pilot of the glider. The continuous dash zone which gave the pre-set value of the glider, did not remain unrestrictedly constant in its position and breadth (reflection on the ground). The method without side signals is not extensive.

II. High Wind Measuring.

For measuring high winds up to 20 km altitude, in particular for high wind velocities, 5 Adcock direction finders were installed about 70 km apart for taking the bearings of radio sounds. Wave length about 11 m. The difficulty in developing the H-Adcock direction finder lay in making the input connections symmetrical. Performance of the direction finder, sharpness of resonance gauge plus or minus 0.1 - 0.2 degrees with sounds 80 km away at 5000 m 1/2 - 1/10 watt capacity. Direction finding errors plus or minus 1.5 degrees on centering. In connection with a series of measurings made on the Luneberger Heide, a very great height of radio sound between 20 and 25 km were measured. Measurements concluded Autumn 1940. Report FB 1321 Folsche Osken "High wind measuring by taking bearing of radio sounds with Adcock direction finders.

III. Aircraft and bombs controlled in accordance with telepictures.

A. Close bombing from aircraft of sea and land targets.

1. To test the apparatus and demonstrate the process, a loaded glider DFS 230 with three axle control, remote control, and remote transmission installation was used. Three axle steering PDS (Build in together with Institute G).

Remote Control: Transmitter and Receiver Strassburg-Kehl.

Command Apparatus: Start-Stop Principle.

Telepicture Apparatus: FB K2 (Ferusch GmbH).

The glider is automatically and rigidly towed from the take-off until released and then remote controlled by the Ju 52 in accordance with the telepicture to its target or landing place. From the take-off until shortly before the target, no interference occurred in respect of the safety pilot in the glider. Flights carried out before the principal of the Technical Office, Col. Vorwald on 10.6.1942.

The numerous tests flights led to a stabilization of the television apparatus, particularly synchronizing. Also the fixing of the optical and electrical ranges of the apparatus. (See also intermediate Report I, II, III, on television transmission between aircraft 1942-43. DFS Report, Author Dr. Folsche and Engelbrecht).

Transmission waves 70-100 cm.
Antenna: Yagi

Co-workers: Gertloff, Wucherer, Reger, Engelbrecht. Several fundamental reports retained. Film handed to Col. Frensch.

2. Streak Disturbance.

During picture transmission on the dm wave between two power driven aircraft, a between bomb Hs 293-D and a power driven aircraft strong streak inference occurs in the picture. The reason was explained on the grounds that the transmitter was frequency modulated by sound noises. With the interference of two frequency modulated beams, which have a difference of path, (a direct beam and one reflected on the ground) there occurs a strong amplitude modulation in the receiver (streakiness). The streakiness was unrestrictedly reproduced in the laboratory direct and over a cable. The sound sensitivity of the transmitter was eliminated by suitable tubes. In connection with the retesting of the function of the diode modulation with this tube, there still remains outstanding:

(a) VM Report: Examination of streak disturbance during television transmission between aircraft and Hs 293-D by T. Folsche dated 26.10.44.

(b) Basis for a comprehensive report on laboratory tests destroyed by H. Engelbrecht.

3. A$_s$ the carrier aircraft should be able to turn about or move as freely as possible after dropping its bombs, a space stabilization of the direction receiving antenna was necessary at least along the longitudinal axis. Illus. 3 shows the principle of a developed and tested Yagi-antenna stabilized about 2 axes. Flight test concluded on 30-9-1944. Fundamental reports have been retained. This is the work of Gertloff and Wucherer.

4. Recognisability of land and sea targets during different weather conditions: with the FB K2 camera with red or blue "IKO"

Sea Target (Ship 130 m long) with clear view.
False light camera view 15 km.
During haze (Natural view 5 km) Camera view 3 km.
Land Target: in Summer with extensive light velocity, red "IKO" (Rotiko) gives better contrast than blue "IKO" (Blaviko); requisite light intensity 200-500 lux.
UM Report: Recognisability of land and sea targets with the FB K2. Folsche 1943.
Co worker: Lutz.

5. In order to increase the disturbance resistance of picture transmission a transmission on the shortest possible carrier waves is interesting, furthermore, many more transmitters can be accommodated in the cm-range. Picture transmission tests with magnet field tube transmitters on the 10.7 cm wave length (RD 2 Mb 0.5 watt capacity). With maximum ausstenering additionally occuring frequency modulation

plus or minus 1.8 MHz, is not noticeable on the ground. Bridged distance on the ground 1 km with normal cones.

UM Report 3564 "Television transmission on the cm-wave". Osken. Muller, end of 1944, Equipment partly seized.

6. Practice equipment for remote picture control.

The apparatus is capable of repeating in particular the conditions as the end of the approach. The picture consists of a model of the target by projection from a spotlight source. The model is correspondingly moved. Suggestion middle of 1943 by Gertloff. Design end of 1944. Executed beginning of 1945. Drawings in existance. The work of Weidenhausen, Matznetter, Draudt. (See also UM 3506, reports on the problem of bomb control by telepictures. A Gertloff. Also House Report No. 66 and UM 3501. Bombing errors when target finding by telepicture and bombing. Klein.

7. Participation in the bombing tests Hs 293-D in Garz and Karlshagen. July and October 1944. Work of Lutz, Reger and Wucherer. Curve flights with gyro stabilized receiver antenna after dropping. Field intensity registration. The Hs 293-D furnished practice apparatus. Bombing tests interrupted. Production of a "Kartesischen" stick to adapt the usual control in the aircraft.

8. Equipment of a Mistel coupled Me 109 (control aircraft) Ju 88 (Bomber) with Seedorf 1 apparatus. Beginning of 1945. Flight tests of the television coupling were not carried out. Television installation by Engelbrecht.

B. Picture transmission and control over long distances. End of 1943 picture transmission to the limit of the electro-optical view. Transfer of pictures from an aircraft approaching a ship to a second aircraft 200 km away at an altitude of 3000 to 4000 m. Transmitter 30 watt 3.5 m. Films and information regarding field intensity completed. Material seized at the time by Captain Campbell.

C. Rockets aimed at air targets controlled by telepictures.

Recognisability of air targets with FB K2 He 111 recognisable with FB K2 against clear sky with arro stratus clouds by a low flying aircraft at about 2.5 - 3 km. (Short circuit picture). Both aircraft were above the haze limit. Co-workers: Edgar Lutz. UM Reports: Folsche "Recognisability of air targets with the FB K2 camera. End of July 1944.

Co-workers necessary for the continuation of the work in the field of flying bodies controlled by telepictures.

Ing. Hermann Engelbrecht
Ing. Edgar Lutz
Electrician Max Vogel
Electro-mechanic Karl Holesak
Mechanic Erwin Amstutz
Dipl. Ing. Rudolf Wucherer
Ing. Heinrich Reger
High Frequency Technician Hugo Busch
Designer Kurt Weidenhausen.

IV. A. Cm antenna with low reflection. For screening enemy jammers during remote control a directional receiving antenna with a low reception factor from the opposite direction is useful on the bomb. The reflection with funnel antennas for 10 cm was measured and fixed in the funnel or dipole in front of it. Within an angle range of about 100°, the receiving field intensity is by this measure lower than 5% of the beam in the front.

Work by Dr. Osken and Ernst Muller. DM 3568 or 823 Ring Funnel Antenna etc. H. Osken. UM 3568 Funnel Antenna with dipoles in front H. Osken E. Muller.

B. Blind landing procedure with rotating cm directional antenna and electric altitude gauge. Suggested January 1944. Work on it beginning in the middle of 1944.

With this procedure, the directions from aircraft were made visible to two transmitters standing on the landing ground on a cathode ray tube as beam from the center point of the screen (synchronized deflecting coils, control of the Wehnelt by the intensity of the receiving field). By the simultaneous transfer of the measuring values given by the electrical altitude gauge on the cathode ray tube as a horizontal stroke at a corresponding distance from the center point, the correct glide path can be read.

For the main production, a double type rotating antenna was used. Adequate sharpening up of the receiver maxima by isolation. Radial recorder and receiver under construction; antenna and transmitter completed. Work discontinued on account of other more urgent problems.

Cm apparatus worked on by Dr. Osken. Sharpening: Engelbrecht and Tasch. Designing radial recorder: Gertloff. Apparatus partly seized.

V. A. Disturbance free command transmission ("Mosaik")

For the purpose of remote control, fighter guidance and signals communications, a transmissionapparatus should be created, which uses on a few high frequency channels and is proof against active jamming.

The transfer of different signals through the same channel can be achieved by using different impulse groups with characteristic distances. Division of impulses on the transmission side by means of supersonic timing links in the impulse group (closing) on the receiving side, combination by means of complementary timing links over a coincidence connection. The freedom from disturbance should be effected by the high keying of the impulses, by differentation after rectifying (cutting out of continuous disturbances) and by the close combination with the self-supercharging process. With the natural supercharging process, the same impulses were transmitted at the frequency. The receiver has no oscillator, but two high frequency circuits tuned to the transmitter frequency. Both high frequencies form the intermediate frequency in a frequency changing tube, so that, thus, one compensates the transmitter, the other the oscillator. The procedure cannot be jammed on one of either frequencies. Jamming tests on an apparatus with a transmitting frequency of 84 and 94 MHz gave no disturbances with a ratio of the jammer to the transmitter of 10^3 to 1. The timing link development for the "Mosaik" used a supersonic frequency of 5-10 MHz, medium alcohol and water. Temperature constancy of the speed of sound of 0.02% per degree, in a favorable mixing proportion of alcohol and water. A transmitting and receiving set for two triple groups was carried out (taken apart or destroyed).

In the report dated 1.6.1943 on the remote control of bombs of projectiles with highly keyed impulse groups, under the authorship of Folsche, the suggestion for "Masaik" is to be found. The suggestion "self-supercharging" by Born, Lutz, Weller, at the end of 1943.

Work completed up to the first quarter of 1945 up to disturbance tests.

B. Procedure against active jamming during radio measuring.

The supersonic time link developed for "Mosaik" is also suitable for solving other problems. Besides using it against passive jamming, a procedure has been taken in hand for cutting out active jamming. The process consists of leading the phase sequested radio measuring impulse over a supersonic link of a length corresponding to the interval between impulses and high frequency addition, while the jammer with this adjustment of the variable timing link does not add up to the right phases. Impulse is taken from the mean value of the jammer. Preliminary tests which show that high frequency addition is possible by reverse coupling over a sound strip (increasing of impulse 1 : 5) have been carried out. (March-April 1945). The equipment has been dismantled and partly destroyed). Co-workers: Lutz and Schnell.

DFS. - ERNST UDET.

REVIEW OF THE WORK OF THE HIGH FREQUENCY DIVISION 1939 - 1945.

PROBLEM	SOLUTION	PARTIAL PROBLEM
1939/41 BLIND TOW OF TRANSPORT GLIDERS (TOGETHER WITH INSTITUTE F).	Short rope in rigid tow.	Testing Ju-52 DFS 230 towing rope length up to 1m rigid tow support with shock absorption.
	Automatic Rigid Tow	Remote control of the bank difference to PDS three axel steering of the cargo-glider.
	Long towing rope with touch-lever-indicator	TESTFLIGHTS
	Tow with direction funder 5 vertical indication.	TESTFLIGHTS.
1939/41 ALTITUDE WIND MEASUREMENTS.	Direction finding by radio soundings from 5 ultra short wave Adcock Stations.	Development of the direction finder and soundings Altitude wind measurements.
		Remote control of a glider from take-off to landing through television from an aircraft, without interference of the pilot, for demonstration and test purposes.
		Removing of the streak interference during television transmission between aircrafts and noise level
		Development of a space-stabilized directional receiving antenna for elimination of minime at take-off.
1941/44 TELEVISION CONTROLLED AIRCRAFTS OR BOMBS.	Close-release from the aircraft on Sea and Land targets.	Recognisability of land and see targets under various weather conditions with the FB camera.
		Television transmission with 10 cm
		Training apparatus for television control (box apparatus). Calculation of the errors.

	...course...of the frame for blind release.	
	Medium tension with television.	
	Television transmission and control over great distances.	Television transmission to the limit of the electro-optical sight.
	Television controlled rockets against air targets	Recognizability of air targets with FBK_2
1943/45 CM ANTENNA WITH NEGLIGABLE REFLECTION. BLIND LANDING PROCEDURE WITH ROTATING CM DIRECTIONAL RECEIVING ANTENNA.	Split ring funnel	Development of a measuring apparatus.
	Front dipole.	Measuring the antenna.
	Glide path through combination of electrical altitude indicator and direction to 2 transmitters on a Cathode ray tube.	Structure of cm equipment, connections to sharpen focus of the direction finding maxima Astral recorder for a demonstration of principles.
1943/45 INTERFERENCE-RESISTANT COMMAND TRANSMISSION (MOSAIK) WITH SOUND STRIPS	High keyed impulse groups pre and deciphering through	Development of supersonic tube-links, not dependent on temperature.
SELF SUPERCHARGING PROCEDURE.	Supersonic strips and coincidence connections	Development of a coincidence connection interference tests.
	Procedure against active interference of radio measuring through phase directional high frequency addition of the succession impulses. (Backcoupling over Supersonic strips).	Examination of the mixed grid plate transceadence dependent on automatic supercharging from the work point.
INTERFERENCE RESISTANT RADIO MEASURING EQUIPMENT.		Circuit for the return and high frequency addition of phase regulated impulses over a changeable supersonic strip. Influence of variuos jammers.
AUTOMATIC NAVIGATION PROCEDURE WITH SOUND STRIPS.	Determination of position in the aircraft, similar to Hyperbel navigation procedure through impulse covering with supersonic delay links.	Determining of a basis with synchronization airborn apparatus with changeable tuning links for testing the principle.

SUGGESTIONS ON BLIND LANDING PROCEDURE, ROCKET CONTROL, COMMUNICATION NAVIGATION PROCEDURE WITH IMPULSES OR IMPULSE GROUPS, SUGGESTION: MAGNETIC KEYING.

To continue the work (reproducing the apparatus) in the field of supersonic delay links and impulse technique (Mosaik etc) my co-workers: Ing. Edgar Lutz, Ing. Peter Schnell, Dr. Hans Weller and Dipl. Ing. Schnebinger are qualified.

C. Navigating procedure by means of timing links similar to the Hyperbol procedure. (With Institute G).

The time intervals of the ground impulses received, which give the position coordinates, were determined by means of timing links and coincidence connections. The signal follows through a normally sentitive instrument. The instrument can be compensated automatically.

Erection of two 50 KW impulse transmitters in Ainring and Salzburg, frequency 45 MHz with synchronization. Completion of an addition to the receiver FuG 135 constantly controllable timing link and instrument indicator.

Flying tests no longer possible. Advantages: Simplified manipulation or automatic control, reduction of expenses.

The testing equipment was dismantled; the fundamentals were destroyed.

This project was worked on from the middle of 1944 to the end of 1945. Dr. Weller being mainly responsible.

- - - - - - - - - -

10. Laboratory for special engines. A report by the director, Eisele, was submitted (enclosure B 3) whose translation follows. See also enclosures A2, A10, A11.

B 3.

Garmische, 9 June 1945.

Schmidt duct.

Experiments by Dr. Ing. Karl Eisele, Physicist, born 25.1.1913 at Warblinger near Stuttgart, head of the independent Institution "Laboratory for Special Engines" (LST) at the DFS Ainring. Present domicile: Tengling near Wagungarm See, approx. 30 km.N.W. Freilassing at Moosburner Sawmill.

1. Professional Activity:

1/12/37 till 31/3/39 scientific assistant at First Physical Institute, Stuttgart Tech. **Activity** - Stratospheric research.

1/12/39 till 29/2/44 Experimental engineer at Forschung Institute fur Kraftfahrwesen, Fahrzeug-n-Flug-motoren, Stuttgart Tech. (Prof. Dr. W. Kamm)

Activity: Work on piezo-electrical pressure measurements, increasing measuring accuracy. From mid 1940 till present date, work on the Schmidt tube. Development of measuring methods to explore the complicated and partly unknown phenomena occuring inside the tube. (Piezo-electrical pressure measurements, mean thrust and thrust variation, analysis of movement of the valve flaps, registering the flame spread, field of sound pressure in the vicinity of the exhaust). Measurements of this type were carried out at all research and development centres in Germany. (P. Schmidt, Munich: original Schmidt tube - DFS, Prien, Darmstadt and Ainring, also

Horsching: manned intermittent ducts working with exmposive and detonating combustion. Measurement of sound pressure on surface of airframe and internal pressure variation in flight, measurement of oscillations and thrust variation in flight - Messerschmidt, Augsburg development of Argus basis, and original Schmidt tube-Argus Motors, Berlin). As a result of this activity, I acquired a probably unique all around experience of the performances and behavior of various types of intermittent ducts, and of their state of development. 1/3/44 to 31/10/44. Experimental engineer and Group Leader of DFS From 1/11/44 Departmental head, Laboratory for Special Engines, DFS.

Activity: Building on past experience gained on various test beds and measuring aircraft, the object was (1) to explore the physical and chemical phenomenon in the duct and to produce the experimental data necessary to build up the theory of intermittent ducts. (2) Further development of the Schmidt duct.
Increase in thrust - Adoption of measuring methods.

Practical Activity

Construction of test beds for high precision measurements both on the ground and in the air. The difficulties attending accurate measurements on intermittent ducts are very considerable. Test beds at Ainring (near airfield) Flying installations for this nearly completed; project worked out by Eng. Edwin Schafer, Ainring). Project for He 219 high speed test bed. The test bed was dismantled and partly evacuated to Tengling. Do 217V flying test bed was left undamaged at Hörschung.

FURTHER DEVELOPMENT OF PHYSICAL AND CHEMICAL MEASURING METHODS.

It was planned to measure thrust, fuel injection pressure, fuel flow, duct temperature, internal pressure variation, movement of flaps, flame pictures, exhaust gas velocity, experiments on fuel injection, exhaust gas analysis, air mass flow, conditions of air induction. Experiments were also made on feeding on GM1 for thrust boosting and on intermittent ducts running on coal dust. These experiments were soon stopped.

FURTHER DEVELOPMENTS AND INCREASE IN OUTPUT

Variations of thrust with length and diameter of duct, experiments with different types of combustion chambers, increasing the ram pressure of the air by fitting a rounded orifice, introduction of a thrust after the combustion chamber, increase in output by reducing the drag on the suction side. This last project of Dr. Ing. G. Dedrich's is probably present in the large wind tunnel at Otztal, Tyrol. Dedrich was formerly with Argus and has probably made the greatest contribution to the development of the intermittent duct, namely the introduction of continuous fuel injection, of a new combustion chamber, and of a throat. New induction cowling, designed by Dipl. Ing. Fishlich of Institute A, Prof. Ruden, DFS.

RESULTS

An experimental test bed was built and in operation, and this gave very accurate readings of thrust, fuel pressure and fuel flow. The flying test bed Do 217 K was ready for use, and the installation for the He 219 nearly completed. As for measuring methods, those for measuring thrust on the test bed and in flight, and for measuring fuel flow were fully developed, whilst the other measuring methods were still in the development stage.

Injection Dept. S1 of DFS, air mass flow at Brunswick, by von Hoffman (DFS). Addition of GM1 did increase the thrust, but the consumption of GM1 was heavy. Practically this is not of great interest, except in very special cases. It was found possible to run a duct on a combination of petrol and coal dust, but thrust was lower than when running it on petrol.

Increase in Output.

Exact figures cannot be given, as all reports have been destroyed, and figures are from memory. Check measurements could be made in one or two months time, after re-erection of the test beds. The cowling would have to be made anew, as it was burned.

See Fig. 1.

Thrust as a function of duct length, static trials.

There is a well defined maximum, not yet explained by theory. This example shows what procedure for further development was intended. It was intended to find the cause of the thrust variation with duct length by measuring all conditions and quantities. Conditions in flight were more involved, on account of air flow and frictional drags.

See Fig. 2.

Behavior in flight of the lengthened duct.
(Argus measurements)

In flight, the increase in thrust is negatived at high speeds, due to increased drag and friction.

See Fig. 3.

Improved valves. Static tests.

Curve 1. Standard Argus valve.
Curve 2. Improved Standard valve. Intermediate ribs removed and entry edges rounded. Larger effective area, better aerodynamically.
Curve 3. DFS Design. Very much larger effective area, but valves have a shorter life.

See Fig. 4.

Improved valves and new cowling.

There was no chance of carrying out the experiments with combustion chambers and restrictions. The experiment with rounded outlet edge of the duct gave negative results. Trials with various diameters of ducts were made. Let d be the diameter of the Standard Argus 014 duct; trials were made with ducts of 5/6 d and 7/6 d diameter. There are maxima in the curves, but the results are not yet fully clear. A combination of a 7/6 d diameter duct with the improved valve gave an

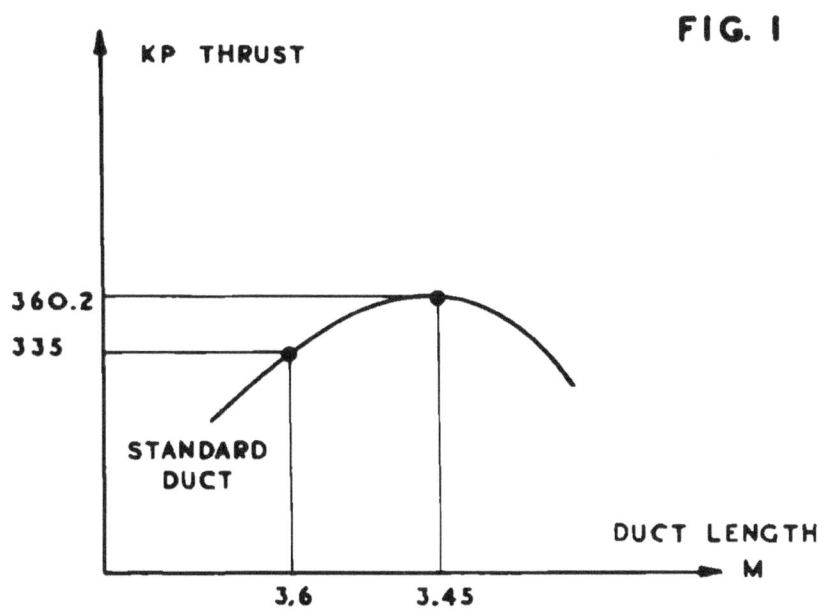

THRUST-DUCT LENGTH CURVE, STATIC

FIG. 1

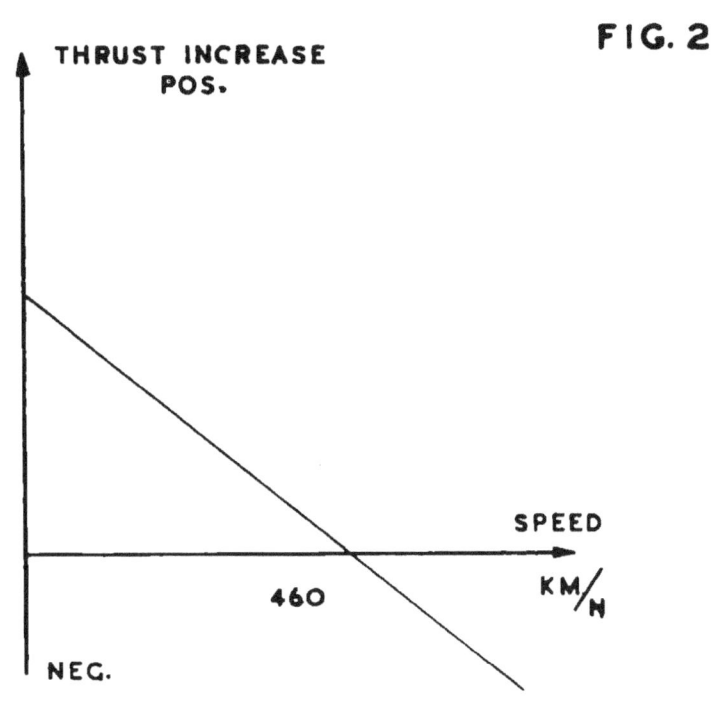

FIG. 2

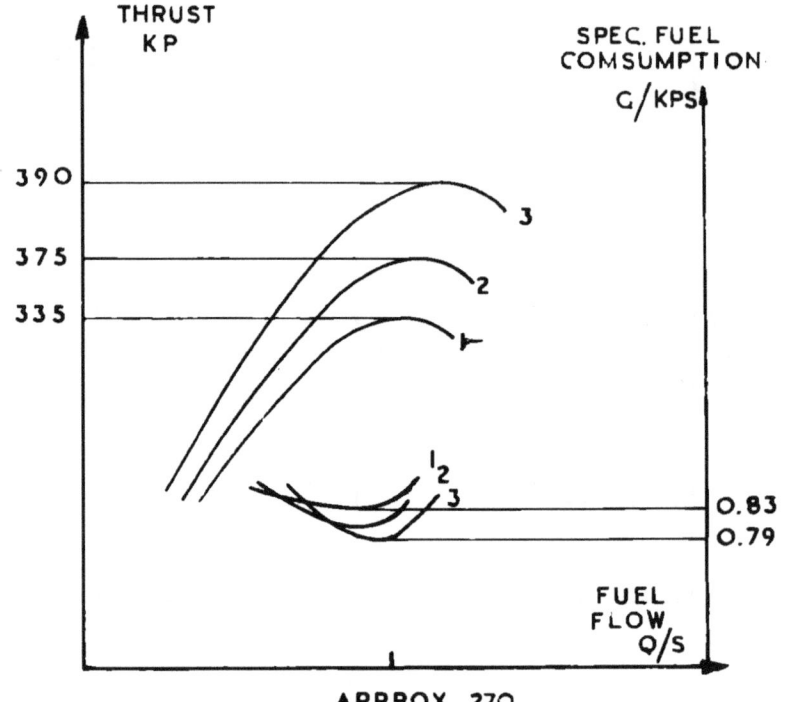

IMPROVED VALVE – STATIC

FIG. 3

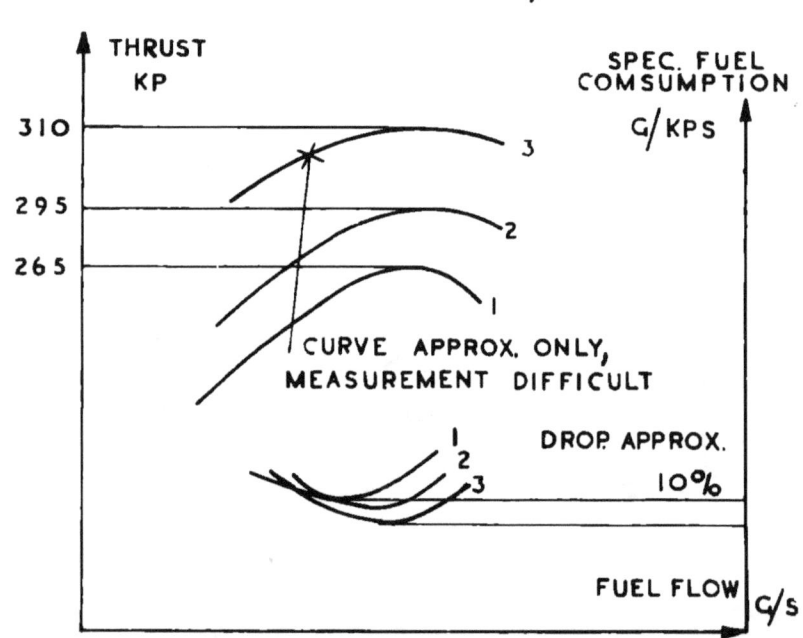

IMPROVED VALVE AND NEW COWLING

FIG. 4

increased thrust (static) of 410 - 420 Kgs. Specific fuel consumption lower than 0.77 gr. (Kg. thrust sec. Length of duct over 4 meters. These trials were made at the very end. Curves are not available. The 5/6 d duct gave no increase in thrust.

As to physical measurements, only a few oscillograms of valve flap movements and of pressures were made at Ainring. Other measurements had to be abandoned on account of the urgency of the development programme. Theoretical work was not carried out. It was to have followed the experimental results on which it would be based.

Theoretical work on the subject has been done by Prof. Bechert-Marz, Prof. Schultz-Grunow (use of graphic gasdynamic methods) and Prof. Lauer. The theorists could only make statements on the spreading of the pressure waves and the suitability of various shapes of ducts.

This report gives a general idea of the development. Further details will be given if required.

Note: (This is a translation of the German by Lt. Block, R.A.F.)

B. 4.

Translation at Garmisch, 10 June 1945 of story submitted by Dr. Ing. Eugen Sanger.

Experiments on Coal Firing for An Athodyd.

Basing on experiments with liquid fuels, the natural sequence for coal firing developments in the athodyd seemed to be: Floating coal-coal dust-solid coal. Orders were given to study the problem of solid coal first.

The first were the main difficulties:

(1) **Feeding and storing the coal.**

The problem of feeding the solid coal to the combustion chamber was avoided by storing the entire coal quantity refined inside the combustion chamber of the athodyd. If the relative size of the diffusor outlet to diffusor inlet is chosen large enough, the loss of thrust caused by the mass of coal blocking part of the free passage inside the athodyd is not very serious. A serious difficulty, however is presented by the problem of how to mount the total coal supply, which can weigh several tons, inside the athodyd. In order to find a solution to this problem of an athodyd flying at 200-300 meters per second with a coal supply exposed to an air stream having a velocity of 20-30 meters per second, model experiments were made with a cylindrical pipe exposed to an air stream dirested along its axis, the diameter of the air stream being approx. 50 cm and the air velocity 25 meters per second. Models of the proposed coal supply mountings complete with coal were burned inside the pipe.

a) **Steel grate cages with uncooled grate bars.**

Approx. 20 x 40 x 60 cm, coal content 40 Kg. See Fig 1. All experiments with this type of grate rise to serious melting of the bars, whatever grade of steel was used. The coal was anthracite, approx. 40 mm. size, and the free gap between grate bars was 30 mm.

b) **Steel grate cages with air-cooled grate bars. See Fig 2.**

Same dimensions and coal content as a). The same serious melting of the bars was observed, and a marked improvement of the cooling air system did not appear practical.

c) **Steel grate cages with liquid cooled grate bars. See Fig. 3.**

These proved very reliable. Water was used for cooling and plain carbon steel for the bars. This type of grate was used for a series of further experiments with a compressor providing the air stream, and

and never gave rise to any trouble. Use in an aircraft would necessitate a special water cooling system, a circulating pump etc.

d) <u>Grate cages with bars made of heat resisting materials.</u>

Such as ceramic or metal-ceramic bars. Experiments could no longer be carried out.

e) <u>Plastic coal</u>

Coal blocks approx. 50 x 50 x 20 cm made of "Skoda Loain Coal" See Fig. 4 These blocks could be mounted in the tube without any trouble in a position that allowed the air to flow by on all sides, thus resulting in complete combustion. The dead weight of the mounting was very low. This plastic coal is a development of Dr. Heinrich Schmitt, of H. Schmidt V.G., in conjunction with Skoda of Prague, and consists of coal particles bound together with synthetic resin.

2) <u>Heat release in combustion chamber.</u>

The importance of the specific heat release in the combustion chamber, H (Kcal $/m^3h$) and of the first differential of H in relation to time, dH/dt Kcal$/m^3h^2$ can be gauged from the following example, the figures for which were taken from an actual project (UM 3509), with a combustion chamber length of 2 meters only, however. See Fig 5. Similar H-t diagrams apply even for athodyds of widely differing types, such as the projected altrodyd developed by us in conjunction with Skoda, having an all up weight of only 3000 Kg. The high values of H and dH/dt required can be met when using liquid fuels. When using lump coal, values of H reading several million Kcal/m3h and of dh/dt reaching several dozen million Vcal/m^3h^2 were measured, using a grate type as described under 1c. It appears therefore that coal can be used for the required conditions of horizontal flight, even when taking the low density of air at say 12 Km. altitude into account. However the conditions demanded for accelerating and climbing, and for combat output require values of F and df/dt which cannot be met by burning of lump coal. For these conditions lump coal burns far too slowly. When using plastic coal, figures were obtained which are slightly below those for lump coal, but improvements are possible, for instance by increasing the exposed surfaces, and according to the manufacturer, by the addition of activating chemical substances, such as oxygen bearing compounds, in this case however at the expense of the calorific value.

In view of this, the Skoda project was designed for combined operation on liquid fuel and coal, the coal being used in throttled back horizontal flight, which represents a large part of the total consumption - see areas of H-t diagram, Fig 5.

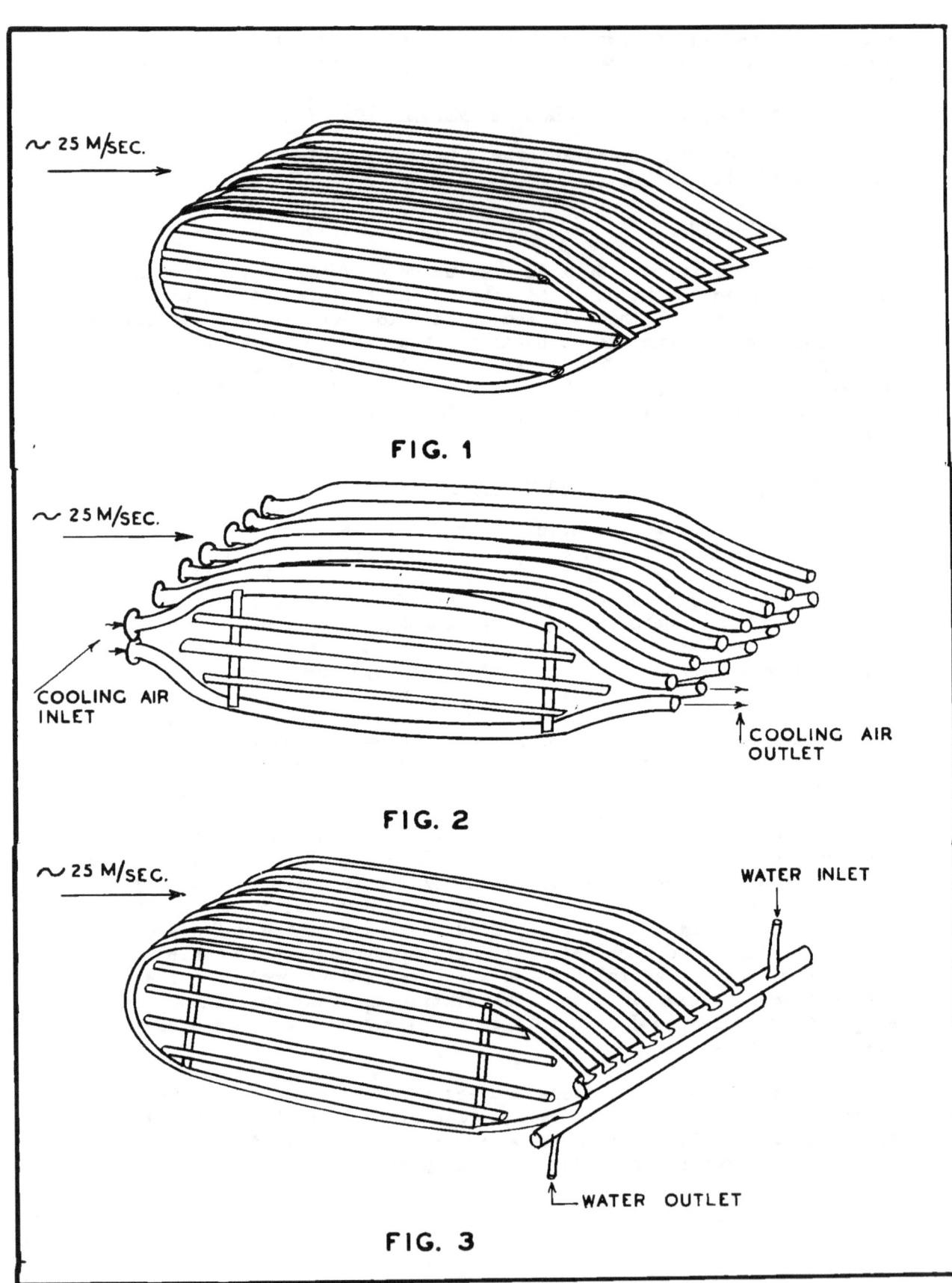

FIG. 1

FIG. 2

FIG. 3

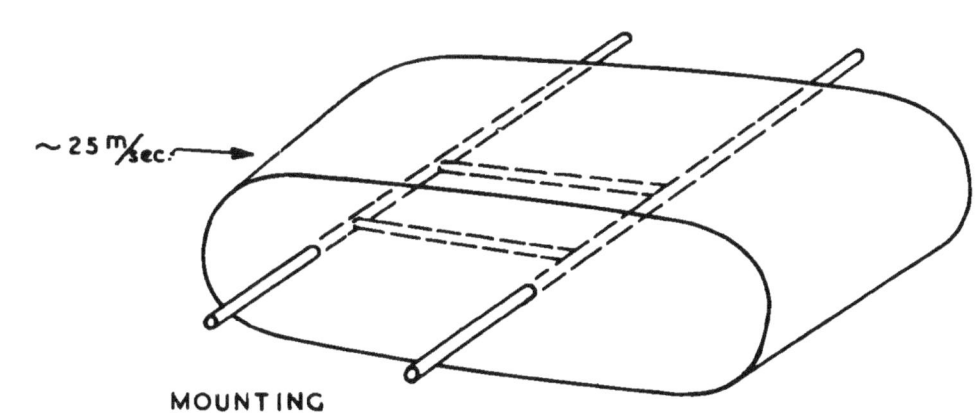

~25 m/sec.

MOUNTING

FIG. 4

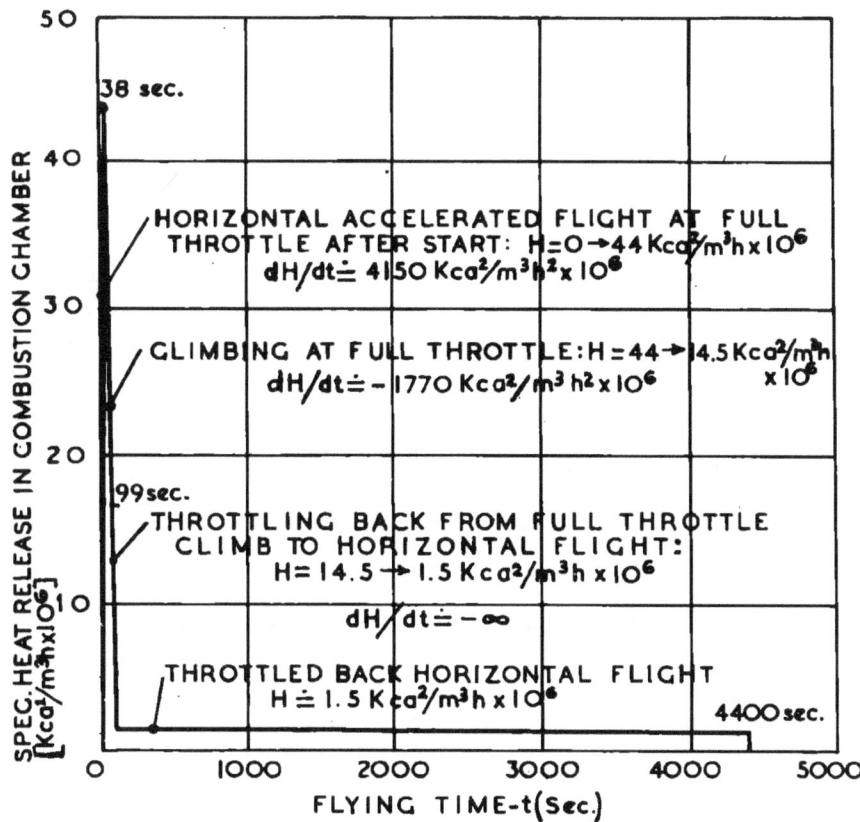

38 sec.

HORIZONTAL ACCELERATED FLIGHT AT FULL THROTTLE AFTER START: $H = 0 \rightarrow 44 \, Kcal/m^3 h \times 10^6$
$dH/dt \doteq 4150 \, Kcal/m^3 h^2 \times 10^6$

CLIMBING AT FULL THROTTLE: $H = 44 \rightarrow 14.5 \, Kcal/m^3 h \times 10^6$
$dH/dt \doteq -1770 \, Kcal/m^3 h^2 \times 10^6$

99 sec.

THROTTLING BACK FROM FULL THROTTLE CLIMB TO HORIZONTAL FLIGHT:
$H = 14.5 \rightarrow 1.5 \, Kcal/m^3 h \times 10^6$

$dH/dt \doteq -\infty$

THROTTLED BACK HORIZONTAL FLIGHT
$H \doteq 1.5 \, Kcal/m^3 h \times 10^6$

4400 sec.

SPEC. HEAT RELEASE IN COMBUSTION CHAMBER $[Kcal/m^3 h \times 10^6]$

FLYING TIME-t (Sec.)

FIG. 5

3) __Ignition__ - of coal was effected without great trouble by using a special pack, in which the following substances set one another alight in the following order:

Electric igniting wire (glowing wire) → chemical ignition core → thermite filled steel tube → wood wool soaked in paraffin → wood shavings soaked in paraffin → coal.

__B 5__

I. __Research Work on a 100 ton Rocket Engine 1939-1942.__

As is known, in the year 1933, my book "The Technique of Rocket Flight" appeared and subsequently several smaller research works in this special field, among others being that published in Astronautics in New York 1936.

As a result of these publications, I was called to Germany from Vienna in 1936 and entrusted with the formation of a Research Institute for the technique of rocket flight, to be built at Trauen.

In 1939, this construction was so far advanced that with about 15 separate buildings (Office Building - Illus. 1, Test Shed - Illus. 2, Oxygen Shed - Illus. 3, Fuel Shed, Electric Supply, Observation benches, Workshop, Hydrogen Laboratory, Ozone Laboratory, Water Supply, Mess, Houses for Lodging, Guardroom, etc.) the research could be undertaken. Its object was to carry out research in a 10 year program on the fundamentals of constructing liquid rocket engines with a thrust of 100 tons and the highest possible exhaust velocity for long distance rocket aircraft, and if necessary, for long distance rocket bombers, and to undertake the construction of 100 ton engines in conjunction with the appropriate industries.

The research work mainly covered the following fields:

(1) Air forces and the form of air frames at Mach. Nos. between 3 and 30.

(2) Gas flow with simultaneous chemical conversion of the flowing medium.

(3) Air forces in a large free path of the air molecule (extreme flight altitudes).

(4) Fuel research (in particular the burning of light metals, the dispersion and properties of liquid ozone).

(5) Research on materials in particular the construction materials for liquid oxygen pumps and high service combustion chambers.

(6) Coolants (suitable cooling and steam making materials for steam cooled combustion chambers).

(7) Construction of a high pressure airborne pumping apparatus for fuel and oxygen for steam turbine propulsion. Illus. 4.

(8) Construction of the ignition apparatus for the rocket engine.

(9) Development of the combustion chambers for extreme fire gas temperatures at 50-100 atu fire gas pressure with cooled walls and steam cooling. (See Illus. 5, 6, 7).

(10) Development of short fire gas jets with cooled walls for these combustion chambers (Illus. 8)

(11) Development of the supersonic catapult device for long distance rocket aircraft.

(12) Development off light mechanics and calculation of trajectories for long distance rocket aircraft.

In 1942, this long term program came into conflict with the prosecution of the war. The work became more and more hindered by the call-up of workers and those in industries lending their support, for war purposes, and by the nedd of valuable construction materials (nickel, copper, chrome) and by my newly undertaken work on the Lorin Engine and on account of this, it was finally broken off in the Summer of 1942 in favor of the Lorin Engine.

Experiences gained up to this time were given in several intermediate reports, particularly in the larger work of Sanger-Bredt: "On rocket propulsion for long distance bombers" Then further representation is planned in the second edition of "Rocket Flight Technique".

FIG. I

Office and Laboratory buildings of the Technical Research Institute for rocket flight in Traven.

FIG. 2

Test Shed of the large Testing bench for liquid fuel - rocket engines at the Technical Research Institute for rocket flight in Traven (with the built in Testing Apparatus in operation).

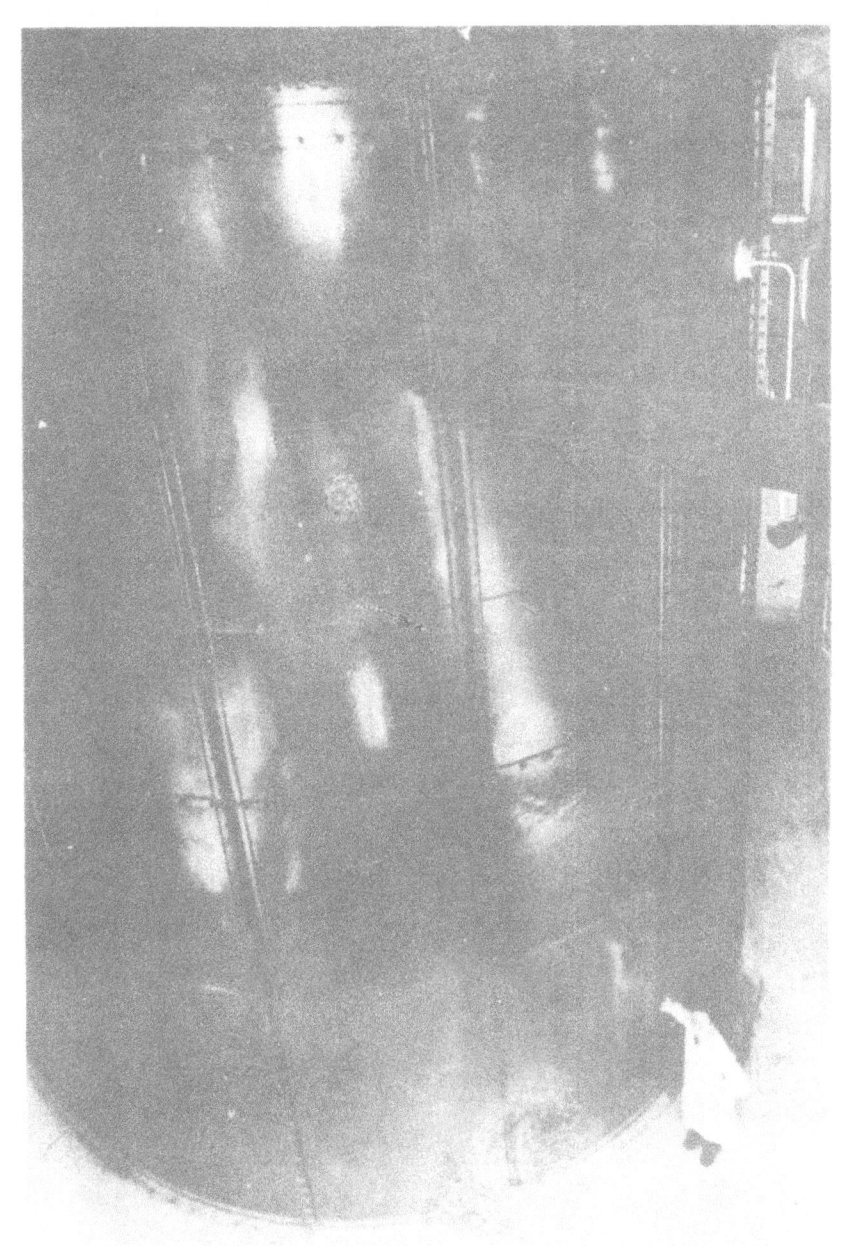

FIG. 3

Liquid oxygen tank for 50,000 kg at the Technical Research Institute for rocket flight at Traven. (The largest tank in Germany).

FIG. 4
Liquid oxygen pump with a supply capacity of
4 liters/second against 150 Atmospheric pressure, at
the Technical Research Institute for rocket flight at Traven.

FIG. 5.
View of the Testing bench in the Test Shed for liquid fuel driven rocket engines at the Technical Research Institute for Rocket Flight at Traven. (Combustion Chamber with 1 ton thrusts gas oil/liquid oxygen supply and water cooling in continuous operation.

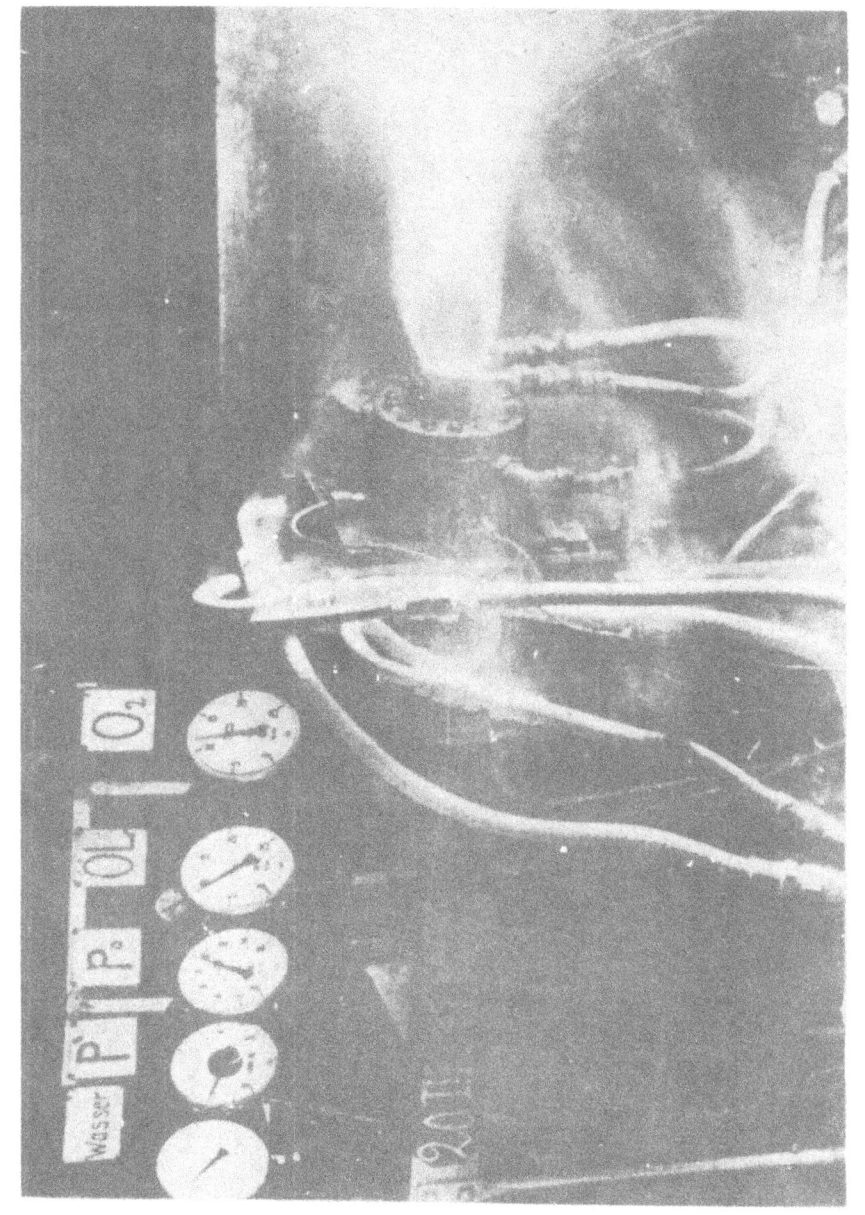

FIG. 6
Combustion chamber with 1 ton thrust, gas-oil, liquid oxygen supply
100 atmosphere fire gas pressure with water cooling in operation.

FIG. 7

Test development of the cooling system of a rocket combustion chamber of 100 tons thrust for burning gas-oil/liquid oxygen.

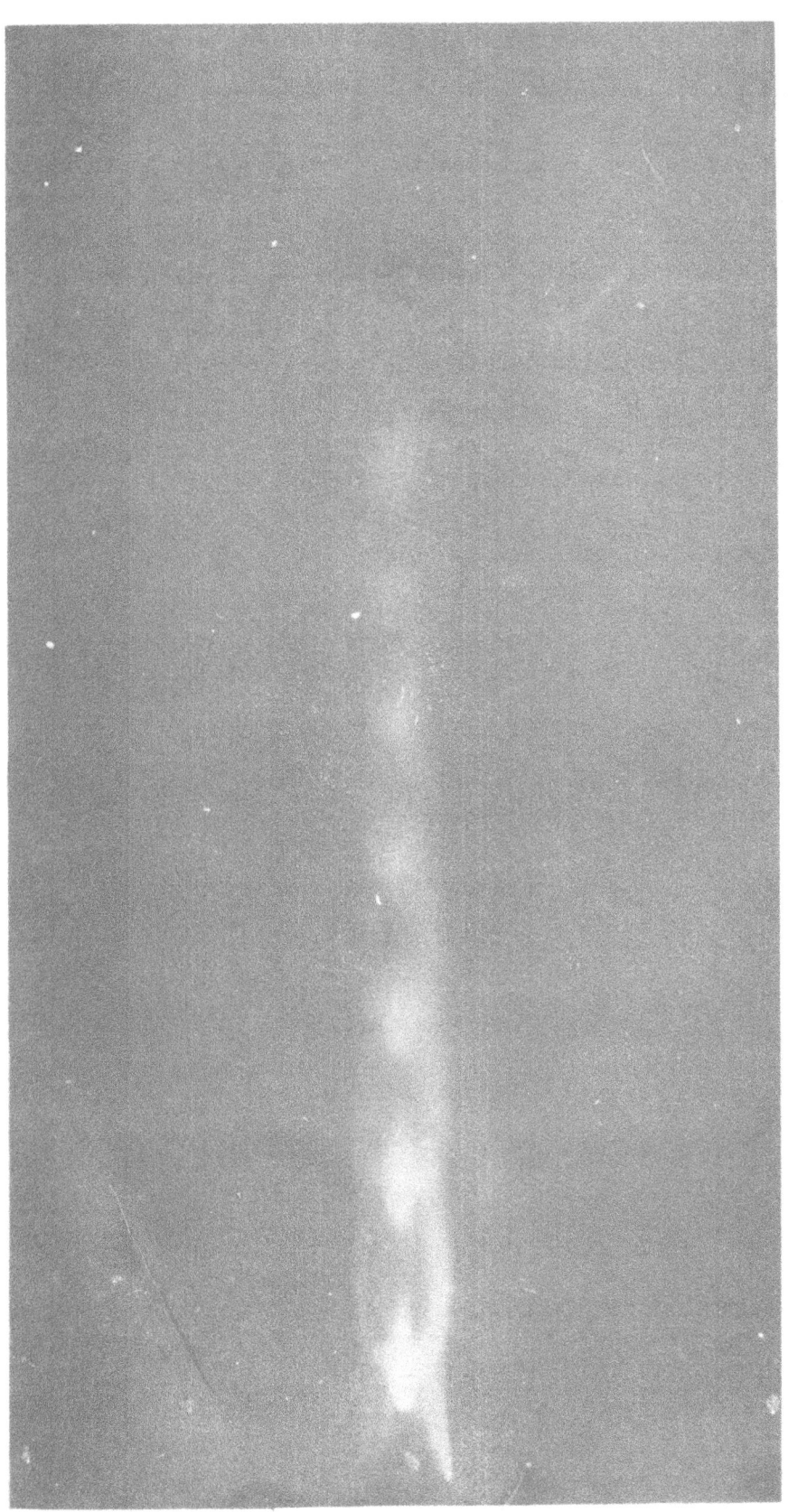

FIG. 8

Fire-gas jet from the jet oilfire from a 1-ton rocket Combustion Chamber with gas-oil/liquid oxygen supply and water cooling.

B 5.

II. **Research Work on an extremely fast climbing Lorin Fighter 1942-1945.**

The propulsion principle for aircraft suggested by Rene Lorin in 1913 should be economically competitive in accordance with tests at very high (supersonic) flying speeds and very low firing temperatures with the usual propellor engine.

In view of the war situation in 1941, I suggested making use of the thrust concentration in a modified Lorin Engine with a high firing temperature, at the expense of rapid climbing and employing this engine in the supersonic flying region in place of rocket propulsion. On account of the fact that it consumed about 5 times less fuel it would have the following advantages:

(a) Extreme climbing capacity e.g. 2 minutes climbing time to an altitude of 12,000 m, as actual rocket fighters.

(b) Considerable horizontal flying time e.g. one hour at great altitudes similar to the jet turbine fighter.

(c) Extraordinarily low cost of construction as a result of the simple engine and thus suitable for the cheapest mass production.

(d) Very suitable for the fuel program of cheap petrols over medium and heavy oils, alcohols, Furfur oils up to liquid coals and pure coals.

B 5.

Jet Fighter

Normal flying speed near the ground: 720 km/h.

Climbing time to an altitude of 12,000 m: 2 minutes (When everything is ready for take-off)

Normal flying speed at 7000-12,000 m: 1000 km/h.

Maximum climbing power at 7000 m: 27,000 h.p. with 5% efficiency and 2300°C fire temperatures.

Maximum thrust when climbing at 7000 m: 7 tons with 1.3 kg/sect petrol consumption.

Highest possible flight duration at 12,000 m with adjustable fire jet section: burning petrol - about 3/4 hr, burning alcohol (colorless flames) about 1/2 hr

Power during horizontal flight at 12,000 m: 3700 h.p. with 10% efficiency and 600° fire temperature.

Thrust in horizontal flight at 12,000 m: 1 ton with 0.65 kg/sect. petrol consumption.

Landing Speed: 150 km/h.

Peak altitude: about 18,000 m.

B 5.

Weight Ratios:

Diffusor	350 kg
Oven with fire jets	300 kg
Cabin	300 kg
Control Surfaces with Carrier	250 kg
Fuel Installation	400 kg
Wing Unit	800 kg
Under Carriage	500 kg
Armament and Munition	500 kg
Weight Equipped	3400 kg
Crew	200 kg
Fuel	2400 kg
All up weight	6000 kg
Take-off Rockets	700 kg
Take-off Weight	6700 kg.

JET FIGHTER

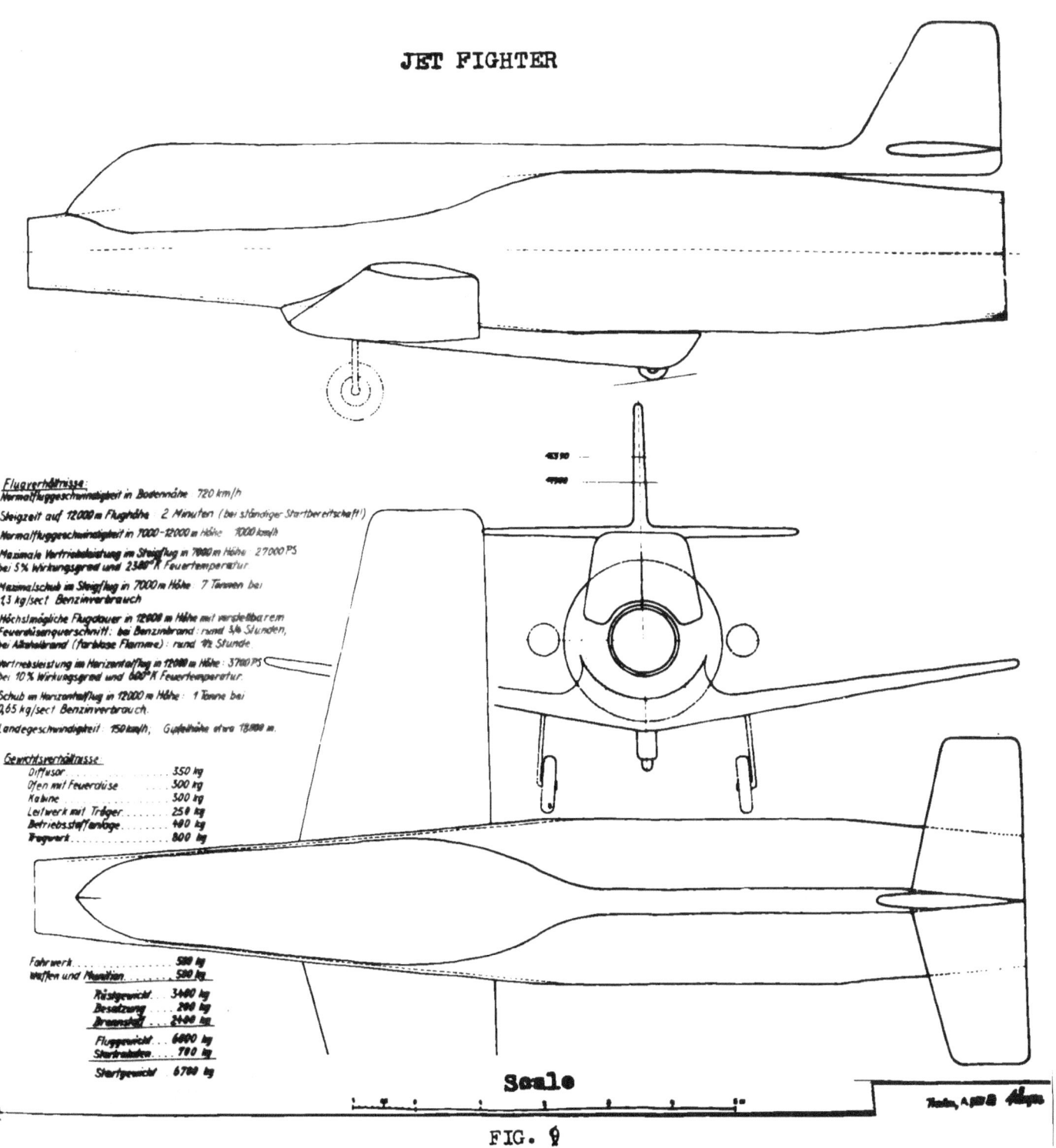

FIG. 9

First design of the Lorin fighter with 6700 kg. Take-off weight including 2400 kg fuel and 700 kg. powder-taker-off rockets. It has a climbing time of 2 mins. to 12,000 m with a 600 kg. fuel consumption, and finally the possibility of 3/4 hr horizontal flight at this height consuming 1800 kg fuel.

FIG. 10

Carrying test on the highway with an 0.5 m high temperature Lorin tube to ascertain the most favorable type of ignition, fuel injection and opening angle of the inlet diffusor.

FIG. 11

High temperature jet tube of 0.5 m diameter, 5.5 m length and C_v = 0.55 propulsion coefficient, consuming petrol on the Do 172 as test carrier.

FIG. 12

High temperature Lorin jet tube of 1.5 m diameter and 10.4 length for flight carrying tests on the Do 217 at a flying speed up to 720 km/h

FIG. 13

Flight carrying test of a 1 m high temperature Lorin jet tube on the Do 217 for measuring the exact pressure distribution in the tube, the actual drag of the tube with impulse calculation and the behavior at a flight altitude of 7000 m.

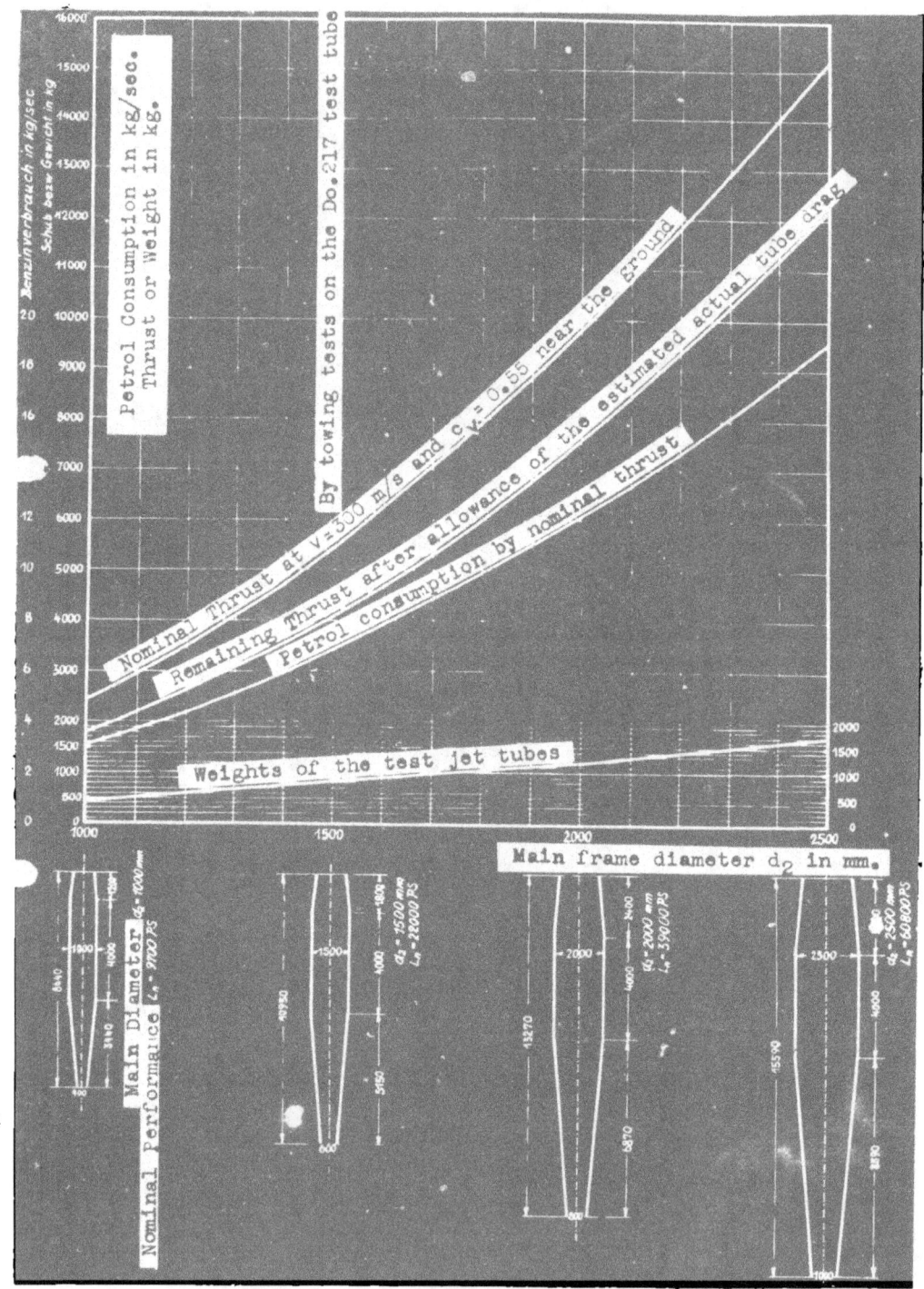

FIG. 14
Weights, measurements, full throttle thrust and fuel throttle petrol consumption of the high temperature Lorin jet tube at 300 m/sec flying speed near the ground. (Weight of the tube in frame about 1/3).

12. Additional information concerning the work at the DFS may be gained, of course, from the publications listed in part 2 of this report in the series 2 c. Since the documents listed in the series 2c represent only material seized at Ainring, they do not give a complete picture. It is to be noted that only five of the eight research divisions of DFS are represented in the series 2c. This seems to indicate that a considerable amount of DFS material was either destroyed or has not bee directed to this office. For convenience, the distribution of the documents in the series 2c amongst the DFS research divisions is given presently, for those who may wish to study in detail the work in just one of these divisions. The serial numbers in the following enumeration refer to the series 2c in part 2.

Institute for glider construction: 50

Institute for aeronautical equipment: 1 through 26.

Institute for physics of the atmosphere: 28, 29, 30, 78, 79.

Department for high frequency: 31, 32, 33, 33a, 34, 35, 36, 47.

Department for engines: 37 through 76.

13. Since the general problem of guided missiles was on of the main topics studied in Ainring, it may be of interest tocall attention to two other places where the same problem was studied. One was the institute for applied mechanics at the university of Gottingen, where in particular the dynamics of guided missiles and gyro controls were investigated. A record place was the CPVA (chemisch-physikalische Versuchsanstalt) in Dänisch Neinhoff, near Kiel, where under the direction of H. Wigge in particular the problems arising in connection with guided torpedoes were studied. These studies included also an investigation of various pursuit curves from a purely mathematical point of view (see part 4 of this report). It is not clear at present whether these two places were given adequate consideration.

Interrogation of Walter Julius Otto Georgii, 28 May 1945.

<u>Career</u> - After serving in the metereological service of the GAF from 17 March 1915 to 20 December 1918, Walter Georgii was discharged as a Lieutenant of the reserves. In 1919 he joined the University of Frankfort as an assistant in the department of physics and mathematics.

In 1924 he became Professor for Geophysics at Frankfort University but later in the same year transferred to the Deutsche Seewarte, Hamburg as a director of the department for "Maritime Meterologie". He also became professor for the same subject at Hamburg University.

In 1926 he was called to the T.H. Darmstadt as professor for "Flugmetereologie und Luftfahrtforchung" remaining there until 1939. It was at the beginning of this period that Prof. Georgii first interested himself in experiments for glider flight taking place in the vicinity of Frankfort. He resolved to dedicate his energies to the creation of a sound scientific basis for the problems of glider flight and to further this new development along scientific lines, by what he terms "Wissensehaftliche Betreung des Segelfluges".

In 1924 the research institute of gliding flight (Forschungs Institute fur Segelflug) was founded on the Wasserkurppe and Prof. Georgii was made a director of this institute. After some time the institute was moved to the airfield of Darmstadt, Griesheim.

The Institute remained in Darmstadt until 1939 and was known as the DFS (Deutsche Forshungsanstanlt fur Segelflug) to which later the name Ernst Udet was added in commemoration of the famous pilot who carried out this flying training on this airfield during the last war.

The original object of the institute was to investigate on a scientific basis all the possibilities of glider motion and to apply and test the scientific conclusions by practical application at glider trials which took place annually near the Rhön.

In the period of 1926 - 1939 the activities of the DFS earned considerable interest abroad.

An expedition led by Dr. Knott demonstrated the possibility of gliding at Boston in 1928 and remained in the USA for 6 months. In 1930-1931 Prof. Georgii visited England as a guest of the Royal Aeronautical Society and selected terrain suitable for gliding in the Chiltern hills. Similar visits took place to Belgium and Holland where gliding was taken up in consequence.

In 1931 the "Internationale Studienkomission fur Motorloesen Flug" was founded and Prof. Georgii elected president, a position he retained until the outbreak of the war.

Other visits by Prof. Georgii took him to Brazil and the Argentine in 1934, and to Portugal in 1936 as a result of which gliding was taken up in all these countries.

In 1939 the DFS moved from Darmstadt to Braunschweig, to the premises of the Luftfahrtforchungsanstalt Herman Göring. After a period of 10 months the DFS was again moved, this time to Ainring, near Reichenhall in the course of the summer of 1940. Only a small wind tunnel for speeds up to 60 m/sec remained in Darmstadt under the direction of Dipl. Ing. Conrad. Prof. Ruden, the principal director of the wind tunnels activities, transferred to Ainring, and directed the research from there. Work carried out at the wind tunnel included investigations of various types of "Mistel" combinations as well as general work for industry. The wind tunnel was damaged by fighter bomber attack in the course of the last operations of this year.

From 1942 onwards Prof. Georgii had to divide his time between the affairs of the DFS and the "Reichisstelle fur Forschung fuhrung der huftfasst" in Berlin. The latter organization was brought into being to guide and foster basic research of air interest throughout Germany and assist various institutes carrying out such work, both with regard to the problems handled as well as financially. The directorate consisted of:

Prof. Prandtle   (President)
Prof. Seewald   (Administrative Head) previously with the DVL Braunschweig and T. H. Aachen.
Dr. Baumbker   (of the "Akademie der Luftfahrt Forschung and the "Lielienthal Gesellschaft fur Luftfahrtforschung")
Dr. Georgii   of the DFS.

In November 1943 Prof. Georgii took over from Prof. Seewald. (Dipl. Ing. Temme joined the RFL in September 1944 as Chief Engineer and assistant of Prof. Georgii).

The members of the RFL met once a month. In the attacks of March 1945 the offices of RFL in Berlin were destroyed together with most of their records. About March 1945 the RFL was dispersed, partly to the Aerodynamic Institute at Goettingen, partly to similar institutes at Luftfahrtforschungsanstalt Hermann Göring, Braunschweig and to the DFS at Ainring.

Various departments of the DFS at Ainring again were dispersed in the Ainring area. A detailed plan with locations of departments and personnel is in the course of preparation by Prof. Georgii and Dipl. Ing Temme.

From Ainring about 10 members of the staff of the DFS were sent by Prof. Georgii to find another dispersal further west. This party was taken over in the neighborhood of Lauterbacher Muhle (near Seeshaupt and Iffledorf at the southern tip of the Starnberger See) but before they could establish any part of their activities.

Activities of the DFS

Prof. Georgii gave the following rapid and general survey of some of the major activities of the DFS. A detailed description of the work done is being prepared separately.

Section for "Konstruktion" (A/C construction) under Dipl. Ing. Kracht.

Theoretical and experimental work on the application of glider principles and the development of towed A/C (Schleppfluzzurge) culminating in the design of the first satisfactory towed glider A/C, the DFS 230. Work on this commenced about 1936 - initially with the object of designing a flying observatory capable of accommodation several experiments and sufficient equipment for air research on meteriological and general flying problems. The A/C was at that time known as DFS OBS.

Parallel work aimed at the development of satisfactory towing methods and necessary cable links and attachments. Then followed about 1940 the development of rigid links (Starrschlepp), although this field had been investigated at an earlier date at Braunschweig. A major problem was the development about 1943 of pick-a-back A/C of the "Mistel" type (According to Prof. Georgii the name was adopted from the name Mistletow.)

The first experiments were with the combination KL 35 mounted on a DFS 230. This combination had the planes towed off the ground by a Ju 52 and was only cast off after reaching height.

Further trials used a STOSSER A/C supported on a DFS 230, this combination was also towed off the ground by a Ju 52, but was cast off at 50 m height and continued alone. Finally experiments were made both with a M 109 on a DFS 230 and a Me 109 on a Ju 188 known by the code name BETHOFEN. Work on this last combination was required for Junkers, who had already carried the steering control problems of such a combination. At the DFS, the flight trials of Pick-a-back combinations were supervised by Ing. Stamer.

Section for Ausrusting (Equipment)

This section was directed by Prof. Fischel and Dipl. Ing. Temme. It concerned itself with a very wide range of control problems of bodies in flight, including air-launched missiles of the Hs 293 type, gyro rudder control systems, automatic steering devices, "Kommando gerate" for A/C (computer devices for use in A/C), W/T impulse control methods (impuls steuring) and factors leading to jamming of the control systems. The latter was done by Dipl. Ing. ERZ.

Section for "Hochfrequency" (High frequency)

This was led by Dr. Foelsche and investigated the development of electrical remote control methods. The DFS 230 was principally used and was found to be ideally suitable for this type of work, being free from many disturbing causes of interference present on or in motorized A/C and having ample space for apparatus and personnel.

One series of experiments, dating from the end of 1942 concerned the control of a DFS 230 A/C by means of a Do 17. The DFS 230 was towed by a Do 17 in the direction of the target. The DFS 230 was equipped in the nose with an optical system which produced a picture of area in the direction of flight of the DFS 230, up to a range of 15 km and over a spread of 1 km at this distance, (about 4°). The picture could show a specific target at this distance, for example a ship, and by means of a television transmitter located in the DFS 230. The picture produced by the optical system was transmitted to a television receiver located in the Do 17. With the aid of this transmission the glider was then steered from the Do 17 A/C by W/T remote control toward the target, while the controlling A/C itself returned on course. The DFS 230 was equipped with automatic pilot control. Applications held in mind were attacks on targets using gliders loaded with explosive or adaption of the Hs 293 type of missile to a similar purpose.

During actual trials a pilot was always present to take over control at the last moment. Experiments were carried out from distances of 15 km from the target, the DFS 230 being taken over by the pilot about 300 m from the target. The target was a house on Ainring airfield. Experiments over sea were carried out at Karlsregen on an airfield on the Rostoch area. Difficulties encountered were due to jamming of the television equipment by the W/T control transmission, also due to interference effects between the television transmission and ground returns. These took the form of horizontal black bands on the presentation screen.

Another series of experiments were concerned with the wire control of the Ju 88 A/C by means of an Me 109. This work was started in view of the experiences already gained with the "Mistel" experiments. A Me 109 and Ju 88 pick-a-back combination was used with the code name "Bethofen". Wire control after separation continued up to 5/7 kms. The experiments were carried out on the airfield on Horsching bei Linz. These experiments were begun in 1944, although earlier experiments had been carried out by Junkers at Dessau. Experiments on wire control method had already been made by Prof. Wagner of Henschel.

Section for AEROLOGIE (Metereological Section)

Directed by Dr. Hohndorf, this section investigated the possibilities of extending gliding to much higher altitudes than hitherto realized, and carried out research on stratospheric glider flight. The highest point said to have been reached was 11,500 m by Ing Klochner at Ainring about 1940/41. Even at this height his vertical speed was 5/m secs, but lack of oxygen supplies forced him to descend.

According to Prof. Georgii, the possibilities of stratospheric glider flight are very real. It is said to have been established that at higher altitudes air currents flow with strong upward components, the amplitude of which increases with height. Sketch shows such a current at over 5000 m level and it is believed similar currents generally form on the leeward side of higher mountain ranges. The flow in the upward component is said to be constant and without turbulence. It is not established as yet whether this effect exists only near mountains or in generally present at higher altitudes. It is the belief of Prof. Georgii that but for the war, heights of 15 to 18 km would have been realized, and that heights between 20-25 km can be achieved. For this purpose a glider with a pressurized cabin, maintaining conditions corresponding to those ruling at 2000 m, was under construction at Ainring and should still be found there partly completed.

Section: FlugAbteilung (Flight Trials)

Dealing generally with flight trails of experimental A/C, this section was working in particular on experimental types to be used for supersonic speeds. As such speeds decrease with height it was intended to explore by means of suitable glider A/C regions between 13 kms and 17 kms and carry out tests on such A/C as apart from wind tunnel experiments. Particularly the critical region or transsonic speeds were to be investigated and the problems occurring at this point. An A/C was under construction for this purpose, by Ing. Cracht. The fuselage was finished, the flying experiments were to be carried out by Ing Ziegler. The A/C was known as the DFS 334 or H 58. For stratosphere research it was intended to use a form of rocket propulsion to gain the initial height (on the Me 103 pattern).

This section was also concerned with experiments on the general electrical effects observed during flight and the relationship between weather conditions and electrical disturbances. For this purpose again glider A/C were particularly suitable on account of the absence of disturbing influences on the glider itself. This work was carried out by Dr. Rossmann and Dr. Weickmann.

Subjects investigated included: Formation of static charges on the A/C, measurements of Air potentials, influence of ice formation on building up of static charges and the subject of ice formation generally. Basic research work was also carried out on the conditions determining the formation of condensation trials, differences between long and short trials etc.

It was found that at altitudes water remained as water up to $50°$, then gradually changed to ice. In the laboratory water remained unchanged to 68°C and only formed ice at 72°. On warming again the change over from ice to water took place at 68°. This work was done by Dr. AUFM KAMPE.

General Notes - Dr. Sanger.

Dr. Sanger conducted experiments at Ainring on the Loring Triebwerk (Athodide), also at Braunnheig (L.F.F.).

The experiments at Ainring were carried out in conjunction with Do 217 A/C and included measurements of outputs obtained. The work was not completed, however, Dr. Sanger is believed to be in the vicinity of Ainring still.

Dr. Lippisch.

In 1937 Dr. Lippisch worked in the section "Konstrucktion" of the DFS at Darmstadt. He was concerned particularly with tail-less gliders and A/C. From 1938 to 1944 Dr. Lippisch was with Messerschmitt and is the originator of the Me 163. In 1944 he is said to have joined the L.F. Forschungsanbalt Munchen - at that time located in Vienna. Recently he is supposed to have left Vienna and to have gone to the Salzkammerfut, but the latter is uncertain. (was working on tail-less A/C since 1924)

Frl. Wildner.

Frl Wildner is the librarian of Prof. Georgii and is believed to be in the Ainring area.

A.4.

INTERROGATION OF Walter Julius Otto Georgii   10 June 1945

Present C.H. Smith, P.W. Wilkinson, J.R. deBaun at Garmisch.

Georgii referred his interrogators to F/Lt. Stokes & F/Lt. Bingham for information and reports from the following:

1. Co. Halder

2. Dr. Fischel- who used model techniques for studing trajectories and to determine the magnitudes of acceleration required and the optimum relative speeds between missile and target.

3. Dr. Kracht - in Prien on the Chiemsee who was connected with BEETHOVEN.

4. Dr. Temme

BEETHOVEN: A wire controlled pick-a-back device utilizing a JU-88(?) as a missile. Junkers and Henschel worked on this. Prof. Wagner made the first tests and Fischel was to conduct flight tests at airfield near Linz. The BEETHOVEN gear was received complete and installed in the planes. The function of Fischel's group was to have been to take the bugs out of the equipment and obtain successful overall operation. Actual flight tests were never conducted. Further work was being done at Junkers Nordhausen. Kracht is our best source of information on this phase.

Georgii could add nothing further to the statements of Temme on investigations of the link between various homing devices and the steering controls of various missiles. He stated that Steinhoff had been transferred to the staff of Gen Dornberger and that we should see Sponder and Fischel for more information.

Georgii was questioned regarding his knowledge of any work on homing devices but could give little information except to recommend the name of Dr. Arenz in Oberpfaffenhofen who is a former Elektroakustik man. Arenz is connected with the Flugfunkforschungsinstitute in Ob.

PROXIMITY FUZE TARGETS:

1. Patentverwertungs Gesellschaft, Salzburg. People from here, names unknown, came to Ainring and borrowed a plane for certain tests. The establishment is located on the Mönchsberg near the elevator.

2. Prof. Madelung od Stuttgart Ruit.
    In Jan. 1945 Dr. Mullers group was transferred to Messerschmidt to work on a homing device for Enzian.

A 10.

DEUTSCHE FORSCHUNGSANSTALT FUR SEGELFLUG (DFS)

June 18 1945

Summary.

The personnel of the DFS, for the most part are still in the Ainring area. The equipment is partly in cellars and barracks at the Ainring airfield, partly in dispersal laboratories and workshops at Reichenhall, Feisendorf, and other neighboring villages, and partly scattered in farmhouses, old castles and the like, in the Ainring area. Dr. Stamer of the DFS is cooperating with Capt. Sannes of ATI in a project to collect all the equipment and documents of the DFS in as few places as possible, to assemble the equipment which has been taken apart, and to complete any unfinished reports on projects which are regarded as important.

This work was undertaken by Capt. Sannes on his own initiative; official approval must be obtained if it is to continue.

In addition the DFS Institute for Aircraft Construction has two experimental aircraft nearly complete, namely the DFS 54, experimental high altitude glider which is at Prien, and the DFS 332, the air frame of which is at Ainring and the propulsion units and drawings for which are at Prien. Dipl. Ing. Felix Kracht, head of this institute is at Prien. If these two aircraft are to be completed, arrangements must be made for materials and workers, either at Prien or at Ainring. The officer in charge of the field at Prien is Capt. Welsh, air officer, 20th Armored Division.

Aircraft of particular interest at Ainring including the first experimental high altitude glider with pressurized cabin, have been removed by the ATI to Stuttgart.

Three cases of documents, dug up during this investigation, contain all the ZWB material from the library of the DFS. These were left in care of Capt. Sannes. They should be listed and micro-filmed as soon as possible.

GENERAL INFORMATION: The DFS is divided into 5 institutes and 2 departments and 1 laboratory, the functions of which are given in a previous interrogation report on Prof. Georgii. This investigation covered the work of the Institute for Aerodynamics (Dr. Ruden), Institute for Flight Tests (Dr. Stamer) Institute for Aerodynamics Equipment (Dr. Fischel), Institute for Physics of the Atmosphere (Dr. Mehnderf) and the Institute for Aircraft Construction (Dipl. Ing

Kracht). The laboratory for Special Propulsion Units and the Dept. for Propulsion Unit Dev. were not covered because their heads, Dr. Eisele and Dr. Sanger were in Garmisch. The Dept for High Frequencies also was not covered since it had already been covered by CAFT Group 1.

INSTITUTE FOR AIRCRAFT CONSTRUCTION   Aircraft planned or under construction by Dipl. Ing. Kracht, are the DFS 54, DFS 228, DFS 346, DFS 1068 and the DFS 332. The first three of these are all part of a program to carry out research at high speeds and at very high altitudes, the 54 being an engineless glider with pressurized cabin and safety features for high altitudes, the 228 being essentially the same aircraft with a Walter propulsion unit, and the 346 being the ultimate design based on the previous one. The 1068 is a series of four aircraft identical except for the angle of sweep-back which was 0, 25, 35 and 45 degrees respectively; the purpose is to check aerodynamic calculations on the effect of sweep-back exchangeable mid-section of wing mounted in such a way that its angle of incidence can be changed during flight and so that lift, drag and moment can be measured accurately, the purpose is to test high performance air foils at high Reynolds numbers in turbulence-free air.

The DFS 54V1 which is in Prien is almost complete except for covering and cabin. Dipl. Ing. Kracht estimates that it would take about ten weeks to complete it if materials were available. About one-third of his workers are in Prien. This aircraft has a wing span of 20 meters, a length of 9 meters and 16-17 Kg sq. meter wing loading.

The powered model, known as the DFS 228 has two variations: one called the V-1 in which the pilot sits in the conventional manner, the other called the V-2 in which the pilot lies down. Both were at Horsching. The V-1 had about forty test flights (towed) and its propulsion system had been tested on the ground. It had never actually been used at high altitudes, however. The V-2 was completely destroyed, only the framework and controls of the pilots compartment being saved. These are at Prien, see photograph Fig 1   It was Kracht's intention to modify the 54V-1 at Prien so that the pilot would lie down as in the 228 V-2. The reason is that the pilots vision is improved, and the pressure sealing is easier. To do this would require 6 months for completion instead of 2 1/2 months as mentioned above. The pilot who flew the 228 V-1 at Horsching was Dipl. Ing. Rudolph Siegler.

The power unit for the 228 V-1 and V-2 is a special Walther unit of the "hot" type, called the R-2203. In this unit the combustion chamber is about three meters from the pump and control unit.

The pressure cabin the 228 V-2 was capable of holding a differential pressure of 0.4 Kg/sq. cm (about 6 lbs/sq. in) with a loss of only 3% in twenty-four hours. The loss through the plywood is said to be negligible, the worst loss being in the rotating joints where the steering controls are taken out.

The final development of this series is the DFS 346 which was to have been built by a firm by the name of Siebel in Halle. Its purpose is the measurement of aerodynamic data at transonic and supersonic velocities and at very high altitudes. Its wings are attached in such a way that six component measurements can be made. It is to be towed to an altitude of 10 km, and then to climb on its own power using two standard Walther 2 ton rocket propulsion units. At altitudes between 20 and 30 km it is hoped that a Mach number to two will be obtained. The outer shape of this model has been decided on: very high sweep-back, 9 meters span. Some of the parts are already designed, drawings which exist being at Seible. Aerodynamic and static data are at Prien.

The four models of the 1068 were completely designed; drawings are available. The 25° sweep-back model was almost completed and the 35° model was partially constructed at the firm Wrede at Freilassing. They were completely destroyed in a recent raid. All four were to be equipped with mountings for four power unit nacelles, wither on the wings or on the fuselage. Either the Ju 004 or the He S0 11 could be used. In addition the 0°, 35°, and 45° models were to have a Walter propulsion unit of 1500 kms thrust in order to get excess speed. A photograph of these four aircraft (models) is shown in Fig 2

As mentioned above the 332 is intended for use in testing high performance airfoils at high Reynolds numbers in turbulence-free air in order to determine the effect on the aerodynamic data of the turbulence which always exists in wind tunnels. It has a mid-wing section which can easily be changed and which can be rotated during flight to produce variations of CL from 0 to 0.5. The aircraft is powered by two Walter R 11 203 units which are now stored at Prien. The airframe is partially completed and is stored in the large workshop at Aimring. It could easily be completed if wanted. A complete set of drawings for it were found at Prien.

Kracht also had at his home in Prien a model of an Me 328, which appeared to be a more or less conventional aircraft with two Argus-Schmidt tubes for propulsion. The project was dropped because the vibration was too great and the high altitude performance too poor. A photograph of the model is shown in Fig. 3

Among the drawings Kracht has at his home is a series showing the operation of the safety cabin for the high altitude aircraft. If the pilot wishes to jettison the aircraft, he presses a button which fires

explosion bolts, detaching the entire pressure cabin from the rest of the
ship. As the cabin descends the pressure seal is automatically broken when
the outside pressure, and at a certain absolute pressure, the nose is
blown off by compressed air and the pilot ejected, his parachute opening
automatically.

Dipl. Ing. Kracht has been asked to make a complete report of the
activities of his Institute as quickly as possible and has promised to
do so.

Institute for Aerodynamics.

The work of this institute is fully covered by the report by
Dr. Ruden attached as appendix I.

Institute for Flight Testing.

Dr. Stamers report, Incl. B. 14, and the photographs, Figs 4 to
18, 15 pictures, gives an idea of his accomplishment.

It is interesting to note that for stable flight with Starrschlepp
the towed aircraft must be less than 1/3 the weight of the towing aircraft
and friction damping must be used. This damping is in the form of brake-
lining in a ball and socket joint at the point of attachment to the
towing aircraft. The attachment to the towed aircraft is a two-gimbal
universal joint without damping.

Institute for Physics of the Atmosphere.

Dr. Hehendorf has written a report on the work of his institute which
is attached as appendix III, the following comments apply:

He did not do experiments in which ice was melted at 72° C but has
heard of them. He believes they were done by Dr. Regener or some of his
group at Freidrichshafen. His only explanation for the possibility of
such a phenomena is that ice formed directly from vapor consists of
isomorphic forms of water which have quite different physical characteristics.

The theory of waves in the upper atmosphere was published in
Beitrage zur Physik before the war. Gliders have reached altitudes as
high as 11.8 km, which was accomplished without pressure cabins;
Dr. Hehenderf believes that an altitude of 16 km can be reached with
pressurized cabins.

Institute for Aeronautic Equipment.

The work done by Dr. Fischel is listed in his report, Appendix IV
The following notes describe items of particular interest to the
investigators:

At the laboratory and workshop in Teisendorf are the parts for a 1000/1 scale model of the flak missile control problem. Although this equipment can be applied generally it has been especially designed for tests on Wasserfall. A tiny model of the missile is mounted in a large frame shaped like an inverted U with motor drives to propel it in a direction normal to its plane.

The model is mounted on wires and can be moved in two directions in the plane of the frame, so that combined motion in three dimensions is possible. The gyroscopic steering control for the missile is mounted in gymbals which are motor driven in such a way that the instantaneous direction of the missile is reproduced.

Control signals are introduced into the system by means of a joystick controller, or by any other device which is to be tested. One computing element determines the effect of this control signal on the angular position of the missile, which information is transmitted to the gymbals by electrical means causing them to be positioned accordingly. A second computing element takes the output of the steering control apparatus and determines the direction of flight of the rocket. A third element determines the velocity of the missile and resolves it into components in accordance with the direction of flight. A fourth element integrates these velocity components and transmits the information to the framework on which the model is mounted.

Two types of computing apparatus have been planned, one a qualitative system which does not take into account the aerodynamics of the missile, and the other a quantitative system which does take the aerodynamics into account and continuously indicates the angle of attack. The first system is essentially complete, the second will require about six months to complete. Reports will be found in the library boxes (which were buried at Ainring).

At the laboratory in Reichenhall is a working model of a missile control system known as "Darmstadt" which transmits five command "up, down, right, left, stop" by means of impulses, and in this system there is a small speed-regulated motor at both the transmitting and the receiving end. A magnetically-operated clutch drives a commutator through one revolution and then stops it. When any command is given the transmitter and receiver clutches are simultaneously operated by an initial impulse so that the two commutators begin to rotate in synchronism. If the command is "up" for example, a second impulse will be sent out by the transmitting commutator at the instant when the receiving commutator is in the correct position to close the "up" relay; other commands are similarly identified. After the "up" signal has been given the missile turns at a constant rate until the stop signal is sent.

Reports on this system an on newer electronic systems to replace it are supposed to be in the boxes which were buried. A manuscript of a long report on "on-off" control has been prepared by members of Fischel's Institute and is in the process of being types and reproduced.

It could be ready in about 2 weeks if photographic reproducing equipment were available. Ing Stamer with the help of Capt. Sannes may have the BFS photographic section operating shortly in a hanger at Aimring.

A sample of one of the little thermal elements used by Dr. Hohener for far infra-red detection was seen at Dr. Hohener's home in Reichenhall. The elements consist of a small molding of synthetic resin in the shape of an I-beam, 3mm by 5 mm, 10 mm long, with a terminal on each end, wound with 90 turns of very fine constanin wire. After winding the wire is silver plated in such a way that plating is applied only to one half of each turn. Each point at which the plating ends acts as a thermocouple so the result is the equivalent of a thermopile of 90 elements. The junctions on one side are blackened to make them better absorbers of radiated energy. The junctions on the other side act as the "cold" junctions. The sensitivity of one of these cells is 10 to 20 millivolts for 2.25×10^{-5} calories per second per square centimeter, and the half-valve time is 0.09 seconds.

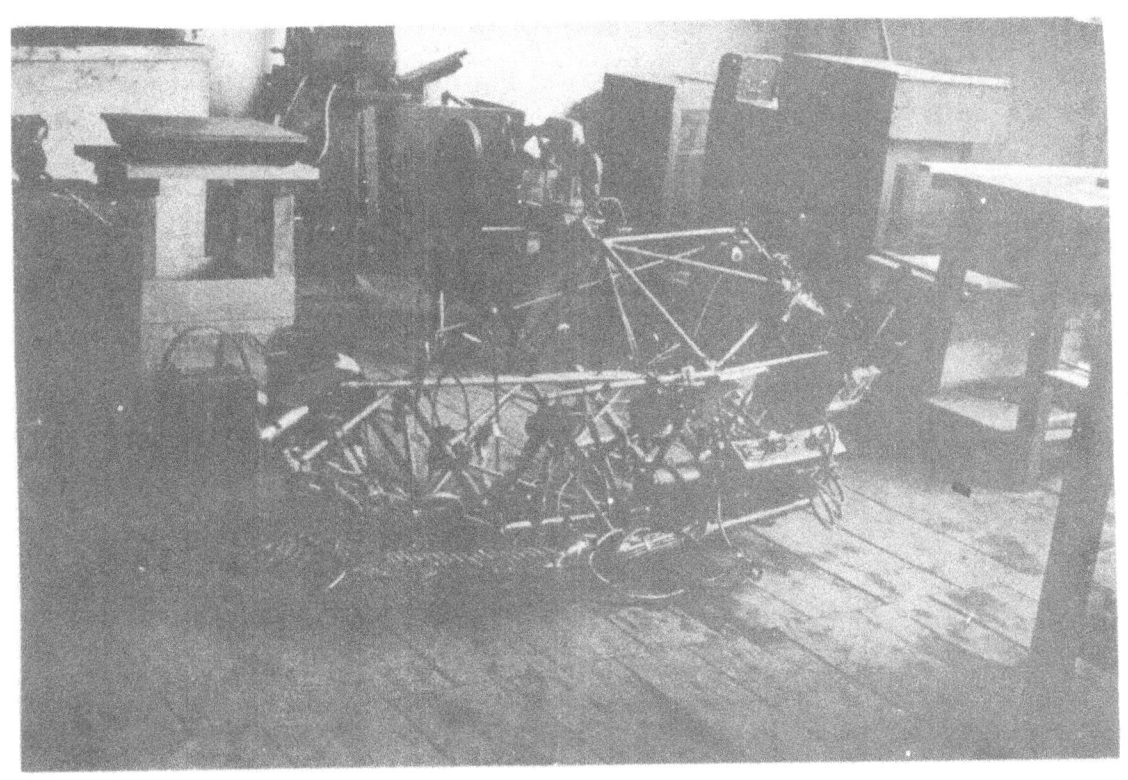

Fig 1.

Frame work and controls of pilots compartment V - 2 (DFS 228)

Four models of 1068 (DFS)

Fig. 3.

Fig. 4.

Rigid Tow in operation.

Fig. 5.

Rigid Tow in operation.

Fig. 6.

Rigid Tow.

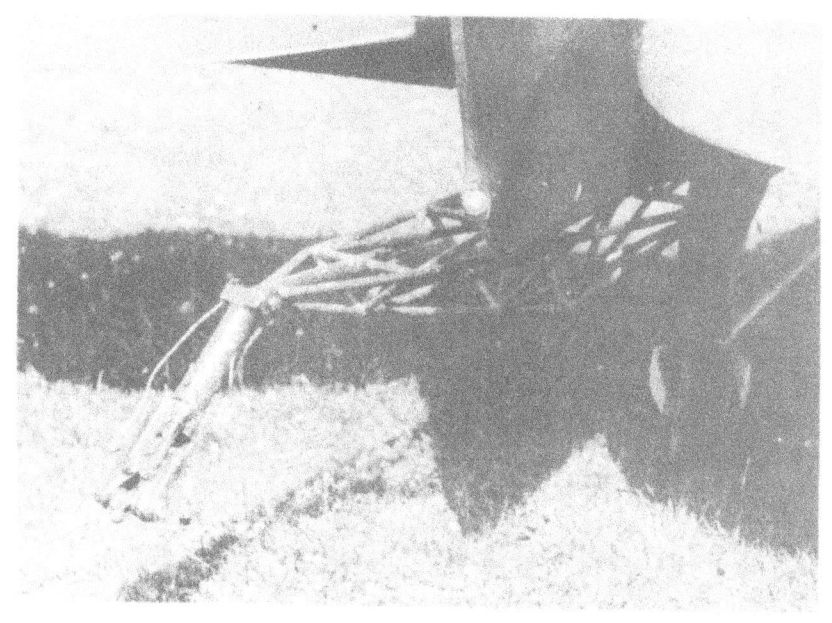

Fig. 7.

Rigid Tow - attachment.

Fig. 8.

Rigid Tow - attachment to tail of aircraft.

Fig. 9.

Rigid Tow - Quick release clamp.

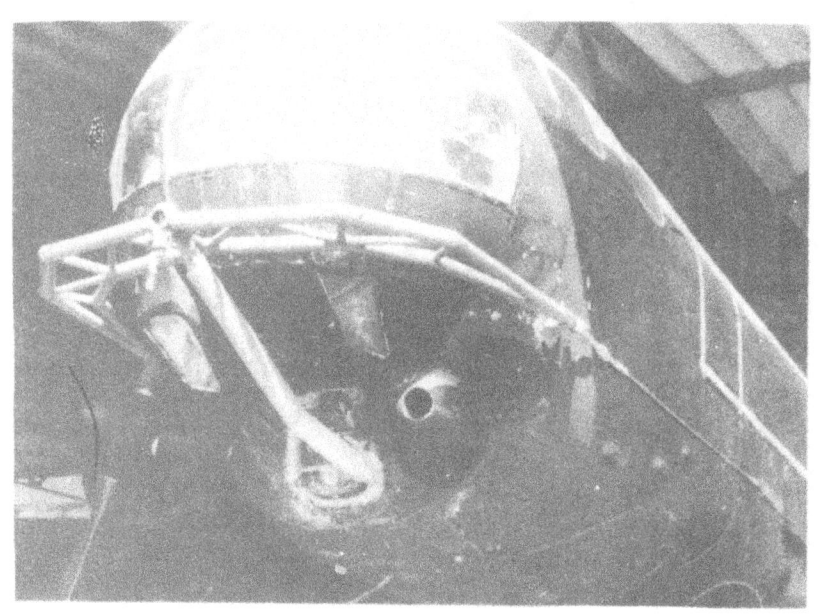

Fig. 10.

Rigid tow - attachment to nose of glider.

Fig. 11.

Rigid tow - attachment to tail of aircraft.

Fig. 12.

Long rigid tow - attachment to tail of aircraft.

Fig. 13.

Carrier tow.

Fig. 14.

Bomb tow - container.

Fig. 15.

Bomb tow container

Fig. 16.

Multiple tow in flight.

Fig. 17.

Starting tow - truck and winch.

Fig. 18.

Starting tow - winch.

A-11

Title: German Glider Research Station (DFS) in Ainring, Ober Bayern.

Director, Prof. E. H. Georgii, Ph.D.Dr. Ing.

Technical Assistant. Dipl. Ing. Temme.

Manager   Ing. Stamer

1. Institute for Aerodynamics, Prof. Dr. Ruden.

1.1. Study of gliding objects. General study of motion of objects, such as Hs 293 through the air. Principal problem was whether to stabilize aerodynamically, or by internal control. Most of the work was done by Dipl. Ing. Vopel who later went to Henschel. Results showed that the best aerodynamic shape was a type of tail-less body (flying wing).

1.2. Flying bridge. This is a narrow foot bridge with pontoons which can be towed by an aircraft to the desired location and landed ready for use. Each section is 18 meters long, 3/4 meter wide and has four pontoons or floats and four wooden wings 2 meters by 3/4 meter which are jettisoned upon landing. The bridge itself is made of light metal alloy tubes and sheets. It is towed with a cable 80 meters long.

Pilot Lettmeyer was the first to test one of these bridges using an Hs 76 or a Ju 52 as the tow plane. The pontoons were mounted on skids, and the bridge was towed off an ordinary runway. On the first two tests the bridge did not take off and was cut loose. On the third trial, Lettmeter climbed as fast as he could and literally lifted the bridge off the ground. As flying speed increased, it gradually attained a flying attitude. Lateral oscillations were bad at first, but were overcome by the addition of vertical stabilizer surfaces at the ends of the wings.

The landing procedure was to head upstream and release the bridge at an altitude of about 30 meters and a speed of 180 km/hr. It then stalls and settles rather easily on the water. At the moment of landing an anchor is fired from a small mortar onto the bank. Experiments in landing were carried out successfully at Salzach, near Ainring. Work was started in 1942. A firm in Westphalia had orders to build some, but apparently these were never finished.

1.3. Rigid towing attachment. Aerodynamic investigation into possibility of rigid attachments to fast aircraft (600 to 700 km/hr). The principle application would have been spare fuel tanks and the like. It was tested and worked all right, but was never applied.

1.4. Retarding descent of dropped containers. Standard containers were used with four 500 kg thrust Rheinmetal Borsig rockets arranged to fire downward. A small parachute is attached to the top to keep the container upright, and a 30 meter chain is attached to the bottom when the chain touches the ground the rockets are fired. At first the rockets were evenly spaced around the periphery of the container, but this method of attachment was found to be unsatisfactory because of the moments introduced by uneven firing of the rockets. The final solution was to group the four rockets together beneath the container.

1.5. Streamlining of diffuser inlet. At study of the best aerodynamic shape for air intake opening was made with application to the cooling system of internal combustion engines and to jet engines.

1.6. Tilting tests (side slipping) of aircraft. This study was made primarily on the Arado 234 at Hershing. Dr. Georgii doesn't know what the purpose was - thinks the work was never completed.

1.7. Wind tunnel studies in Darmstadt (2 meter tunnel, 50 m/sec velocity) for DFS and industrial problems.

2. Institute for glider construction, Dipl. Ing. Kracht.

2.1. Cargo glider. This glider was known as the DFS-230, and was the first large towed glider in Germany. It was actually finished in 1937, but no one was interested until 1939. Late in 1939 or early 1940 the designs were handed over to Gotha Waggon-fabrik. Subsequently this glider and later modifications were called Gotha gliders. Other gliders, both larger and smaller have been designed by Gotha.

2.2. Fighters with jet propulsion. Experiments to determine whether Argus- Schmidt motors could be used to propel very fast aircraft (up to 600 km/hr) were made using DFS 228 with two Argus tubes mounted as shown in the following sketch:

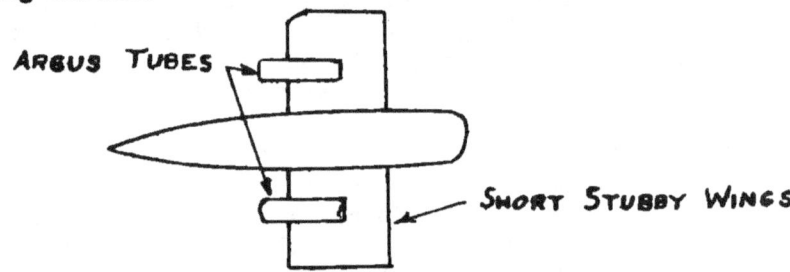

Two planes of this type were built after initial tests on a DFS-230 which fell apart from the vibration. Tests were made by mounting the 228 on a Do 217 and releasing it at the test altitude. The DFS 278 was piloted, and could land at the completion of its tests. The Argus tubes used had a thrust of about 300 kg and a frequency of 50 Hg. Dr. Georgii thinks they were about the same as were used on the V-1.

2.3. High altitude glider known as HS 7 or 8 to be used for experiments at altitudes between 13 and 17 km. One of these gliders was completed at Ainring and was ready to be tested. It had a pressurized cabin which would maintain a pressure altitude of 3000 meters inside. With this plane, preliminary experiments were to be made preparing the way for projected work on high-speed, high altitude research. For example an instantaneously operating oxygen mask was needed in case the cabin pressure failed or the pilot had to bale out. A delayed action parachute was needed so the pilot would not freeze to death in the stratosphere. Very little was known about aerodynamics of such aircraft, and it was hoped that preliminary work at least could be done on this model.

For the later experiments a Walter propulsion unit was to be used, after release at 7 km from a tow ship. Ascent would be in easy stages, such as 7-12 km, 12-15 km and finally 15 to 17 km. It was believed that speeds up to $M = 1$ could be reached at 13-17 km. Eventually they even hoped to attain an altitude of 24 km.

2.4. Research glider with laminar-flow wings. This was a twin-fuselage aircraft which was being constructed at Prien. The central part of the wing (between the two fuselage sections) was to be adjustable in flight. The object was to parallel wind-tunnel work being done on very thin wing sections.

2.5. Mistle (pick-a-back) experiments with Ju 188 and Me 109. Described in report of interview with Georgii by F/Lt H. M. Stokes, 28.5.45.

2.6. Preliminary experiments on motorless aircraft for exploring the behavior at $M = 1$. Refers to the work mentioned in 2.3.

2.7. Coupling between two aircraft in flight. Experiments were made with an F.S. Weibe and a small, two engined Gotha for the purpose of studying the process of establishing a rigid link between two powered aircraft in flight. The Weibe had a funnel-shaped fitting on its tail. The Gotha flew up to within about 3/4 meters behind the funnel; the pilot then pressed a button and a rod with an anchor shot forward and made junction in with the tail of the Weibe. The object was to enable an aircraft to refuel in the air, and to enable a fighter escort to be carried and fuelled from a bomber.

3. Institute for Flight Tests, Ing. Stamer.

3.1. Cable and rigid bar towing. Towing experiments began with 90 meter cables, which were gradually reduced to 40 meters, at which length violent oscillations occurred. The shortening continued to 9 meters and finally down to 1 meter. The towing seemed to be quite safe at 1 meter, so they finally tried a rigid link. According to Dr. Georgii only one degree of freedom was needed, and in fact only one pivot point was used. It seems impossible that two airplanes coupled in this way could take off or fly stably; the writer believes that at least two pivot points must have been used, having axes as shown in the following sketch:

DR GEORGII'S IDEA — ONE PIVOT

MORE PROBABLE ARRANGEMENT — TWO PIVOTS

For towing aircraft Hs 46, Ju 56 and Do 17's were used. Towing a DFS 230, a DFS 230, a Do 17 could attain a speed of 180 km. It was noticed that when towing a glider, an aircraft could fly much slower without stalling, than it could normally, because of the extra lift of the glider. Also it could attain nearly the same altitude; for example the Flamingo could reach 3600 m normally, and could reach 3200 m towing a glider.

3.2. "Pick-a-Back" procedure. These tests are covered in F/Lt Stokes report on interrogation of Georgii, 28.5.45.

3.3. Lift-towing. This is a technique for getting a glider off the ground by lifting it, so to speak with an almost vertical cable. The towing aircraft climbs very steeply and the glider flies off the ground with a very low angle of attack, its lift being almost all supplied through the cable, which is attached in the following way:

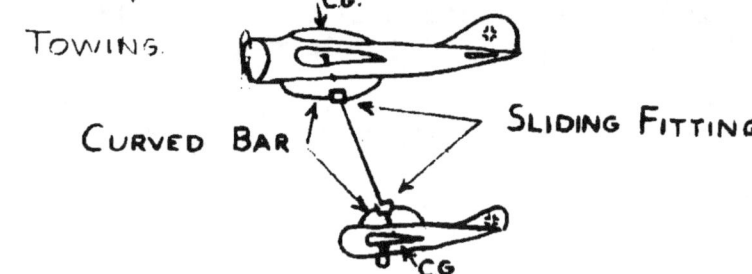

In the beginning the glider was towed in the conventional manner and then dived in order to get into the position shown. Later it was pulled off the ground in this attitude.

3.4. Hook-towing. In order to pick up a heavy glider from a condition of rest on the ground, some means must be provided for absorbing the sudden impulse or shock. DFS worked out a device for this purpose using a box containing steel cable wound back and forth over fragile wooden forms. When the acceleration impulse came some of the pieces of wood broke, releasing as much cable as necessary to take up the shock. This device was tested using the DFS 230 and worked satisfactory.

3.5. General flight testing for the other Institute.

4. Institute for Aeronautic Equipment, Prof. Dr. Fischel.

4.1. Infra red test equipment. Thermocouples were used with a mirror objective for detecting sources of heat or for infra red energy. An aircraft could be detected at about 5 km, but was badly confused by clouds and other stray sources. It was hoped it might be useful in detecting warm air currents, but apparently was never used much. Dipl. Ing. Hohenner worked on it.

4.2. General research on compasses in steel aircraft. Object was to determine position and method of mounting for least error. Dipl. Ing. Geiling should be informed about this work.

4.3. Automatic stabilization of pilotless flying objects (Theoretical). This theoretical study was made in connection with the more general problem mentioned in 1.1.

4.4. On-off control procedure (Theoretical)

4.5. Development of gyro-control for flying objects.

4.6. Gyro stabilization of telescope. This project would have had a general application to observation work, gunsights, driftmeters etc.

4.7. Stabilization of Torpedoes (theoretical). This work was done about a year ago in connection with model experiments at Gottenhafen.

4.8. Model studies for solving remote control problems. The model consisted of (a) a ship model moving slowly or stationary (b) a motor driven object with a point of light representing the flare of an Hs 293 and (c) a control carriage in which the control operator rides with apparatus for controlling the motion of (b). As can be seen, this makes an ideal training device, and it is understood that Henschel copied it as a trainer for Hs 293 bombardiers.

4.9. Connection of target seeking devices to the automatic control (theoretical). This work has fundamental importance in the case of flak missiles.

4.10. Apparatus for disturbance-free control signal transmission. A new method of control using impulses instead of continuous keying has been developed. (Dipl. Ing. Temme is writing detailed description of the work done in connection with 4.4., 4.5., 4.9., and 4.10.

5. Institute for Physics of the Atmosphere, Dr. Hohndorf.

5.1. Soaring in the stratosphere. Dr. Georgii believes that some day it may be possible to attain higher altitudes in sail-planes than in powered aircraft. For details see interrogation report 28.5.45. Dr. Hohndorf was studying the conditions under which rising air currents can occur in the stratosphere.

5.2. Condensation-trail research. A group of scientists, some of whom were Prof. Regener of Friedrichshafen, Dr. Weickmann of Ainring, and Dr. Vollmer of Berlin were studying the problem of formation of condensation trails by aircraft at high altitude. Some of this work is contained in Prof. Vollmer's book "Die Phasen des Wassers". The important fact, according to Dr. Georgii is that the process of ice formation is always water-vapor water-ice. Never direct transition from water vapor to ice.

5.3. Physical researches on the supercooling of water at low temperatures. This heading refers to laboratory tests in which a small sample of air was compressed, cooled mixed with a definite amount of water and then suddenly expanded. At the low temperatures thus produced water droplets and ice crystals formed on a microscope slide and could be photographed. According to Dr. Georgii under these conditions the condensation consisted entirely of water droplets at -68°C, was a mixture of ice and water particles from -68° to 72°C and was entirely ice crystals below -72°C. On adding heat, water droplets again appeared at -68°C. (Note - explanation of these seemingly impossible facts may be lack of equilibrium). Tests were also made in high altitude aircraft, air samples being drawn in through a tube and photographed. At -50°C both ice crystals and water droplets were observed. The equipment of these tests and photographs should be at Ainring.

5.4. Icing of aircraft. Flights were made under all sorts of icing conditions and photographs were made of ice formation.

5.5. Atmospheric electricity research at high altitudes with DFS 230. Formation of static charge on the aircraft and the way in which it is affected by condensation, ice formation, precipitation, dust, etc. is best studied in a motorless aircraft according to Dr. Georgii because the disturbing factor of the motors and their exhaust need not be reckoned with.

6. Department for High Frequency, Dr. Folsche.

6.1. Direction-finding procedures for measuring wind velocity of great heights without optical sight. In 1940-41 trials were made in which balloons were D/F'd by five stations on the ground. Previous experiments based on clear weather observations had led to the assumption that the wind velocity became less in the stratosphere, but these experiments showed winds of 200 km/hr and more at an altitude of 18 km.

6.2. Flight tests with television for the purpose of improving the clarity of the received image. The principal source of disturbance was rapid fading caused by interference between the direct and the ground-reflected waves, particularly as the transmitter approached the earth. A second source of difficulty was the presence of dust and water droplets in the air which made the optical image at the transmitter end less distinct. Blue and red filters were found helpful under certain conditions. The television equipment was supplied by Fernser, G.m.b.H., Berlin.

6.3. Remote control using television apparatus tests were made using a DFS 230 in which was installed a television transmitter and remote steering apparatus, controlled from a Do.17 in which was the television receiver. Tests were made both over land and over water, the latter being the more successful.

6.4. (Not on chart). Wire control of missiles. Dr. Folsche's assistant, Dr. Engelbrecht worked with Dr. Kracht on this project during the last two months. The story we had heard about using wire control for a distance of 1000 km is regarded as preposterous by Dr. Georgii.

7. Laboratory for Special Propulsion Units, Dr. Eisele. Improvement of jet propulsion motors. Tests on various ideas to improve the performance and life of the Schmidt-Argus motor:

(1) Life of flapper valves, design and materials.
(2) Better aerodynamic shaping of the valve supports
(3) "   "   "   of the air intake.
(4) Effect of length and other dimensions of resonating combustion chamber.
(5) Attempts to improve output by adding coal dust to intake air. Prof. Kamm of Daimler Benz in Stuttgart also carried out experiments along this line, and Prof. Lutz of Braunschweig experimented with the introduction of GM-1 and other oxygen carriers.

The only real improvement obtained was through the shaping of the air inlet and valve supports. This work was reported to have increased the efficiency by 10-15%. (Prof. Lutz was to have gone to the Luftfahrtforschungsanstalt, Munchen, Ottabrunn, but it was not yet completed at the end of the war).

8. Department for Propulsion Unit Development, Dr. Sanger.

8.1. Development of a Lorin motor. This unit was tested on a Do-17 with considerable success. A Me 262 was to be furnished for further testing but did not arrive in time. For further details see interrogation report.

8.2. Development of a coal burner for Lorin motor use. In this connection he worked with Dr. Lippisch. Work not considered very successful.

9. Photographic Section, Dipl. Ing. Harth.

10. Central Workshop, Ing. Erbskorn.

11. Administration, Herr Rauber.

Miscellaneous Notes:

Dr. Esan. President of the Physikalische Technische Reichsanstalt, Berlin, formerly head of the Phys. Tech. Inst., U. of Jena, in charge of all high-frequency problems in the various Technical Institutes of the Reichsforschungsrats, was last heard of at Inntal between Rosenheim and Kufstein at an Institute there. Dr. Georgii thought that Prof. von Hantl had an Institute on the Wendelstein part of which was at the foot of the Wendelstein in neighborhood of Brannenburg. This is German territory, but near the border of Austria.

Prof. Hahn may be in Urrach in Wurtenburg. Prof. Hersenberg might be there with him.

PART II.

A Preliminary Survey of German Studies of Mathematical Pursuit Curves.

The following survey is based solely on documents seized at Ainring plus two interrogations at Gottingen; thus further relevant contributions, made either in the Allied countries or in Germany, could not be taken into account. Hence, the following presentation is probably very incomplete On the other hand, the documents used include several German reports which seem to represent work on a high level.

1. The use of pursuit planes and of guided missiles leads to a variety of problems some of which belong, at least if stated in an oversimplified form, into pure mathematics. Since various aspects of the general problem of guided missiles were studied intensively at Ainring, it may be in order to supplement the information on this work, given in the preceding portion of this report, by a brief survey of some of the purely mathematical questions involved.

2. In the sequel, T will refer to a target (enemy aircraft or ship) that travels in a straight line with constant speed c. A pursuer P (guided rocket or torpedo, or a pursuit plane) pursues T, where P is assumed to have a constant speed v but generally a curilinear path. It is assumed that P travels in a fixed plane that contains the rectilinear path of T. Depending upon the tactical situation, various types of trajectories may be advantageous for P. The path of P will be termed a pursuit curve.

Example 1. P is an anti-aircraft rocket with a target seeking (or homing) head that determines instantaneously the direction from P to T (by reflected radio waves, for instance) and is connected with a steering mechanism that turns P instantaneously into the direction toward T. Mathematically the path of P is a curve whose tangent passes, at each moment, through the point T. In connection with the assumption that T and P have constant speeds, the path of P is then the oldest known pursuit curve, the so-called hound curve (Hundekurve).

Example 2. P is now a rocket, fired from a point O on the ground, and guided from the point O (by radio beam) in such a way that the points O, P, T are always on a straight line. The trajectory of P is then the co-called three point curve, where it is understood that the further conditions stated above are complied with.

3. The curves referred to in the preceding examples will be termed the ordinary hound curve and the ordinary three point curve respectively. Indeed, they are special cases of more general pursuit curves that will be reviewed presently.

4. **Acoustic pursuit curves.** In this case, P is a missile with an acoustic target-seeking head. That is, P always travels in the direction from which the noise originated by the target P seems to come. A study of the resulting acoustic pursuit curves is contained in the following report.

Gerbes, W. Über Verfolgungskurven, speziell "akustische" (On pursuit curves, especially acoustic ones), Arbeitsprotokoll Nr. 100, Flugfunk Forschungsinstitut Oberpfaffenhofen e.v.

Changing the notations of Gerbes to suit the English-speaking reader, let the target T move upward on the y-axis with the constant speed c, while P represents the pursuing missile which travels with the constant speed v along its path (see figure). Let v_s denote the speed of sound, and let T_1 be that previous position of the target T whose noise just reaches P at the moment considered. Then the line $T_1 P$ is by assumption the tangent at $\bar{P}$ of the acoustic pursuit curve. If τ is the time it took the noise from T_1 to reach P, then $E = v_s \tau$, $a = c\tau$, and hence $E/a = v_s/c$. Putting $v_s/c = \sigma$, $v/c = \epsilon$,

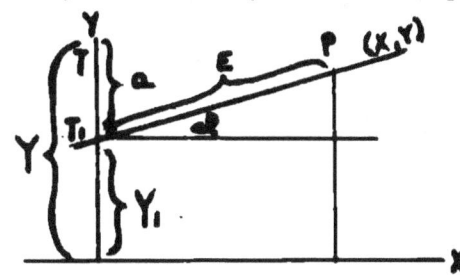

σ and ϵ are two positive constants, and $\dfrac{E}{a} = \sigma$ (1)

The differential equation of the pursuit curve follows now readily. Putting $\rho = dy/dx$ we have successively

$$\rho = \frac{dy}{dx} = \tan \alpha = \frac{Y-Y_1}{x}, \quad Y_1 - y = -\rho x, \quad Y_1 = y - \rho x$$

$$E = [(y-Y_1)^2 + x^2]^{1/2} = (1+\rho^2)^{1/2} x$$

$$a = Y - Y_1 = Y - y + \rho x.$$

In view of (1) there follows the equation

(2) $(1+\rho^2)^{1/2} x = \sigma(Y - y + \rho x)$

Now $v = (\dot{x}^2 + \dot{y}^2)^{1/2}$, $c = \dot{Y}$, where the dots denote differentiation with respect to the time t.

We have thus

$$\epsilon^2 = \frac{v^2}{c^2} = \frac{\dot{x}^2 + \dot{y}^2}{\dot{Y}^2} = \frac{1 + \left(\frac{\dot{y}}{\dot{x}}\right)^2}{\left(\frac{\dot{Y}}{\dot{x}}\right)^2} = \frac{1+\rho^2}{\left(\frac{dY}{dx}\right)^2}$$

(Since (cf. figure) Y increases as x decreases, it follows that

(3) $\dfrac{dY}{dx} = -\dfrac{1}{\epsilon}(1+R^2)^{1/2}$

Differentiating (2) with respect to x and then replacing dY/dx by the expression (3), there follows the differential equation of the acoustic pursuit curve

(4) $\left(\dfrac{1}{(1+R^2)^{1/2}} - \dfrac{1}{G}\dfrac{R}{1+R^2}\right) R' = \left(\dfrac{1}{\epsilon} + \dfrac{1}{G}\right)\dfrac{1}{x}$

where $R = \dfrac{dy}{dx}$, $R' = \dfrac{dR}{dx} = \dfrac{d^2y}{dx^2}$

5. The equation (4) arises, as pointed out by Gerbes, in still another connection. Let now P denote a pursuit plane, with a fixed cannon which fires a projectile that travels at the constant speed v_g (gravity, air resistance are neglected). P is desired to travel with constant speed v in such a manner that if the cannon is fired at any moment, then the target T is hit, where T travels along a fixed straight line with constant speed c. Using again the notations $G = v_g/c$, $\epsilon = v/c$, a reasoning entirely analogous to that used in 4. yields for the path P the differential equation

(4*) $\left(\dfrac{1}{(1+R^2)^{1/2}} + \dfrac{1}{G}\dfrac{R}{1+R^2}\right) R' = \left(\dfrac{1}{\epsilon} - \dfrac{1}{G}\right)\dfrac{1}{x}$

The equation (4*) differs from (4) only by the sign of G. If the path of P, as considered at present, is terms a <u>pursuit curve with firing lead</u>, then it appears that these curves may be considered as acoustic pursuit curves corresponding to <u>negative</u> sound speed. Thus equation (4) covers both types of pursuit curves if G is not restricted as to sign.

6. If v_g is taken, either in 4. or 5. as $+\infty$, then clearly we obtain the ordinary hound curves (f. 2). Thus the ordinary hound curves are accounted for by taking $1/G = 0$ in (4), and hence we have the differential equation $\dfrac{R'}{(1+R^2)^{1/2}} = \dfrac{1}{\epsilon x}$.

7. The integration of (4), formally, proceeds as follows. Regarding p as the unknown function of x, (4) is a first order ordinary differential equation in which the variables can be separated immediately. Thus one quadrature yields p in terms of x, and a second quadrature yields then y in terms of x, since $p = dy/dx$. Disregarding for the moment complications that may arise on account of vanishing denominators, we introduce a new independent variable u by means of the formula

$$p = \text{Sin } u$$

where

$$\text{Sin } u = \dfrac{e^u - e^{-u}}{2}$$

denotes the hyperbolic sine of u. Other hyperbolic functions to be

used are
$$\cos u = \frac{e^u + e^{-u}}{2}, \quad \tan u = \frac{\sin u}{\cos u} = \frac{e^u - e^{-u}}{e^u + e^{-u}}$$

Then $1 + p^2 = 1 + \sin^2 u = \cos^2 u$, $p' = u' \cos u$, and (4)

yields $\left(1 - \frac{1}{\epsilon} \tan u\right) u' = \left(\frac{1}{\epsilon} + \frac{1}{\delta}\right) \frac{1}{x}$

(5)

Denoting by m a constant, (5) yields by integration

(6) $\quad u - \frac{1}{\delta} \log \cos u = \left(\frac{1}{\epsilon} + \frac{1}{\delta}\right) \log \frac{x}{m}$

Putting $\frac{\delta}{\delta + \epsilon} = \alpha$.

(6) yields

(7) $\quad x = m \, e^{\alpha \epsilon u} \cos^{\alpha - 1} u$

Theoretically, (7) should yield u in terms of x, but explicit solution of (7) for u is impractical. Thus we prefer to find also y in terms of u, thus obtaining the solution curve in parametric form

Now $dy/du = p \, dx/du$. (7) yields, by differentiation, dx/du, and since $p = \sin u$, there follows the formular (k a constant of integration)

$$y = k + \int \frac{dx}{du} \sin u \, du = k + x \sin u - \int x \cos u \, du$$

and thus in view of (7)

$$y = k + m e^{\alpha \epsilon u} \cos^{\alpha - 1} u \sin u - m \int e^{\alpha \epsilon u} \cos^{\alpha} u \, du.$$

Explicit solution of the indefinite integral in (8) does not seem feasible, but a rapidly convergent series expansion may be readily obtained. In this manner, (7) and (8) yield the solution curves in parametric form. Gerbes proceeds on this basis to discuss the following questions: location of the curves, actual hits, curvature, number of curves through a given point in a given direction, and other matters relevant for the applications. However, the subject seems to need a great deal more attention. It should be also noted that every step of the formal calculations used must be carefully discussed.

7. As noted above, for $1/\delta = 0$ we are in the case of the ordinary hound curves. The equations (5) reduces then to the simple form

$$u' = \frac{1}{\epsilon x}$$

and the explicit equations of the hound curves follow readily. A detailed discussion of this case is given in the paper: Hasse, H. Ebene Verfolgungs-kurven, Marine-Forschung, Forschungsbericht Nr. 8.

8. The ordinary hound curve, as closer study shows, has generally very large curvature near the target. For this and other reasons, the

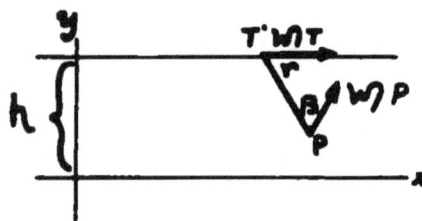

following modification is used (see figure). The target T moves along the line $y = h$ at constant speed c, while the pursuer P (in the sequel a torpedo) travels at constant speed v in such a way that the tangent to its path encloses a fixed angle β with the line TP. The resulting pursuit curves are the <u>hound curves with constant lead angle</u> ($=\beta$). These curves were studied in great detail by R. Hosemann in the following reports:

1) Mathematische Grundlagen der Schussbahnen von eingelenkten Torpedos bei radialem Steuereffect und konstantem Vorhalt (mathematical foundations of the trajectories of guided torpedoes with radial steering effect and constant lead), Bericht Nr. 4, Jan 22, 1945 Arbeitsgruppe Leukverfahren bei T.V.A. Gotenhafen.

2) Berechnung der Schussbahnen etc. (Calculation of the trajectories etc), Marine Forschung, Forschungsbericht Nr. 27.

These two reports are practically identical. A brief survey of the methods follows. Denoting by (X,h) the coordinates of T and by (x,y) the coordinates of P, X is of the form $X = a + ct$, where a is another constant. The method of Hosemann is based on using a coordinate system (ξ, η) that is fixed relative to the moving target T, as indicated in the figure

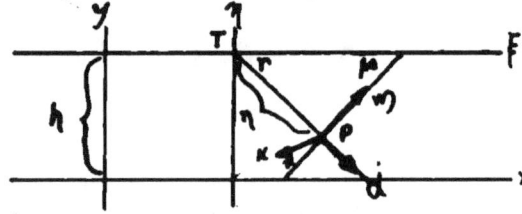

If (ξ, η) are the coordinates of P in this system, then $\xi = x - X = x - a - ct$, $\eta = y - h$

Hence if the path of P is described in terms of ξ, η then the description in terms of x, y is immediate. Thus we shall work with the relative coordinates ξ, η, and in fact with the relative polar coordinates r, ρ indicated in the figure. Introduce the unit vectors j, k as in the figure. Let ξ, η be thought of as functions of the time t, and let w be the vector with components $\dot\xi, \dot\eta$ relative to the system ξ, η (that is w is relative velocity vector of P). Let μ, ψ be determined as in the figure. Then

$$\xi = r \cos\rho, \quad \dot\xi = \dot r \cos\rho - r\dot\rho \sin\rho,$$
$$\eta = r \sin\rho, \quad \dot\eta = \dot r \sin\rho + r\dot\rho \cos\rho,$$
$$\tan\mu = \frac{\dot\eta}{\dot\xi}, \quad \frac{\pi}{2} = \psi + \mu + \rho = \pi, \quad \psi = \mu + \rho - \frac{\pi}{2}$$

These formulas yield, after elementary calculations,

$$\tan \psi = \frac{-\dot{\eta}}{\eta \dot{r}}$$

$$|m| = (\dot{\xi}^2 + \dot{\eta}^2)^{1/2} = (\dot{\eta}^2 + \eta^2 \dot{r}^2)^{1/2}$$

$$\cos \psi = \frac{\eta \dot{r}}{|m|}, \quad \sin \psi = -\frac{\dot{\eta}}{|m|}$$

From the figure there follows for m the representation

$$m = \eta \dot{r} \, k + \dot{\eta} \, j$$

Now let m_T, m_P denote the velocity vectors of T and P respectively, relative to the fixed coordinate system x, y. Then (see figure)

$$m_T = c(-\sin r \cdot k + \cos r \cdot j)$$
$$m_P = v(-\sin \beta \cdot k - \cos \beta \cdot r)$$

On the other hand $m = m_P - m_T$, and by a previous formula, $m = \eta \dot{r} k + \dot{\eta} j$. Comparison of these formulas yields

$$\eta \dot{r} = c \sin r - v \sin \beta$$
$$\dot{\eta} = -c \cos r - v \cos \beta$$

Putting $\lambda = v/c$ there follows by division the formula

$$\frac{\lambda \cos \beta + \cos r}{\lambda \sin \beta - \sin r} = \frac{\dot{\eta}}{\eta \dot{r}} = \frac{\frac{d\eta}{dt}}{\eta \frac{dr}{dt}} = \frac{1}{\eta} \frac{d\eta}{dr} = \frac{d}{dr} \log \eta,$$

and hence

$$\boxed{\log \eta = m + \int \frac{\lambda \cos \beta + \cos r}{\lambda \sin \beta - \sin r} \, dr} \qquad *$$

Note that the lead angle β is constant by assumption, and λ is also a constant. Thus the integral in * is of the form

$$** \int \frac{a + \cos r}{b - \sin r} \, dr,$$

where $a = \lambda \cos \beta, b = \lambda \sin \beta$ are known constants.

This is an elementary integral; thus r follows in terms of r, and the

$$\xi = \eta \cos r, \quad \eta = -\eta \sin r \qquad \text{yield the parametric}$$

equations of the solution curve, in terms of the parameter r, relative to the system ξ, η. The integral may be solved by the usual real methods, but Hoseman proceeds in a manner more suited for the actual discussion of the solution curves. Introducing the complex variable $z = e^{ir}$, the integral ** becomes after simple calculation

$$-4 \int \frac{z^2 + 2az + 1}{z(z^2 - 2bz - 1)} \, dz,$$

where the integration is extended over a suitably chosen arc of the unit circle $|z| = 1$. In this form, the integral can be solved by using the method of partial fractions, and the existence of singular values of z, and hence of τ, becomes evident. Thus the study of these pursuit curves is reduced to a discussion of explicit elementary formulas.

This discussion is carried out by Hosemann in great detail, and it appears that a large number of possibilities exist, some of which may be described as unexpected. For details, the reader must be referred to the original documents.

9. A generalization of the three point curves (see 2) has been studied in the following report.

   Hasse, H. Eine Verallgemeinerung des Dreipunkdeckungsverfahrens (a generalization of the three-point alignment method), Marine Forschung, Forschungsbericht Nr. 20.

The following situation (suggested by the use of guided torpedoes) is

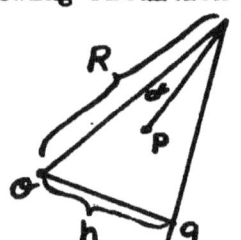

studied by Hasse (see figure) The target T moves along a straight line g at uniform speed c, while the pursuing torpedo P travels at constant speed v in such a way that the lines that join T to P and to a fixed point O form a constant angle α (for $\alpha = 0$ we are in the case of the ordinary three-point curve). Put $\gamma = c/v$ and let h be the shortest distance from V to the line g. By proper choice of units, it can be assumed that

$$v = 1, \quad \gamma = h, \text{ and hence also } \gamma = h = c.$$

The situation is further simplified by choosing axes x, y as indicated in the figure.
Let f be the line P T; thus while P travels, the line f and the angle α vary. The equation of f is readily obtained in the form
$$x \sin \alpha - y \cos \alpha = R \sin \alpha$$
The figure shows that $\angle BOT = \alpha$ and hence from the triangle OBT
$$\tan \alpha = \frac{BT}{h}$$

If t is so measured that for $t = 0$ the target T is in the position B, then $BT = ct$, and hence, since $g = c = h$,

$$\tan \psi = \frac{ct}{h} = t.$$

It follows that

$$\cos \alpha = \frac{1}{(1+t^2)^{1/2}} \qquad \sin \alpha = \frac{t}{(1+t^2)^{1/2}}$$

Since P, with coordinates x, y, lies on f, with equation $x \sin \alpha - y \cos \alpha = R \sin \alpha$, substitution of the preceding expression for cos (sin yields the formular

$$xt - y = (1+t^2) g \sin \alpha$$

Further, by assumption,

$$\dot{x}^2 + \dot{y}^2 = v^2 = 1,$$

where dots denote differentiation with respect to t. Thus the coordinates of P, as functions of t, satisfy the system

$$(S) \begin{cases} \dot{x}^2 + \dot{y}^2 = 1 \\ xt - y = R(1+t^2) \end{cases}$$

where we put

$$g \sin \alpha = R = \text{constant}$$

The solution of the system (S) was to be given in a subsequent report of Hasse which is however not available at this time. The present report of Hasse gives a discussion of the solution curves based directly on the system (S). This study is based on a parabola, termed by Hasse the <u>limit parabola</u>, which is associated with the system (S) as follows. For a given point (x, y) to be located on a solution curve, the second equation (S) must be satisfied by some real value of t. That equation being a a quadratic equation for t, it follows that we must have the inequality

$$x^2 - 4p(p+y) \gtreqless 0, \text{ ot equivalently } y \lesseqgtr \frac{1}{4p} x^2 - p$$

In other words, all the solution curves of (S) are located below the "limit parabola" with the equation

$$y = \frac{1}{4p} x^2 - p$$

This parabola has various other remarkable relation ships to the solution curves. For example, itfollows easily that all the lines f are tangent to this parabola. Hasse derives a number of fundamental facts for the solution curves of (S), by using the limit parabola, which cannot be reproduced here. A full discussion of the system of (S) is however dependent upon the solution of (S) which is made, as stated by Hasse, in terms of elliptic functions in the second (not available) report of Hasse.

10. In 8, the hound curve with constant lead angle were discussed in a coordinate system fixed relative to the moving target T. For completeness, we add the differential equation of these curves, relative to a non-moving coordinate system (see figure). Using the notations and assumptions of 8. let is put further $\mu = \frac{dy}{dx}, \frac{c}{v} = q, \tan\beta = m$

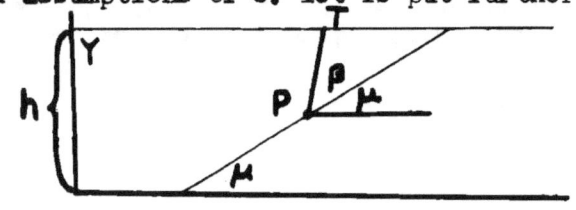

The figure yields
$$\tan(\beta + \mu) = \frac{h-y}{X-x}$$

Also
$$\tan(\beta + \mu) = \frac{\tan\beta - \tan\mu}{1 - \tan\beta \times \tan\mu} = \frac{m+p}{1-mp}$$

Hence

(a) $$\frac{m+p}{1-mp} = \frac{h-y}{X-x}$$

Now
$$\frac{dx}{dt} = v\cos\mu, \quad \frac{dy}{dt} = v\sin\mu, \quad \frac{dX}{dt} = c$$

$$\cos\mu = \frac{1}{(1+\tan^2\mu)^{1/2}} = \frac{1}{(1+p^2)^{1/2}}$$

and hence $\sin\mu = \frac{\tan\mu}{(1+\tan^2\mu)^{1/2}} = \frac{1}{(1+p^2)^{1/2}}$

(b) $$\frac{dx}{dt} = \frac{v}{(1+p^2)^{1/2}}$$

(c) $$\frac{dX}{dx} = \frac{dX}{dt} \cdot \frac{dt}{dx} = \frac{c}{\frac{dx}{dt}} = \frac{c}{v}(1+p^2)^{1/2} = q(1+p^2)^{1/2}$$

Differentiating (a) with respect to x, and then replacing $\frac{dX}{dx}$, X by their expressions resulting from (a) and (c), there follows the differential equation of the hound curves with constant lead angle in the form

(d) $$\frac{dp}{dx} = \frac{(m+p)(1+p^2)^{1/2}\left[m(1+p^2)^{1/2} - q(m+p)\right]}{(h-y)(1+m^2)}$$

This equation may be transformed by using y as the independent variable.

Since
$$\frac{dp}{dx} = \frac{dp}{dy}\frac{dy}{dx} = p\frac{dp}{dy}$$

the equation (d) becomes

(e) $$\frac{dp}{dy} = \frac{(m+p)(1+p^2)^{1/2}\left[m(1+p^2)^{1/2} - q(m+p)\right]}{p(h-y)(1+m^2)}$$

Here m, q are given constants, while p is thought of as an unknown function of y. In (e) the variables can be immediately separated, but the resulting integration seems to be more involved than that arising in par. 8. In any case, one quadrature yields, theoretically, $p = dy/dx$ as a function of y, and a second quadrature yields y as a function of x. This procedure seems to be inferior to that in par. 8 as far as discussion of the solution curves is concerned.

11. The system (S) in par. 9 can also be readily reduced to an ordinary differential equation. Using again the notation $\dot{x} = \frac{dx}{dt}$, $\dot{y} = \frac{dy}{dt}$, we have (since $\dot{x}^2 + \dot{y}^2 = 1$)

(α) $$\dot{x} = \frac{x}{(\dot{x}^2 + \dot{y}^2)^{1/2}} = \frac{1}{(1+\dot{y}^2)^{1/2}}, \quad \dot{y} = \frac{dy}{dt}$$

(β) $$\frac{dt}{dx} = \frac{1}{\dot{x}} = (1+\dot{y}^2)^{1/2}$$

Differentiating the second equation of the system (S) with respect to x, and replacing dt/dx by the expression (β), we get

$$t + (1+y')^{1/2} x - y' = 2t(1+\dot{y}^2)^{1/2}$$

This equation yields t in terms of x and y, and substitution in the second equation of the system (S) yields the desired differential equation.

12. The reports of Gerbes, Hasse and Hosemann, considered above, seem to represent the best of the Ainring material from the purely mathematical point of view. As regards applications, the over-simplified assumptions made in these reports should be changed to give a closer approximation of actual conditions. The Ainring material contains several reports that make contributions in this direction. These reports are listed below, with brief comments on the contents.

13. Fricke, A verfolgungskurven in Luftkampf (Pursuit curves in aerial combat) ZWB, UM 732. This report contains valuable additions to the theory of the pursuit curves with firing lead, studied by Gerbes (see par. 5. The case studied by Gerbes is that os a weightless projectile

travelling in vacuum. Fricke, considers the actual ballistical
situation, and gives at least brief indications concerning other
relevant issues (for example, the case of a target moving along a non-
rectilinear path).

14. Vogg, K. Untersuchung einer Einrichtung zur Erliegung des Rammkurses
(Study of an arrangement for flying the ramming course) is a report
prepared in the institute for flight equipment at Ainring. This study
is concerned with a rocket, equipped with a target seeking head, that
directs the rocket along a lath which may be described as a <u>hound curve
with variable lead angle.</u> More precisely, the tangent t (see figure
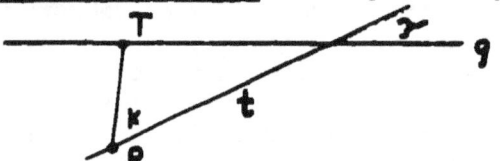
of the path of the pursuing
rocket P forms an angle K
with the line TP such that
K is a linear function of
the angle γ.

In the special case k = constant, we are in the case considered in
par. 8. The purpose of the present generalization is to obtain trajectories
that are more favorable from the aerodynamical point of view.

15. (1) Greinel, Flugbahnen eines Geschosses mit elektromagnetischen
Zielsuchkopf (trajectories of a projectile with electro-magnetic target-
seeking head, ZWB, UM 3547.

(2) Greinel, Uber Bahnkurven von Flugkorpern mit akustischen
Zielsuchkopf (On the trajectories of flying bodies with acoustic target--
seeking head) ZWB, UM 3544.

Theoretically, in the first case the trajectories are ordinary hound-curves
(cf par.2) and in the second case they are the acoustic pursuit curves
considered in par. 4. However, if the rocket is either too far or too
close to the target, then for obvious technical reasons the homing devices
will cease to function. Furthermore, if the trajectory assigned to the
rocket has too large curvature, then the rocket will not be able to follow
it. The two reports of Greinel are concerned with these complications.
It appears that the trajectories will be made up of straight segments, arcs
of circles, and of ordinary hound-curves and of acoustic pursuit curves.
respectively.

16. Schlögl and Walker, Spezielle Dreipunktkurven fur Raketengeschosse
mit stark veranderlicher Geswindigkeit (Special three-point curves for
rocket projectiles with rapidly varying speed) ZWB, UM 3512.
The following general situation is considered (see figure) The target
T travels along an
arbitrary, but known,
curve with arbitrary speed.
The pursuing rocket P is

is guided from the point of observation O in such a manner that
O, P, T, are always collinear. Furthermore, the speed of P is an
assigned function $v(t)$ of the time t. The differential equation of
the trajectory of P is set up as follows. Using spatial polar coordinates
r, ϑ, ω as indicated in the figure, let r, ϑ, ω be relative to
P, R, ω_1, ϑ_1 be relative to T. From the three-point condition
$\omega = \omega_1, \vartheta = \vartheta_1$ and thus ω, ϑ are known functions of t.
Hence $r = r(t)$ is the remaining unknown function. By elementary
calculations

(a) $\quad \left(\dfrac{dr}{dt}\right)^2 + r^2 a(t)^2 = v(t)^2$

where $v(t)$ is the assigned speed of P, and

$$a(t)^2 = \left(\dfrac{d\vartheta}{dt}\right)^2 + \left(\dfrac{d\omega}{dt}\right)^2 \sin^2\vartheta$$

Thus, in (a), $a(t)$ and $v(t)$ are known functions, and hence (a) is an
ordinary first-order differential equation for the trajectory of P. The
equation is brought into a more convenient form by introducing $\omega = \omega(t)$
by the equation

$$\dfrac{d\omega}{dt} = a(t)$$

and then introducing ω as a new independent variable. The equation (a)
becomes then

(b) $\quad \left(\dfrac{dr}{d\omega}\right)^2 + r^2 = w(\omega)^2$

where

(c) $\quad w(\omega) = \dfrac{v}{\frac{d\omega}{dt}} = \dfrac{v}{a}$

is a known function of t and hence of ω.

A different transformation of (a) is as follows:
Let β be the angle between the radius vector OP and the tangent to the
trajectory of P.
On introducing $u = \tan\beta$ as a new unknown function and using the above.
as the independent variable, simple calculations yield for $u = u(\omega)$
a differential equation of the Abelian form

(d) $\quad \dfrac{du}{d\omega} + g(\omega) u^3 - u^2 + g(\omega) u - 1 = 0$

where (cf. (c))

(e) $\quad g(\omega) = \dfrac{1}{w}\dfrac{dw}{d\omega}$

is a known function of ω. Once $u(\omega)$ is determined, r follows from the
relations $r = (v/a)\sin$, $\tan\beta = u$. Thus the problem is reduced to the
study of the Abelian differential equation (d).

Actually though, the Schloge-Walker report gives, in its first part, only fragmentary information about very special cases, while in the second part, for uniform rectilinear motion of T and for $v(t) = c_1 \; t + c_2 + 2$ (c_1, c_2 constants) approximate solutions are discussed, based on the first few terms of series expansions.

16. Elementary and quite incomplete (and at times erroneous) discussions of the various pursuit curves considered above are contained in the reports.

(1) Dobbrack-Knothe, Über einige Arten von Verfolgungskurven (On certain types of pursuit curves) ZWB, UM 650.

(2) Leisegang, Bahnkurven der nach dem Deckungs verfahren gelenkten Flugkorper ZWB, FB 1923. (Trajectories of flying bodies guided by the three-point alignment method). These reports are of interest primarily as introductory elementary studies.

17. Assuming that the purely mathematical studies, whose nature has been briefly outlined in what procedes, were complete (which is not the case) they would represent merely a first step in the study of guided missiles. Indeed, once the theoretical trajectories are fully known, there arises the problem of their evaluation from the point of view of aerodynamical suitability, and next, the question of the instrumental equipment that should be used for the guiding of the missiles. One result of the purely mathematical investigations should be mentioned here. No matter what type of pursuit curve is used, a direct hit is possible, even theoretically, only in restricted cases, especially since too strongly curved trajectories cannot be followed by an actual missile P. However, it will be possible, generally, to assign aerodynamically acceptable trajectories that will take P close to the target T. Hence the importance of providing P not only with a guiding device but also with a proximity fuze.

18. The information concerning pursuit curves, presented above, has been supplemented by interrogations of the German mathematicians H. Hasse and W. Magnus. Reports of these interrogations are enclosed (see enclosures B 20, B 21). As regards control mechanism used in guided missiles, see also the report of the interrogation of M. Schuler, enclosure B 22. A few remarks will be made presently about these reports; for more details, the reader is referred to the enclosures B 20 and B 21.

19. The integration of the system (S) in par. 9 may be carried out, according to Hasse, as follows. First the curvature of the solution curves is calculated. We have by a well known formula (ϱ radius of curvature)

$$\frac{1}{\varrho} = \frac{d\psi}{ds}$$

where s denotes the arc-length and ψ is the angle between the tangent of the solution curve and the positive x-axis. Now since by assumption $v^2 = \dot{x}^2 + \dot{y}^2 = 1$ and $v = ds/dt$, there follows the formula

(1) $\quad \dfrac{1}{v} = \dfrac{d\psi}{ds} = \dfrac{d\psi}{dt}\dfrac{dt}{ds} = \dfrac{d\psi}{dt}$

and similarly

(2) $\quad \cos\psi = \dfrac{dx}{ds} = \dfrac{dx}{dt}\dfrac{dt}{ds} = \dfrac{dx}{dt}, \quad \sin\psi = \dfrac{dy}{dt}$

Using again dots to denote differentiation with respect to t, and noting that $\tan = y/x$, $\psi = \arctan(y/x)$ we obtain

(3) $\quad \dot{\psi} = \dfrac{\dot{x}\ddot{y} - \ddot{x}\dot{y}}{\dot{x}^2 + \dot{y}^2} = \dot{x}\ddot{y} - \ddot{x}\dot{y}$

since $\dot{x}^2$ plus $\dot{y}^2 = 1$. The expression on the right of (3) is further evaluated as follows. From the system (S) in 4.ϱ we obtain, by differentiation with respect to t, the formulas

(4) $\quad \dot{x}\ddot{x} + \dot{y}\ddot{y} = 0$

(5) $\quad -t\dot{x} + \dot{y} = x - 2pt$

(6) $\quad -t\ddot{x} + \ddot{y} = 2(\dot{x} - 2p)$.

We now calculate (cf. (3))

$$(\dot{x} + t\dot{y})\dot{\psi} = \begin{vmatrix} \dot{x} & \dot{y} \\ -t & 1 \end{vmatrix} \begin{vmatrix} \dot{x} & \dot{y} \\ \ddot{x} & \ddot{y} \end{vmatrix} =$$

$$= \begin{vmatrix} \dot{x}^2 + \dot{y}^2 \\ -t\dot{x} + \dot{y} \end{vmatrix} \begin{vmatrix} \dot{x}\ddot{x} + \dot{y}\ddot{y} \\ t\ddot{x} + \ddot{y} \end{vmatrix}$$

In view of (2), (3), (4), (5), (6) we obtain

(7) $\quad \dot{\psi} = \dfrac{2(\cos\psi - p)}{\cos\psi + t\sin\psi}$

Introducing ψ as independent variable, and considering t as the unknown function of ψ, (7) yields for t the linear differential equation of the first order

(8) $\quad \dfrac{dt}{d\psi} + Pt = Q$.

Where

(9) $\quad P = -\dfrac{\sin\psi}{2(\cos\psi - p)}, \quad Q = \dfrac{\cos\psi}{2(\cos\psi - p)}$

According to well known methods, the general solution of (8) is obtained in the form

(10) $$t = e^{-R} \int Q e^{R} d\psi$$

where R is any function such that $dR/d\psi = P$.
In view of (9) we can choose

$$R = \log |\cos\psi - p|^{\frac{1}{2}},$$

and then t appears in the form

(11) $$t = \frac{1}{2} \frac{1}{(\cos\psi - p)^{1/2}} \int \frac{\cos\psi \, d\psi}{(\cos\psi - p)^{1/2}}$$

Let us note that once t is known in terms of ψ, ψ can be determined as a function t, and since $x = \cos\psi$, $y = \sin\psi$ by (2), x and y follow in terms of t by quadratures. As regards (11), the integral

$$y = \int \frac{\cos\psi \, d\psi}{(\cos\psi - p)^{1/2}}$$

can be reduced, according to Hasse, to standard elliptic integrals by means of appropriate substitution. Taking for example, the case $0 < p > 1$ let us put, with Hasse, $p = \cos\gamma$.
Then his substitution

$$\sin\frac{\psi}{2} = \sin\frac{\gamma}{2} \sin\frac{z}{2}$$

where z is a new independent variable, leads to the formular

$$\frac{\cos\psi \, d\psi}{(\cos\psi - p)^{1/2}} = \frac{\cos\psi \, d\psi}{(\cos\psi - \cos\gamma)^{1/2}} = \frac{1}{\sqrt{2}} \frac{1 - 2k^2 \sin^2\frac{z}{2}}{\sqrt{1 - k^2 \sin^2\frac{z}{2}}}$$

writing $$1 - 2k^2 \sin^2\frac{z}{2} = 2(1 - k^2 \sin^2\frac{z}{2}) - 1$$

there follows the relation

$$\frac{\cos\psi \, d\psi}{(\cos\psi - p)^{1/2}} = \sqrt{2} \sqrt{1 - k^2 \sin^2\frac{z}{2}} - \frac{1}{\sqrt{2}} \frac{1}{\sqrt{1 - k^2 \sin^2\frac{z}{2}}}$$

Thus the integral

$$y = \int \frac{\cos\psi \, d\psi}{(\cos\psi - p)^{1/2}}$$

is reduced to a linear combination of the elliptic integrals

$$\int \frac{d\frac{z}{2}}{\sqrt{1 - k^2 \sin^2\frac{z}{2}}} \quad \text{and} \quad \int \sqrt{1 - k^2 \sin^2\frac{z}{2}} \, d\frac{z}{2}$$

For values of p outside of the range (0, 1) analogous calculations are used to reduce the integrals y to elliptic integrals.

Hasse also studied the hound curve with constant lead angle, discussed in par. 8 above. His manuscript on this subject was destroyed shortly before the Germans collapsed, but B 20 contains a brief report by Hasse on his manuscript. In contradistinction with Hosemann (see par. 8) Hasse works with a fixed coordinate system and with real variables. He feels that his treatment is superior to that of Hosemann, which is not quite evident to the writer. In any case the integration of the differential equation of the problem depends upon elementary explicit functions, and the burden of the work lies in the discussion of the solution curves which Hasse does not consider in his brief report in B 2). He stated however that he would be willing to write up a detailed presentation He also stated that in his opinion the best treatment of this subject was given by a German mathematician named Wunderlich, whose manuscript also went to the Chemisch-physikalische Wersuchsanstalt. An effort should be made to locate this manuscript also.

21. For further details, the reader is referred to the enclosures B 20, B 21. In particular, B 21 gives a review of the various pursuit curves and of their actual or projected applications from the German point of view.

Note on Practical Application.

The control system developed at Ainring with the assistance of Dr. Wigge, physicist, Dr. Magnus, applied mathematician, and Dr. Hasse, algebraist, was called Feldmühle. It was brought to the point of practical application ahead of rival systems and full-scale comparative tests were carried out with a number of guided missiles near Kiel in July and August 1944.

The planned trajectory called for a climb to a precomputed altitude and then direction from the ground in a glide path towards the target to a point where an infra-red electro-magnetic homing device took over and steered the missile on a simple hound curve to the hit or nearest approach point.

In spite of a number of simplifications such as assuming constant missile speed disregarding parallax between firing and aiming stations, and limiting the missile-target ratio to values between 2 and 10 the basic theory was found to be at fault in such fundamentals as control in roll axis.

Dr. Rado in the above report developed the German theory well beyond the point at which it was applied to Feldmühle in 1944.

JOHN A. O'MARA
Lt. Col.   AC.

Interrogation of Dr. Hellmuth Hasse.   B-20

Prof. of Maths. at the University of Gottingen.

Date: Gottingen, 12 Sept. 1945.

Interrogation by Dr. T. Rado, Tech. Rep., Prof. of Maths. of The Ohio State University.

    Hasse is a prominent German mathematician, who was very active in productive research in pure Mathematics before the war. During the war, he served as a corvette captain in the German Navy, and was assigned to the Chemisch-Physikalische Versuchsanstalt (Chemical-physical research institute), referred to by the letters CPVA in Danisch Nienhoff, near Kiel, where he worked on mathematical problems that arose in the theory of guided missiles, in particular guided torpedoes. The engineering aspects of the problem were studied by a group under the direction of Prof. Heinrich Wigge at the CPVA.

    a) Hasse has been previously interrogated late in June and early in July of 1945, by Klemperer, Chairman, Joint Chiefs of Staff, Guided Missile Committee and Hartogs of ALSOS. These interrogation reports should be compared, if available, with the present report.

    b) The main purpose of the interrogation was to get additional information concerning his work on the trajectories of guided missiles. The information obtained from Hasse follows:

    c) Hasse prepared a report on the ordinary hound curve which is available at the ADRC in London, with the title:

    Ebene Verfolgungskurven (Hundekerven), Marine-Forschung, Forschungsbericht Nr. 3, 16. April 1944.

    He supplemented this study by an investigation of the following case. The missile is guided along an ordinary hound curve, subject to the following two assumptions.

1) If the radius of curvature drops to a certain value G^*, then the missile continues along the oscillating circle.

2) If the missile gets within a certain given distance d from the target, then it is detonated by a proximity fuze. His study of this case was submitted to the CPVA in two notes which should be available there. His main results are summarized in the following statement (contributed by Hasse himself at the request of the interrogator).

Let a projectile P follow a target T on an ordinary hound-curve (fixed leading angle $\alpha = 0$). If the velocity ratio $q < \frac{1}{2}$, the radius ϱ of curvature tends to 0 as P approaches T. For $q = \frac{1}{2}$ this limit is > 0, but also tends to 0, as a function as the starting angle ψ_o, for $\psi_o \to \frac{\pi}{2}$.

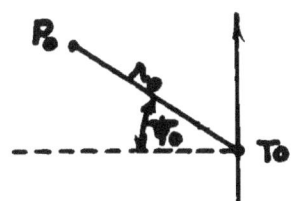

Suppose now $q \leq \frac{1}{2}$, and suppose that P shall continue to move on the circle C of curvature from the moment when ϱ decreases below a given value $\varrho^* > 0$.

Further say that there is a "d-hit", when P come within the given distance $d > 0$ from T.

Then the following two theorems hold:
I. <u>There is a d-hit already on H itself, for any ψ_o, if and only if $d \leq q \varrho^*$</u>
II. <u>There is a d-hit on the combined curve H&C, for any ψ, if and only if $d \leq Q \varrho^*$</u>

where
$$Q = q \arcsin q - 1 - \sqrt{1-q^2}$$

q	0.05	0.10	0.15	0.20	0.25	0.30	0.35	0.40	0.45	0.50
Q	0.0012	0.0050	0.0116	0.0204	0.0314	0.0454	0.0619	0.0811	0.1031	0.1278

Furthermore: If $d < Q \varrho^*$, there are two fixed angles $\overline{\psi}_o, \overline{\overline{\psi}}_o$ (depending in a rather complicated way - that may be expressed explicitly however, on the ratios $d: \varrho^*: \Lambda_o$), such that a d-hit on H plus C occurs, if and only if

$$-\frac{\pi}{2} \leq \psi_o \leq \overline{\psi}_o, \quad \text{or} \quad \overline{\overline{\psi}}_o \leq \psi_o \leq \frac{\pi}{2}$$

For $q = \frac{1}{2}$ this latter statement has to be slightly modified.

d) Hasse contributed an excellent report on the following generalization of the three-point curve, which seems to be more favorable for torpedoes than the ordinary three point curve: if O,M,T, denote the (stationary) observer, the missile and the target respectively, then the angle enclosed by the lines OT and MT is equal to a given constant angle. This report is available at the ADRC in London title: Eine Verallgemienerung des Dreipunktdeckverfahrens, Marine-Forschung, Forschungsbericht Nr. 20, 24 June 1944). In this report Hasse studies the trajectories directly from the differential equation, and states that a more refined study as well as the explicite solution of the differential equation will be given in a subsequent report. Questioned about this subsequent report, Hasse stated that the manuscript was submitted to the CPVA in Danisch Nienhoff, where it is probably available. However, at the request of the interrogator, he prepared a condensed discussion of the integration of the differential equation of the generalized three-point curve. This discussion follows (the references relate to the Hasse report mentioned above in the present section).

Integrals for the generalized three point problem.

(By Helmut Hasse, Göttingen).

Differential equation (see par. 3 in part I):

$$\frac{dt}{dx} = \frac{1}{t} \frac{t \sin x + \cos x}{\cos \psi - p} \qquad (p = q \sin \alpha)$$

Well known method of integration for linear diff. equ.s leads to following general integral (apart from the special straight-line integrals $x = \pm y = $ for $p \leq 1$, $p = \cos y$:

$$t\sqrt{|\cos x - p|} - t_0\sqrt{|\cos x_0 - p|} = \frac{\cos x - p}{|\cos x - p|} \cdot \frac{1}{t} \int_{x_0}^{x} \frac{\cos x \, d\psi}{\sqrt{\cos x - p}}$$

Case A (Hyperbolical case): $0 \leq p < 1$, $p = \cos y$, $0 < y \leq \frac{\pi}{2}$

Type A^+: $-y < x < y$. Choose $\psi_0 = 0$ (i.e., starting points of the integral curves on the isocline $P_0 = P_r$, as defined in part I, § 13).

Type A^-: $y < x < 2\pi - y$. Choose $\psi_0 = \pi$ (i.e., starting points on the osocline $P_\pi = P_R^+$).

Substitution $\tilde{x} = x - \pi$, $\tilde{y} = \pi - y$, hence $\frac{\pi}{2} \leq \tilde{y} < \pi$, $-\tilde{y} < \tilde{x} < \tilde{y}$

leads to form analogous to type A^+

$$t\sqrt{\cos \tilde{x} - \cos \tilde{y}} - t_0\sqrt{1 - \cos \tilde{y}} = \frac{1}{t} \int_0^{\tilde{x}^2} \frac{\cos \tilde{x} \, d\tilde{x}}{\sqrt{\cos \tilde{x} - \cos \tilde{y}}} = F_{\tilde{p}}(\tilde{x}) \text{ with } \tilde{p} = \cos \tilde{y} = -p, \therefore -1 < \tilde{p} \leq 0$$

Case B (Elliptical case): $1 < p^2 < \infty$, $p = \cos y$, y imaginary.

Only one type: $-\alpha < x < \alpha$ Choose $\psi_0 = \pi$ (starting point on $P_\pi = P_R^+$).

$$t\sqrt{p - \cos x} - t_0\sqrt{p + 1} = \frac{1}{t} \int_\pi^x \frac{\cos x \, dx}{\sqrt{p - \cos x}}$$

Substitution $\tilde{\psi} = \psi - \pi$ leads to

$$t\sqrt{\cos \tilde{\psi} - \tilde{p}} - t_0\sqrt{1 - \tilde{p}} = F_{\tilde{p}}(\tilde{\psi}), \text{ with } \tilde{p} = -p, \text{ hence } -\infty < \tilde{p} < -1$$

Case C (Parabolical case): $p = 1$, $p = \cos y$, $y = 0$

Only one type: $0 < \psi < 2\pi$ Choose $\psi_0 = 0$ (starting point on $P_\pi = P_R^+$).
Substitution $\tilde{\psi} = \psi - \pi$ leads to

$$t\sqrt{\cos \tilde{\psi} + 1} - t_0\sqrt{2} = F_{-1}(\tilde{\psi}) \text{ with } \tilde{p} = -1$$

Reduction to the Legendre normal elliptic integrals.

Definition (as well-known)

$$E(\theta, \phi) = \int_0^\phi \sqrt{1 - k^2 \sin^2 \theta} \, d\phi, \quad F(\theta, \phi) = \int_0^\phi \frac{1}{\sqrt{1 - k^2 \sin^2 \theta}} d\phi$$

with modulus

$$k^2 = \sin^2 \theta \qquad (0 < \theta < \frac{\pi}{2}).$$

Case A.

Types A^+, A^- combined, by putting $\widehat{p} = \pm p$ according to case $A^\pm$ hence
$$-1 < \widehat{p} < 1; \widehat{p} = \cos\widetilde{\gamma}, 0 < \widetilde{\gamma} < \pi; -\widetilde{\gamma} < \psi < \widetilde{\gamma}.$$

Transform the variable angle ψ into a new one $\widehat{\xi}$ by
$$\sin\frac{\widetilde{\psi}}{2} \Big/ \sin\frac{\widehat{\gamma}}{2} = \sin\frac{\widehat{\xi}}{2} \qquad (-\pi < \widehat{\xi} < \pi).$$

Then
$$F_{\widehat{p}}(\widetilde{\psi}) = \sqrt{2}\; E\left(\frac{\widetilde{\gamma}}{2}, \frac{\widetilde{\xi}}{2}\right) - \frac{1}{\sqrt{2}}\; F\left(\frac{\widetilde{\gamma}}{2}, \frac{\widetilde{\xi}}{2}\right)$$

with modulus
$$k^2 = \frac{1-\widehat{p}}{2} = \sin^2\frac{\widetilde{\gamma}}{2}, \quad \theta = \frac{\widetilde{\xi}}{2}$$

Case B.

$$-\infty < \widehat{p} < -1; -\infty < \widetilde{\psi} < \infty$$

Define a new parameter angle $\widetilde{\gamma}'$ by $(0 < \widetilde{\gamma}' < \pi)$
$$\frac{2}{1-\widehat{p}} = \sin^2\frac{\widetilde{\gamma}'}{2}$$

Then
$$F_{\widehat{p}}(\widetilde{\psi}) = \sqrt{1-\widehat{p}}\; E\left(\frac{\widetilde{\gamma}'}{2}, \frac{\widetilde{\psi}}{2}\right) + \frac{\widehat{p}}{\sqrt{1-\widehat{p}}}\; F\left(\frac{\widetilde{\gamma}'}{2}, \frac{\widetilde{\psi}}{2}\right)$$

with modulus
$$k^2 = \frac{2}{1-\widehat{p}} = \sin^2\frac{\widetilde{\gamma}'}{2}, \quad \theta = \frac{\widetilde{\psi}}{2}$$

Case C.

$$\widehat{p} = -1; \widetilde{\gamma} = \pi; -\pi < \widetilde{\psi} < \pi$$

The elliptic integral degenerates into a trigonometrical integral:
$$F_{-1}(\widetilde{\psi}) = -\frac{1}{\sqrt{2}} \log \operatorname{tg}\frac{\widetilde{\psi}+\pi}{4} + \sin\frac{\widetilde{\psi}}{2} \sqrt{2}$$

With the help of those explicit representations of the integrals a very interesting discussion of the integral curves - as to cusps, behaviour in infinity etc - can be given. Details see in ms., available at the CPVA, Danisch-Nienhof near Kiel. For p = 0 (ordinary three point problems) there are also numerical tables available at the CPVA.

c) Hasse also studied the hound curve with constant lead angle. He feels that his work was superior to that of Hosemann (Mathematische Grundlagen der Schussbahnen etc., TVA Gotenhafen, Bericht Nr. 4, 22 January 1944, available at the ADRC in London). On the other hand, Hasse feels that the best treatment is due to a mathematician called Winderlich, whose manuscript on this topic should be available at the CPVA in Danisch Nienhoff. The report of Hasse on the same topic, which was only in manuscript form, was dest5oyed a few days before the occupation of Gottingen, but the interrogator Hasse prepared the following abstract of his destroyed manuscript, (due to the lack of notesand the pressure of time, minor errors may be present).

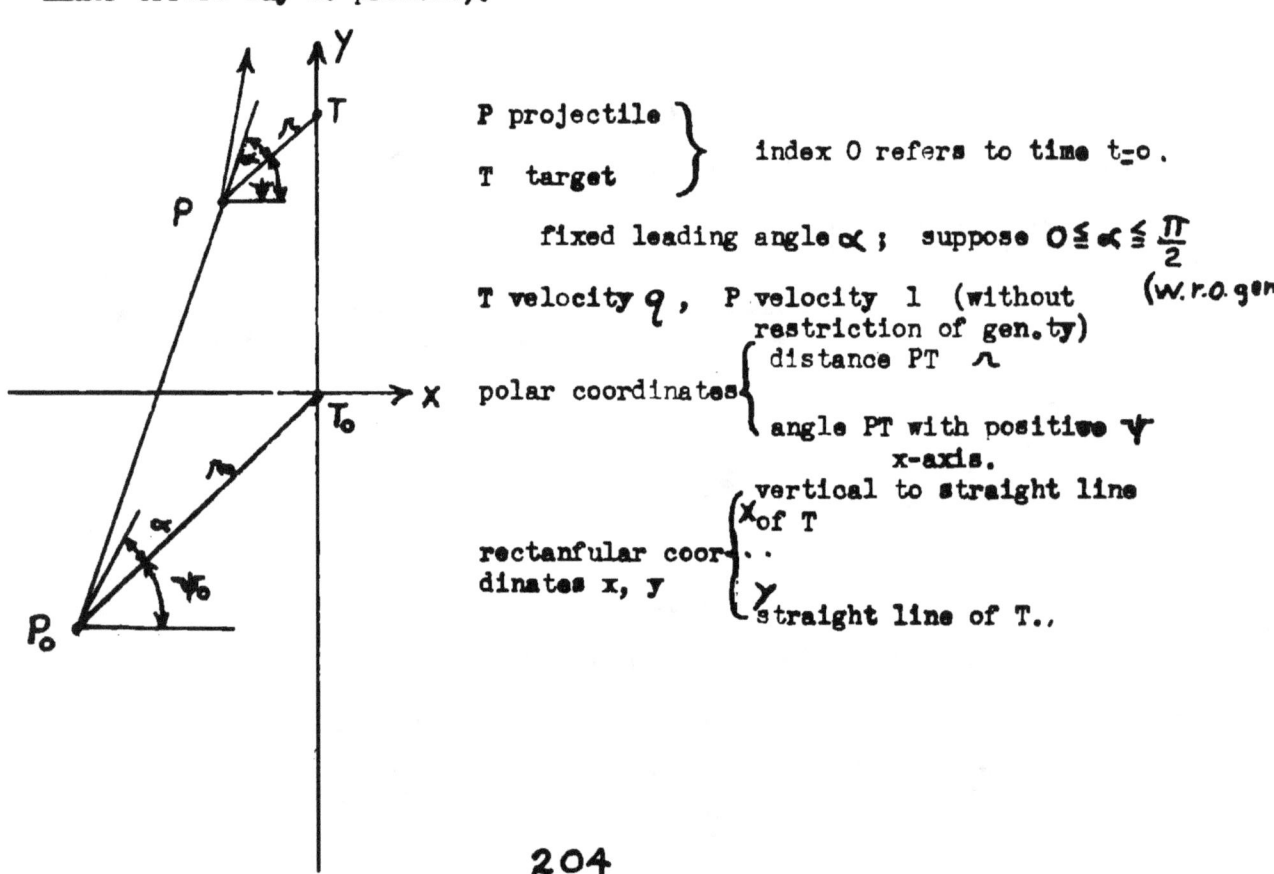

P projectile
T target
} index 0 refers to time $t=0$.

fixed leading angle α; suppose $0 \leq \alpha \leq \frac{\pi}{2}$ (w.r.o.gen)

T velocity q, P velocity 1 (without restriction of gen. ty)

polar coordinates
- distance PT r
- angle PT with positive x-axis ψ

rectangular coordinates x, y
- vertical to straight line of T
- straight line of T.

Fundamental equations

(i) $\begin{cases} -x = r\cos\psi \\ gt - y = r\sin\psi \end{cases}$ (geometrical situation).

(ii) $\begin{cases} \dot{x} = \cos(\psi + \alpha) \\ \dot{y} = \sin(\psi + \alpha) \end{cases}$ (velocity condition)

Differentiate (i) and compare with (ii)

(iii) $\begin{cases} \cos\psi\, dr - r\sin\psi\, d\psi + \cos(\psi+\alpha)\, dt = 0 \\ \sin\psi\, dr + r\cos\psi\, d\psi + (\sin(\psi+\alpha) - g)\, dt = 0 \end{cases}$

Hence

$dr : d\psi : dt = \begin{vmatrix} -r\sin\psi & \cos(\psi+\alpha) \\ r\cos\psi & \sin(\psi+\alpha)-g \end{vmatrix} : \begin{vmatrix} \cos(\psi+\alpha) & \cos\psi \\ \sin(\psi+\alpha)-g & \sin\psi \end{vmatrix} : \begin{vmatrix} \cos\psi & -r\sin\psi \\ \sin\psi & r\cos\psi \end{vmatrix}$

or

(iv) $dr : d\psi : dt = r(g\sin\psi - \cos\alpha) : (g\cos\psi - \sin\alpha) : r$

Formal integration in two steps:

(v) $\dfrac{dr}{r} = \dfrac{g\sin\psi - \cos\alpha}{g\cos\psi - \sin\alpha}\, d\psi$ — gives first integral: $r\,\mathcal{F}(\psi) = C$

(with constant $C = r_0\,\mathcal{F}(\psi_0)$).

(vi) $dt = \dfrac{r}{g\cos\psi - \sin\alpha}\, d\psi = C\dfrac{d\psi}{(g\cos\psi - \sin\alpha)\mathcal{F}(\psi)}$ gives second integral

The second integral turns out to have the form:

$$t = r_0\,\mathcal{G}(\psi_0) - r\,\mathcal{G}(\psi)$$

with a comparatively simple function $\mathcal{G}(\psi)$. This formula allows a rather interesting geometrical construction of the radius ρ of curvature: $\rho = \dfrac{r}{g\cos\psi - \sin\alpha}$ with a comparatively simple function ($\mathcal{G}$).

Lists of functions F, G see of p.

For carrying out the integration, introduce new variables and parameters in different ways according to case.

Case A (Hyperbolical case): $0 \leq \sin\alpha < q$

Put
$$\sin\alpha = q\cos\gamma \quad \left(\tfrac{\pi}{2} \geq \gamma \geq 0\right)$$
$$\cos\alpha = pq\sin\gamma, \text{ hence } p = \operatorname{ctg}\alpha\operatorname{ctg}\gamma = \frac{\cos\alpha}{\sqrt{q^2 - \sin^2\alpha}} \geq 0$$

Introduce uniformizing variable for trig. fcts of ψ as follows:
$$z = \frac{\operatorname{tg}\tfrac{\gamma}{2} + \operatorname{tg}\tfrac{\psi}{2}}{\operatorname{tg}\tfrac{\gamma}{2} - \operatorname{tg}\tfrac{\psi}{2}} = \frac{1 - \cos(\psi + \gamma)}{\cos\psi - \cos\gamma} \quad \left[\begin{array}{l}\text{so that to } z = 0, 1, \infty \\ \text{correspond } \psi = -\gamma, 0, \gamma\end{array} \;\bigg|\; \begin{array}{l} z \to z^{-1} \\ \psi \to -\psi \end{array}\right]$$

with
$$\frac{dz}{z} = \sin\gamma \, \frac{d\psi}{\cos\psi - \cos\gamma}$$

Then (V) becomes
$$\frac{d\pi}{\pi} = \frac{\sin\psi}{\cos\psi - \cos\gamma} d\psi - p \frac{dz}{z}$$

Hence the first integral:
$$\frac{\pi}{\pi_0} = \frac{\cos\psi_0 - \cos\gamma}{\cos\psi - \cos\gamma} \cdot \frac{|z_0|^p}{|z|^p}$$

Now by comparison of values for $\psi = -\gamma, 0, \gamma$:
$$N(z) = \tfrac{1}{2}(z + z^{-1}) + \cos\gamma = \frac{\sin^2\gamma}{\cos\psi - \cos\gamma}$$

Hence
$$\frac{\pi}{\pi_0} = \frac{N(z)}{N(z_0)} \frac{|z_0|^p}{|z|^p}$$

Then (VI) becomes
$$dt = \frac{1}{q\sin\gamma} \frac{|z_0|^p}{N(z_0)} \cdot \frac{N(z)}{|z|^p} \frac{dz}{z}$$

Hence the second integral:
$$t = \frac{1}{q\sin\gamma} \left[\pi_0 \frac{P(z_0)}{N(z_0)} - \pi \frac{P(z)}{N(z)}\right]$$

with
$$P(z) = \tfrac{1}{2}\left(\tfrac{1}{p+1} z + \tfrac{1}{p-1} z^{-1} + \tfrac{1}{p}\cos\gamma\right)$$

This second integral is not valid for $p = 1, 0$ ($q = \sin\alpha = \tfrac{\pi}{2}$) in those special cases one of the terms in $P(z)$ is to be replaced by a logarithmical term.

By elementary transformation one finds the fcts. F.G. as defined
above after (V), (VI) as follows:

	$p \pm 1, 0 (q \pm 1, \alpha \pm \frac{\pi}{2})$	$p = 1 (q = 1, \alpha \pm \frac{\pi}{2})$	$p = 0 (q > 1, \alpha = \frac{\pi}{2})$
$F(\psi) =$	$(q \cos \psi - \sin \alpha)\|z\|^p$	$1 + \sin(\psi - \alpha)$	$q \cos \psi - 1$
$G(\psi) =$	$\dfrac{1 + q \sin(\psi - \alpha)}{(1 - q^2)\cos \alpha}$	$-\dfrac{\sin(\psi - 2\alpha)}{2\cos^2 \alpha} - \dfrac{F(\psi)}{2\cos \alpha} \log\|z\|$	$-\dfrac{q \sin \psi}{q^2 - 1} - \dfrac{F(\psi)}{\sqrt{q^2 - 1}^3} \log\|z\|$

Note: Apart from this solution there is a trivial solution $\psi = \pm \xi$ which
means geometrically a pair of straight lines, of which one is stable,
the other instable. The asymptotic behavior of the general solution
can be elegantly described by these two straight lines. All this
turns out to be a far reaching analogy to corresponding theories
in my treatment of the integrals of the generalized three-point
problem; see the ms. part II.

Case B. (Elliptical case) $0 < q < \sin \alpha (\leq 1)$

Put $\quad p = \dfrac{\cos \alpha}{\sqrt{\sin^2 \alpha - q}} \geq 0 \qquad$ (i.e., replace the above by ip).

Define Z as above; then ζ defined by

$$z = e^{i\zeta}$$

is real. The argument under A may easily be adapted in such a way,
as to cover the present case B as well. By expressing the results,
in real terms one finds:

	$p \pm 0 (\alpha \pm \frac{\pi}{2})$	$p = 0 (\alpha \pm \frac{\pi}{2})$
$F(\psi) =$	$(q \cos \psi - \sin \alpha) e^{-p\zeta}$	$q \cos \psi - 1$
$G(\psi) =$	$\dfrac{1 + q \sin(\psi - \alpha)}{(1 - q^2)\cos \alpha}$	$\dfrac{q \sin \psi}{1 - q^2} - \dfrac{F(\psi)}{\sqrt{1 - q^2}^3} \zeta$

Case C (Parabolical case): $0 < g = \sin\alpha\ (\leqq 1)$

Put $p = \text{ctg}\,\alpha = \dfrac{\sqrt{1-g^2}}{g} \geqq 0$

and define $z = \dfrac{1}{\text{tg}\,\frac{\psi}{2}}$

Then by methods similar to those under A one finds:

	$p \gtrless 0\ (g<1, \alpha \pm \frac{\pi}{2})$	$p=0\ (g=1, \alpha=\frac{\pi}{2})$
$F(\psi) =$	$(1-\cos\psi)\,e^{pz}$	$1-\cos\psi$
$G(\psi) =$	$\dfrac{1+\sin\alpha\sin(\psi-\alpha)}{\cos^3\alpha}$	$-\dfrac{1}{3}\dfrac{(1+\cos\psi)(2-\cos\psi)}{\sin\psi}$

General Remarks.

1) It is easy to reduce the problem to $0 \leqq \alpha \leqq \frac{\pi}{2}$ remarking that substitutions $\alpha \to -\alpha$ and $\alpha \to \alpha - \pi$ have an obvious geometrical significance.

2) All curves for a fixed pair of parameters g, α are similar to each other. In case A this only holds by dividing the curves into two types, according to whether ψ ranges in $-\chi<\psi<\chi$ or in the complementary interval of the circle. Those two types are separated by $z > 0$ or $z < 0$ with regard to this we had to introduce the absolute values $|z|, |z.|$ in the expountial, logarithmical and power terms.

3) The first integral is the equation of the curve in a "moving" polar coordinate system: the second integral gives by means of formulas (i) a representation in the fixed system.

4) The terms "hyp., ell., parab" become a real geometrical meaning by the method of Wunderlich.

f) According to Hasse, a great deal of important research on guided missiles was carried on at the CPVA in Danisch Nienhoff, under the direction of Heinrich Wigge. As far as Hasse is aware, the CPVA is practically intact.

B 21.

Interrogation of W. Magnus, Dr. Prof. of Mathematics at the
University of Konigsberg.

Date: Göttingen, Sept. 12, 1945.

Interrogator: Dr. T. Rado, Tech. Rep., Prof. of Mathematics, The
Ohio State University.

- - - - - - - - - -

Magnus is presently employed by the British as interpreter at the
AVA in Göttingen. His attitude is one of full cooperation. He
started out as a pure mathematician, and during the war he took up
the study of electronics, in connection with the German war effort.
During the war, his position was essentially that of a go-between for
the engineering group working at Danisch Nienhoff under the direction
of H. Wigge on the one side, and pure scientists like the mathematician
Hasse on the other side, in connection with problems of guided missiles
(rockets and torpedoes). The purpose of the interrogation was three-
fold: 1) to determine whether our information concerning the various
types of pursuit curves, considered by the Germans in connection with
guided missiles, was complete. 2) To obtain information about the
actual tactical applications of the various pursuit curves.
3) To determine the importance and relevancy, in the opinion of the
Germans, of the mathematical study of pursuit curves. A summary of
the information gained from Magnus follows:

1. Types of pursuit curves. In this connection, reference should
be made to a report by Magnus, "Vergleich der Bahnkurven gesteurter
Raketen bei verschiedenen "Genkungsverfahren" (Comparison of the
trajectories of steered rockets with different guiding methods), Marine
Forschung, Forschungbericht Nr. 10, April 1944, which is available
at the ADRC in London. On the basis of present information, this
report of Magnus seems to contain a complete list of pursuit curves
considered by the Germans, except for the so-called acoustic pursuit
curves studied by W. Gerbes: Über Verfolgungskurven, speziell
"akustische" (On pursuit curves, especially acoustic ones), Flugfunk-
Forschungsinstitut Oberpfaffenhofen e V., Arbeitsprotokoll Nr. 100,
14 June 1944, available at the ADRC in London. Thus the reports of
Magnus and of Gerbes, both available at the ADRC in London, seem to
give a complete list of the types of pursuit curves considered by the
Germans. As regards detailed mathematical discussions of the various
pursuit curves, reference may be made to an interrogation of H. Hasse,
by the same interrogator on Sept. 11, 1945. The report of that
interrogation contains references and supplementary details concerning
what appears to be the most important German contribution. At the

request of the interrogator, Magnus prepared a brief discussion of the so-called BR curves (bomb rocket curves) on which no reports seem to be otherwise available. As far as Magnus is aware, no use was made of these curves, whose theory is also quite elementary. Still, for completeness, the following discussion, contributed by Magnus, is inserted:

Differential equation and curvature of the so-called BR curves.

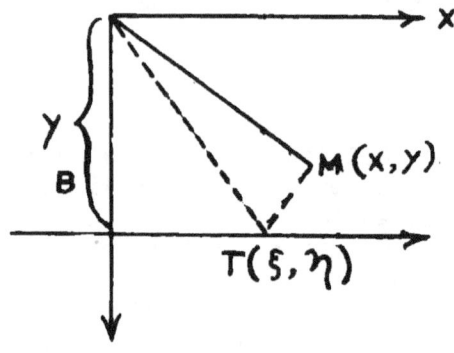

Notations:
O Observer
M Missile
T Target

t time $\varphi = \frac{y}{x}$
c velocity of M
v velocity of T
B shortest distance of O from the line on which T moves

Assumptions: 1) $\overline{OM} = \overline{OT}$
2) Velocity of M and T is constant
3) T moves in a straight line.

A point · denotes the differential quotient for the time.

Differential equations:

From 1) we have $x^2 + y^2 = \xi^2 + \eta^2$
"   2) "   " $\dot{x}^2 + \dot{y}^2 = c^2$
"   3) "   " $\xi = vt \quad \eta = B$

reckoning the time from the instant when the distance OT is a minimum.

Polar coordinates $x = r \cos\varphi$, $y = r \sin\varphi$

I $r^2 = v^2 t^2 + B^2$

II $\dot{r}^2 + r^2 \dot{\varphi}^2 = c^2$

Radius of curvature R, determined by -

III. $\frac{1}{R} = \frac{\dot{x}\ddot{y} - \dot{y}\ddot{x}}{(\dot{x}^2 + \dot{y}^2)^{3/2}} = \frac{1}{c^3}(\dot{x}\ddot{y} - \dot{y}\ddot{x})$

IV $\frac{1}{R} = \frac{1}{c^3}(-\ddot{r}\dot{\varphi}r + 2\dot{\varphi}\dot{r}^2 + \dot{\varphi}^3 r^2 + \ddot{\varphi}\dot{r}r)$

$= \frac{1}{c^3}(-\ddot{r}\dot{\varphi}r + c^2\dot{\varphi} + \dot{\varphi}\dot{r}^2 + \ddot{\varphi}\dot{r}r) = \frac{c^2 - v^2}{c^2 \cdot r^2 \dot{\varphi}}$

From I and II we have as a differential equation for (by eliminating both γ and $\dot{r}$)

$$\text{V.} \quad \dot{\varphi} = \sqrt{\frac{v^2(c^2-v^2)t^2 + c^2 B^2}{v^2 t^2 + B^2}} = \frac{\sqrt{q^2(1-q^2)t^2 + B^2/c^2}}{q^2 t^2 + B^2/c^2}$$

from where φ may be determined explicitly. Therefore the equations I, II may be solved by elementary functions.

From IV and V we have

$$\frac{1}{R} = \frac{c^2 - \gamma^2}{c r^2 \dot{\varphi}} = \frac{c^2 - v^2}{c\sqrt{v^2(c^2-v^2)t^2 + c^2 B^2}}$$

Introducing again $q = \frac{v}{c}$ we get

$$\frac{1}{R} = \frac{1-q^2}{\sqrt{v^2(1-q^2)t^2 + B^2}}$$

and from this equation we have

$$\frac{1-q^2}{B} \geq \frac{1}{R} \geq \frac{1-q^2}{r}$$

2). In the following remarks, it is assumed that the reader has consulted the reports of Magnus and Gerbes, referred to above, as well as the interrogation report by Hasse, concerning the definitions of the various pursuit curves that will be mentioned. It should be also stated that the following information, contributed by Magnus, is based mainly on his experience gained while working with the group directed by H. Wigge, at the CPVA (Chemisch Physikalische Versuchsanstalt = Chemical Physical Experimental Institute) in Danisch Nienhoff near Kiel. This group was concerned with guided missiles, especially torpedoes.

The ordinary hound curve was not actually used, as far as Magnus knows, but the German Navy planned to use it for rockets, primarily as regards rockets fired from the shore against landing craft, and also from submarines against shipping. Further, use for torpedoes was also considered.

The acoustic hound curve was used both by the Navy for torpedoes and by the Luftwaffe for rockets from aircraft to aircraft. The acoustic homing devices employed started to operate at a distance of.

about 1 km from the target. This project was started only in 1943 and probably did not get beyond the experimental stage.

The hound curve with constant lead angle seemed to offer many advantages (better angle of impact, reduced curvatures) and in fact with this method of steering it was theoretically possible to achive a rectilinear trajectory. However, no combat use was made, as far as Magnus knew, of this method.

The ordinary three-point curve was used for anti-aircraft rockets. A series of reports by Hoch, partly in collaboration with others, is concerned with the dynamical problems arising in this method of control (the Hoch reports are available in the ZWB series at the ADRC in London). The studies of Hoch were carried out at the institute for applied mechanics in Gottingen (if the Schuler interrogation report).

The generalized three-point curve (cf. the Hasse interrogation report) gives rise to the following remarks. In this method, the missile M is guided by a stationary ground observer O toward a proving target T in such a way that the segments OT and MT enclose a given constant angle. The project concerned with this method of guiding was termed the project Tasso, and it was one of the problems of the Wigge group at the CPVA (see above).

The target T was a ship at sea, and the missile M was a torpedo launched from the shore. The generalized three-point curve of the Tasso project was, mathematically, a curve lying in a fixed plane (the surface of the sea). Actually this was merely an approximationg, since the torpedo was meant to travel above the water surface (at a maximum altitude of about 200 yards), to insure better radar control, and also the proper angle of incidence when the torpedo struck the water. The generalized three-point curve was also termed the Wigge curve (after Wigge who first proposed its use) and also the TR curve (torpedo rocket curve). Again, this project did not seem to have been carried beyond the experimental stage.

Summing Up: As far as the Navy was concerned, it seems that no extensive combat use of the various pursuit curves could be made, due to reduced research facilities. In anti-aircraft missiles, actual combat applications were made. The development of the dynamical and technical problems was however carried on persistently, especially by the Fischel group at the DFS in Ainring (cf. the Ainring report) by the Schuler group in Gottingen (see the Schuler interrogation report) and by the Wigge group at the CPVA in Danisch Nienhoff.

3. The question of the relevancy of a purely mathematical study of the various pursuit curves arises naturally if one notes that these pursuit curves correspond to greatly oversimplified physical and technical assumptions (for example, the guided missile is assumed to travel at constant speed). On the other hand, it is clear that some a priori insight into the nature of the trajectory is indispensable, to estimate the stability of the missile and to select and to design the target-seeking head, the control mechanism and the necessary proximity fuze. According to Magnus, the purely mathematical study of the various pursuit curves was considered by the German engineering groups, engaged in work on guided missiles, as an important preliminary step in the designing of guided missiles. In view of the manifold aspects of the problem of guided missiles (mathematics of pursuit curves, stability studies, remote control, homing devices, proximity fuzes) frequent conferences took place between the specialists involved, and in fact go-betweens like Magnus were used.

APPENDIX C.

Index of Scientific papers published by DFS, Ainring, research workers prior to Allied occupation.

On deposit with ADRC.

C.1. Erz, J. Development of remote Action Devices at the Institution for Flight Equipment (Director Prof. Fischel) of the DFS UM 353a, ZWB, Aug. 1944.

Description of work and of present results on the remote control devices "Darmstadt" and "Mosel". The principles involved, methods of operation, and details of control devices and construction and of wiring are given.

C.2. Fischel, Edward. Gyroscopic problems in the airplane. Feb. 10. 1939. This is a paper read on the gyroscope and its application in many aircraft instruments such as compass gyro, position indicator, artificial horizon, automatic pilots, etc. The gyroscopic effect of the rotating masses in an airplane, such as the propeller, are briefly considered.

C.3. Fischel, Edward. Schriften der Deutschen Akademie der Luftfahrt forschung, 1941. p. 25-37. Artificial Longitudinal Stability. Artificial stabilization of an airplane requires operation of the elevators in proportion to a change of the position of the plane and to the speed of such change. Simultaneously, changes of the speed which are caused by the change of position are to be balanced. The report discusses the details of the problem and its solution. An apparatus for automatically stabilizing a plane is described.

C.4. Fischel, E. Automatic steering and remote control of flying bombs. Schriften der deutschen Akademie der Wissenschaften, 1942, pp 11-53. A paper read on the studies made at the DFS on flying bombs. It appears that stability can best be attained by actuating the ailerons under the control of a gyro with backwardly tilted measuring axis. In steering a bomb, the method according to which change of direction is attained by turning the flying body through an angle is preferable to a method by which an angular velocity is forced on the bomb. The controlling may be accomplished either continuously or stepwise. An apparatus for stepwise control is described.

C.5. Fischel, E. On the steering of two-winged rockets. March 1, 1945. Suggestions are made for steering the two-winged rockets as efficiently as the rockets with cross-wise arranged wings.

However, the required amount of apparatus is justified only if the rocket is used against approaching and changing course targets. The solution is found in the application of a steering stick universally swingable and transmitting its motion to a converter which transforms the motion according to polar coordinates. The stick is free to move up and down but locked against lateral movement. In order to release the stick it must be turned about its axis. The rocket follows such motion, that means it must turn about its axis before a change of its course can be attained by actuation of its elevator.

C.6. Fischel, E. Letter to Reichsfuhrer S.S. S.B.2 March 23, 1945. The letter is a critical answer to the question which of two definite designs of target sounding heads for rockets is preferable. The answer states, that a stabilized platform is necessary, that the platform of Kreiselgerate G.m.b.H. is preferable to that by Rauk. Both platforms are useful for project "Wasserfall" only. A third type apparatus is suggested for development. The merits of the various methods of target-sounding cannot yet be judged since required data has not yet been received.

C.7. Fischel, E. Guided bombs UM 3542, ZWB, Aug. 1944. A talk on the construction, tactical use, technical problems, apparatus for study and training, defense. The talk concludes with remarks on the trends of further development.

C8. Gerbes, W. A method of evaluation for multiple bearings. FB 1732, ZWB, Nov. 1942. In a number of situations where several bearings are used (several direct in finding radio stations) there arise mathematical problems which cannot be solved by elementary problems which cannot be solved by elementary methods in a limited time. It is proposed to meet such difficulties by using methods of higher geometry. Some possibilities are discussed in detail.

C.9. Klein. Switching in of target seeking missiles in pursuit plane projects. (Appendix to reports 77 Lg I - E 1086) June 20, 1944. This report contains the memoranda of 15 meetings on the problem of sel-aiming missiles automatically controlled to find and follow the target. Various principles are treated viz., ultra-red accoustical, radio. In general, it is intended first after the firing, to direct the missile by remote control. Only after the missile is properly directed the automatic aiming device should be switched in. The devices are to be developed for use with the project "Wasserfall"

The suggested accoustical device operates with accelerations of course alterations of .7 to 2 g; mean velocity of 165 m/sec and a limit of response of at least 500 m.

C 10. I. Meixner. Theory of deflection of ellipsoids of revolution. I Scalar theory of the deflection on small ellipsoids of revolution. 1944. This is a mathematical treatment of the problem of the deflection of vanes caused by an ellipsoidal surface. The results are given for great wave lengths and for very great wave lengths and applied to the limits of a thin wire and a thin disc.

C.11. Ramsbrock. W. Substitution of an electrical device for the damping gyroscope used in automatic control. UM 3516 ZWB Feb. 1944. The purpose is to reduce the technical complexities of automatic control. The mechanical processes induced by the gyroscope can be replaced by electrical processes. The necessary electrical units, as well their dimensions are discussed. An example is used to illustrate the necessary theoretical reasonings and numerical calculations.

C.12. Ramsbrock, W. Device for the representation of coupled vibrations in mechanical systems with multiple linkages. UM 3534, ZWB, Aug. 1944. The vibration started in the mechanical system is transformed into an electrical oscillation, where the couplings between the individual mechanical vibrating systems are effected electrically. The switching elements used there arise opportunities for errors which cannot be neglected. The applications lie in the field of stability problems in flight mechanics.

C.13. Schedling, J. The apparatus for the laboratory study of the cross-winged missile, with special regard to the "Wasserfall" UM 3558, ZWB, Jan 1945. The purpose of the apparatus is to permit the derivation of qualitative and quantitative statements concerning the flight of guided anti-aircraft rockets. After a theoretical study of the requirements upon such an apparatus, the technical problems of the construction of the apparatus are considered.

C.14. Schlogl F, and Walker R. Special three point curves for rocket missiles with widely variable speed. UM 3514, ZWB Jan. 17 1944. The differential equation is set up and solved for the three point curve with predetermined change of speed of the pursuing flying body. A graphical method for determining the path and the calculation of the turning speed for two dimensional flight paths are discussed and applied to an anti-aircraft rocket. The second part of the paper gives an approximation solution of the equation and the calculation of the turning speed, curvature and winding of the pursuit curve for selected cases.

C.15. Sponder. Investigation of the yawing stability of glider bomb with automatic control. FB 1819, ZWB May 1943. The yawing stability of an automatically controlled glider bomb dependent on the variable values of the system and the control are investigated. Under certain simplified assumptions, the influence of the oscillations of the path in a vertical plane on the yawing stability is also considered.

C.16. Sponder. On the dynamic stability of the yawing not in automatic Flettner control. FB 1990. ZWB, Sept. 1944.

Aircraft control of greater ease can be achieved by using a Flettner flap, provided that adequate dynamic stability can be maintained. This question is studied, by means of the Lagrage equations of the second kind, for large airplanes with automatic rudder control.

C.17. Thiry and Fischer in collaboration with Stinshoff. Equipment of pursuit plane projects with target seeking apparatus (ZSG) June 20 1944. The report discusses the four possibilities for a solution of a target sounding apparatus by accoustical, optical, ultra red and radio methods. The radio method appears to be the most advantageous one; however, it is very bulky and very limited in its application. The next best method is the accoustic. No apparatus ready for actual use is available at the time of the report.

C.18. Vegg. Karl. Investigation on a device for steering a ramming course in flight.

The conventional pursuit curve (Hundekurve) is unfavorable owing to the large curvatures shortly before reaching the target. The ramming course is aerodynamically the most favorable one. The report tends to prove by calculation of the problem in a two-dimensional system, that it should be possible to design a device for steering a ramming course of a curvature decreasing towards the end of the path.

C.19. Walker R. On the calculation of cam discs and cam bodies. UM 3540 ZWB Sep. 6 1944. Exact and approximate formulae for the shape of the edge of a cam disc and approximate formulae of the surface of a cam body are set up for a given shift of the center of the follower roller or ball. It investigates what conditions the function of the given shift must fulfil in order to be capable of being represented by cam discs or bodies.

C. 20. Weidmann-Seebach. Investigation on the deviation of a gimbal-suspended, free gyroscope under the effect of the nutation. FB 1965, ZWB July 25, 1944. The deviation of a gimbal suspended free gyroscope due to nutation is investigated theoretically and by experiment and measures to prevent the deviation are discussed.

C.21. Greinel H and Leisegang, H. Oscillations of the control circuit in the On-Off control of systems with one degree of freedom of control motion. The investigations of the oscillations are carried through for systems without natural dampening, with dampening without restoring force, and with restoring force and with natural dampening. In each case with influence and angle of lost motion will be considered through which the steering element has to turn and also the influence of a transmission delay. The pertaining differential equattions are set up solved, and their result in oscillation curves are plotted in graphs therefrom the conditions can be determined under which these oscillations decrease are invited, and increased. Examples are the On-Off control of a flying body with and without stabilization by means of a dampening gyro or other stabilizing device.

C.22. Greinel. The path of flight of the missile X4 from the moment the operation of the target - sounding head is started, under considerations of the response characteristic and response frequency of the sounding device. Feb.24 1945. The path of the missile is calculated and plotted with the assumption that both missile and target move in the same horizontal plane. Furthermore definite assumptions are made as to speeds, the range of the sounding device, the velocity of sound, and the response frequency of the sounding device. The missile reaches the target within 12 sec.

C.23. Greinel. The remote control of the HS 117 from the point of its firing on the ground, and the range of the angle necessary to pick up the target at a distance of 2000 m. The investigation aims to determine whether the aperture angle of the target sounding device is sufficient to pick up the target at a distance of 2000 m. from the missile. The calculation finds that the optical device should have an aperture angle of + 25°

C.24. Greinel, H. On the trajectories of flying bodies with an accoustic target locating device. UM 3544, Oct/ 1944. A theoretical study of the pursuit curves and of the ballistic arising in connection with a pursuit plane equipped with an accoustic target locating device.

C.25. Greinel, H. Trajectories of a projectile with electromagnetic target-seeking head UM 3547, ZMB, Oct. 1944. The various trajectories are described. In various initial distances, flight angles and ranges the projectile are constructed and the conditions for destroying the enemy are determined.

C.26. Leisegang. Trajectories of flying bodies with remote control by the method of three point curves. FB 1923, ZWB, March 1944. In guiding anti-aircraft rockets and flying bombs, a knowledge of the theoretical trajectories is necessary. The mathematical formulas are derived, and the curvatures of the trajectories are determined. The use of very fast flying bodies requires special study due to their slight maneuverability.

C.27. Gerbes, W. On pursuit curves, particularly "accoustic" pursuit curves. June 14, 1944. Those curves are dicussed which originate by directing the pursuer according to the noise of the pursued target. The results of the solution of a differential equation set up for constant speeds and a straight path of the target are discussed. One of the main conclusions drawn therefrom is the statement that the accoustic pursuit curves are more favorable as to their curvatures that the conventional (Hunde) curve.

C.28. Weickmann, H. Experimental studies on the formation of ice and water or nuclei at low temperature. Nov. 1942. The purpose was to devise laboratory conditions which were sufficiently similar to those prevailing in the natural atmosphere. A detailed account is given of the methods and results. The report contains an extensive bivliography and a large number of fine photographs.

C.29. Hohndorf. letter to "Forschungsfuhrung. March 26 1945. The letter states the various problems and projects on which the Institute for physics of the atmosphere, department of the DFS is working. The problems comprise certain studies of the atmosphere and investigation and development of instruments for measuring or responsive to conditions of the atmosphere.

C.30. Bickenbach A, and Weickmann H. The range of various thermal direction finder in fog. UM 3556, ZMB, Jan 1945. The purpose is to determine the most favorable instrument for warning of the approaches of a heat-radiating object in fog. To this end, properties of clouds were studied (distribution of raindrops and total water content) and the penetrating power of infra-red radiation measured. The report includes: 1 Comparative measurements in infrared direction finder instrument in the Wasserkuppe mountain upon visibility, raindrop radius and water vapor content. 3. Comparison of theoretical and experimental results. 4. A report on fog measurements.

C. 31. Ahrens. letter to Forschungsfuhrung Re: Eliminating influence of "duppeln" (Windows). Jan 22, 1944. At wavelengths of about 2 m the American "Liberator" shows a very strong and regular reflection of about 60 H_2. In view of this phenomenon it is suggested to use the "Nurnberg" board method with new apparatus filtering a very narrow low frequency band of about 60 H_2. Several suggestions are made for the application of such apparatus.

C.32 Born, H. Guide beam system for anti-aircraft rockets. May 20 1944. The system described in the reports forms two intersecting guiding planes through four impulse transmitted frequencies. The common curve of the two planes constitutes the guide beam. The system offers the advantage of simple conditions for the actuation of the control elements of the rocket. The receiving apparatus in the rocket is small.

C.33. Folsche. Application of impulse groups for the remote control of bombs or missiles. June 1 1943. In order to prevent jamming of radio control of bombs it is suggested to convert an original single impulse of the transmitter into a group of e.g. three impulses of very rapid sequence but differently spaced as to time. The receiver in the bomb is to be equipped with a device delaying the first and the second impulse according to the arrival of the last one, and conducting the impulses to the three grids respectively of a tube permitting passage of current only when all grids receive a positive voltage simultaneously.

C.33(a) Osken, H. Funnel shaped antenna with ring for reducing the reflection UM 3568 Oct. 12. 1944. In order to reduce the reflection of a funnel-shaped antenna it is suggested to apply a conical ring at a certain distance from the funnel rim. Measurements on such an assembly are stated for opening angles of 40, 50 and 60°. Reflection can be reduced very considerably.

C.34. Oaken H. and Muller. Reduction of the reflection of funnel-shaped antennas with a dipole arrangement in front of the opening. UM 3566 ZWB, March 23, 1945. In order to reduce the reflection of funnel-shaped antennas, the influence of a dipole arranged in front of the funnel opening on the radiation diagram is investigated. Measurement results are given on the decrease of the reflection of a short funnel-shaped radiator with 50° opening angle with various dipole distances and dipole lengths.

C.35. Roessler, Erwin. Schriften der Deutschen Akademie der Luftfahrtforschung pp 41-48. Apr. 17. 1943. Remarks on a method of taking bearings of transmitters of equal wave length is always possible owing to the occurrence of four definite points of intersection of the resulting bearing curves.

C.36. Weller, H. Broadcasting method by means of self-superimposed impulses to prevent jamming. June 6, 1944. A broadcasting method is disclosed in which the possibility of jamming is greatly reduced. It operates according to the principle of self-super imposed impulses, i.e. two impulses of carrier frequency are transmitted and superimposed in the receiver without additional oscillator frequency. Several possibilities of modulation are discussed and the applicability of the method for guiding pursuit planes is indicated.

C.37. Petersen, W. Calculation of the horizontal flight behavior of an extremely fast climbing Lorin fighter plane. UM 3558, ZWB, April 1944. In UM 3509, certain climbing and horizontal flight paths of a definite model of an extremely fast climbing Lorin fighter plane were calculated in the way of examples, while the more accurate study of the optimal flight conditions was reserved for subsequent publications. The present calculations deal with the same model, and is restricted to the horizontal flight paths at the tactically most important altitudes of 6000, 8000, 10,000 and 12,000 m (use as fighter bomber) where the primary topics of interest are maximal range (use as fighter bomber) and maximal flying time (use as fighter plane with proximal combat time) Further, the optimal flight altitude is briefly considered, and the minimal velocities in the vicinity of the ground are determined at which the jet plane is still able to accelerate.

C.38. Sanger E. Brief presentation of rocket technique FB 828, Nov 1936. Topics covered include: general definitions, application, exhaust velocities, nozzle, wings, velocity, fuselage, fuels, cooling, engine, combustion chamber, range. efficiency.

C. 39. Sanger, E. High exhaust velocities in rocket drive. FB 829, ZWB, Nov 1936. Starting with well established results, the report goes on to consider as yet unexplored possibilities of construction, operation and use.

C. 40. Sanger E. Gaskinetic of very high flying speeds. FB 972, ZBW, May 31, 1938. The conventional laws of the gaskinetic are not applicable at very high flying speeds. The report develops and discusses a method whereby satisfactory results can be obtained by calculation.

C. 41. Sanger E. Efficiency and dimension of Lorin engines. FB 996, ZWB, Aug.1938. The jet engines with continuous operation, proposed by Lorin 25 years ago, are still without practical importance. The reason for this is mainly the very low pressure in the combustion chamber. As a consequence, the device must have very large dimensions and possesses very low efficiency. These facts are verified by detailed calculations. It follows that without appropriate modifications, the original Lorin engine is impractical.

C. 42. Sanger E. and Bredt, I. On a Lorin drive for jet propelled pursuit planes. UM 3509 ZWB Oct. 1943. The report gives the calculation of performances obtainable with the Lorin drive and of the dimensions and form of the jet tube. It states the technical qualities of the tubes operating at high temperatures. Towing experiments have been carried out with a 2400 H.P. and a 20,000 H.P. tube. Finally, the fields of application of the Lorin-drive are discussed.

C. 43. Sanger E. The position of the Lorin fighter in the family of jet fighter planes. UM 3536, ZWB Aug. 1944. A comparative study of the following four jet drives, turbine, Lorin, rocket, P. Schmidt. The main topics of interest are flight performance and fuel economy.

C. 44. Sanger E and Bredt J. On a rocket drive for long bombers. UM 3538, ZWB, Aug. 1944. This is a voluminous condensation of a book whose publication had to be delayed on account of the war. The main difficulties in the use of a pure rocket drive result from the limitations on exhaust velocity and flight velocity due to problems of construction. On the basis of detailed physical and chemical studies, various possibilities of developing a pure rocket drive for long range combat planes are considered.

C. 45. Sanger E. Increase of the performance of the Me 262 by Lorin additional drive. UM 3557, ZWB, Jan 31 1945. The Lorin engine is not well suited to be used as an additional driving means. However, the investigation shows that by its application the climbing performance and the ceiling can be increased. The report does not deal with the question whether or not the flying qualities of the Me 262 are impaired by the attachments.

C. 46. Sanger E. High temperature jet drive. For 30 years, essentially fruitless studies were carried out on the Lorin jet tube. The main difficulty was that adequate efficiency could be achieved only at high flight velocity and simultaneous low combustion temperature. The present study discusses an invention which permits to achieve high efficiency at high combustion temperature.

C. 47 Fölsche, T. A method against active enemy jamming in radio measurements and in signal transmission, Feb. 23. 1945. The method is based on the use of delaying elements in the receiving circuit.

C. 48. First registrations of the atmospheric electric field and of the electric charge in the aircraft by means of field intensity miles. (Feldstarkenmuhlen) in the glider. FB 1845, ZWB. For measuring the atmospheric electric field, the glider is superior to powered aircraft, but still the change carried by the glider is to be taken into account. The device used to achieve this is called the field intensity mill (Feldstarkenmuhlen). It makes it possible to study separately the atmospheric electric field and the charge carried by the aircraft. Detailed results of measurements of both are given.

C. 49. Aufn Kampe. Humidity measurements in high altitude aircraft flights by the psychometer method. UM 737, ZWB. The method used is based on the psychrometer principle. It permits continuous registration during the ascent of the aircraft, and is applicable in the upper troposphere and in the lower stratosphere for temperatures as low as $-50°C$.

C. 50. Kracht, F. Ideas on the development of an aircraft for use at extreme altitudes, Schriften der deutschen Akademie der Luftfahrtforschung 1944. Before the war, it was discovered that in certain regions there exist upward wind currents extending to extreme altitudes. Thus there was given a possibility of ascent by glider to very great altitudes, provided that protection of the pilot against the hazards involved could be achieved, and proper aerodynamic shaping of the glider is developed. Comments are made on these topics whose intensive study was interrupted by the war.

www.ingramcontent.com/pod-product-compliance
Lightning Source LLC
Chambersburg PA
CBHW080411230426
43662CB00016B/2367